PENGUIN BOOKS

SPEAK TO THE EARTH

Vivienne de Watteville was born in England in 1900. She first visited Africa at the age of 24, accompanying her father on a hunting trip. He was tragically killed by lions on the trip, but Vivienne, who had fallen in love with the landscape, returned on a solo safari in 1928–29 to seek solace and "make friends with the animals." In addition to *Speak to the Earth,* she wrote two other books on Africa—*Out in the Blue* and *Seeds That the Wind May Bring.* In 1930 she married General George Goschen in England, with whom she had two children. She died in 1957.

SPEAK TO THE EARTH

Wanderings and Reflections
Among
Elephants and Mountains
by
VIVIENNE DE WATTEVILLE

With an Introduction by
ALEXANDER MAITLAND

PENGUIN BOOKS

PENGUIN BOOKS
Published by the Penguin Group
Viking Penguin Inc., 40 West 23rd Street,
New York, New York 10010, U.S.A.
Penguin Books Ltd, 27 Wrights Lane,
London W8 5TZ, England
Penguin Books Australia Ltd, Ringwood,
Victoria, Australia
Penguin Books Canada Ltd, 2801 John Street,
Markham, Ontario, Canada L3R 1B4
Penguin Books (N.Z.) Ltd, 182–190 Wairau Road,
Auckland 10, New Zealand

Penguin Books Ltd, Registered Offices:
Harmondsworth, Middlesex, England

First published in Great Britain by Methuen & Co. Ltd 1935
This edition first published by Methuen London Ltd 1986
First published in the United States of America by
W. W. Norton & Company, Inc., 1987
Published in Penguin Books 1988

LIBRARY OF CONGRESS CATALOGING IN PUBLICATION DATA
De Watteville, Vivienne.
Speak to the earth.
Reprint. Originally published: London:
Methuen, 1935.
1. Kenya—Description and travel.   2. Kenya, Mount
(Kenya)—Description and travel.   3. De Watteville,
Vivienne—Journeys—Kenya.   I. Title.
DT433.527.D4   1988   916.76'2043   88-4056
ISBN 0 14 01.1086 0

Printed in the United States of America by
R. R. Donnelley & Sons Company, Harrisonburg, Virginia
Set in Bembo

PREFACE

When you gave me *Out in the Blue*, dear Vivienne, I remember exclaiming after I had read it: 'Oh, please write another book as enchanting as this one, but in which nobody wants to kill an animal, and they all live happily every afterward!'

A rash request, I thought on reflection; not that I doubted your ability to produce another enchanting book, but that I feared there might be little more to say about big game untroubled by human violence than about countries similarly blessed. . . .

Well, my fears were unfounded, and I ought to have known it; for after all (and unless you guessed it, I can't imagine why you chose me for this preface), after all, I too, have lived that life and stammered that language, though my mountain tent was only the library lamp-shade, my wilderness a garden, my wildebeest stealing down to drink two astute and arrogant Pekingese; and as one of the initiated I was aware that those who know how to talk with animals know also how to talk about them.

And beautifully indeed you have proved it in these sunlit windswept pages. From the elephants romping with their friends, or twinkling at you ironically through the trees, to the least little bird hopping in at your hut door, they all had so much to tell that they had evidently been awaiting such a confidant for ages; and you would never have been able to pack all their yarns into one book if the Angel of Fire had not suddenly driven you out of the Paradise where you and

v

they had lain down so happily around the Remington.

But what a pity that he drove you out so soon! I resent the too hurried reporting of those slow shy approaches to communion; I long for the subsequent history of creatures just glimpsed and lost again in your crowded pages, like the tantalizing acquaintances made and lost in the rush of travel. You had found—or so it seems to me—the exact language in which to tell us of these desert and mountain friendships; elusive, wary phrases, shifting and shimmering like their own forest leafage, and words held out to them like coaxing hands. Since Farrer's sylvan language I have met none that seemed so made for its subject; and then, just as you were drawing nearer to the mysterious heart of your theme, as flower and bird and wild-hoofed creature were pressing about you to tell you their last secrets—just, in short, as you were about to 'stroke the elephant's ear'—the crash came, the sky grew black, and the golden gates clanged shut. . . .

But luckily, thanks to you, not on us, your happy readers. For we are there again, in your innocent Bestiary whenever we open your book; or even without opening it, merely when we walk out and see through your eyes and hear with your ears the tireless messages of Nature.

Many will say this to you, many more will think it, and wish they had the courage to tell you. I count myself privileged to have been the first to walk with you in your wild places, and to have been asked to say what I found there, and invite in others to share my delight.

EDITH WHARTON

Sainte Claire le Château,
    January, 1935

CONTENTS

Part I

AMONG THE ELEPHANTS

Part II

THE MOUNTAIN (MOUNT KENYA)

LIST OF ILLUSTRATIONS

INTRODUCTION

IN June 1923, twelve years before she published *Speak to the Earth*, Vivienne de Watteville and her father set off from Nairobi on safari, travelling north across Kenya to the Tana River. Vivienne was in her early twenties and filled with 'glorious anticipation' for the eighteen-month expedition whose purpose was to collect African big game specimens for the Berne Natural History Museum.

Until then, Vivienne had led a varied, colourful, yet in some respects sheltered, life. 'I had gone out as a stranger,' she wrote, 'knowing nothing of what Africa held in store for me.' She found excitement and romance far beyond her wildest dreams, but the safari ended tragically when Bernard de Watteville was killed by a lion near Lake Edward in the eastern Congo. Vivienne's widely-praised account of their adventures, *Out in the Blue* (1927)—a modest, remarkably unsentimental book—contained a brief but deeply moving description of her father's last hours. The fact that *Out in the Blue* had been written by a girl was unusual rather than unique. An Englishwoman, Agnes Herbert, had published the record of an African shooting trip in 1908, entitled *Two Dianas in Somaliland*, while the daring exploits of the young glamorous huntress Osa Johnson—the wife of America's most famous wildlife photographer Martin Johnson—were glorified in books and films.

Vivienne's journal, however, offered more than an exotic tableau of hunting adventures, primitive tribes and natural history, a well-worn formula repeated over and over by earlier generations of hunter-naturalists, among them Selous, Chapman and Stigand. Its red-blooded thrills were tempered by many subtler, reflective passages which revealed insights into the writer's innermost thoughts and feelings. Together these combined to portray a way of life which has vanished forever. They gave a tantalising foretaste of *Speak to the Earth* and clearly showed how much she had been appalled and inspired by the African wilds.

Vivienne had not been ashamed to confess bitter feelings of remorse as she knelt beside the carcass of an impala, the first animal her father killed, and wept as she stroked its sleek, bloodstained flanks. But that same evening, as she munched roast impala liver by their camp fire on the Tana, Vivienne regretted having shed tears over the delicate creature whose tender meat magically revived the dispirited and weary caravan. The distressing experience forced her to admit the reality of this primeval world where beauty and harsh cruelty existed side by side. Vivienne's readers were thus confronted with an enigmatic young woman who had cried for a dead antelope, yet stood unflinchingly by while her father shot buffalo and elephant or faced the savage charge of a wounded lion.

The same brave, tender-hearted girl who delighted in wild flowers and birdsong rose from her sick-bed to nurse her dying father heroically for thirty hours, while she herself was ill with spirillum fever, a disease capable of causing blindness or even death. Such episodes, which Vivienne invariably dismissed in a few sentences, suggest that she possessed great reserves of hidden strength and passion. Her nature was charmingly intricate, sometimes contradictory, and it would help us to understand Vivienne better if at this point we were to examine the early decades of her life.

Her family background was distinguished and firmly rooted in tradition, although her upbringing combined rigid formality with an altogether extraordinary degree of freedom. Vivienne's father, Bernard Percival de Watteville, the eldest of Louis and Eléonore de Watteville's four children, was born on 23 October 1877. Bernard was an aristocratic Swiss from the Bernese Oberland, a keen sportsman and amateur landscape painter of independent means, whose family home, the picturesque fifteenth-century Château de Gingins, stood near Lake Geneva. Vivienne's mother, Florence Emily Beddoes, was the only daughter of a retired naval captain, Henry Willoughby Beddoes, of Hesterworth, Hopesay, in Shropshire. Florence's great-grandfather, Dr Thomas Beddoes, had been a friend of Coleridge and a colleague of Sir Humphry Davy. Her great-grandmother's sister was Maria Edgeworth, the novelist.

Florence and Bernard met and fell in love soon after Bernard arrived in England in 1897 to study drawing under Sir Hubert von Herkomer RA, an artist nowadays best remembered for his sombre portraits of the Victorian working class. Maria Edgeworth would have thoroughly approved. She observed in *Castle Rackrent*, 'a love match was the only thing for happiness, where the parties could any way afford it.' Florence and Bernard were married two years later, on 13 October 1899. They settled at Hopesay in a house close to Florence's parents, where Vivienne, their only child, was born on 19 August 1900.

Judging by photographs, Florence was slender and a little above average height, with light-brown wavy hair and placid, oval features. Vivienne's grey eyes reflected her mother's dreamy wistfulness. Like Florence, she had a full, firm mouth with a little twist at one corner which suggested quiet determination and a gently provocative sense of humour. As she grew older, Vivienne began to resemble her father more and more, especially her profile with its long nose and purposeful chin. She and Bernard had the same distinctively curved lips and the same tranquil, direct gaze which betrayed unworldliness and introspection. When she was little, Vivienne called her father 'Dadboy', and later on, in her teens, 'Brovie'. Both names suited Bernard well, for like Peter Pan, he had never quite grown up and being young at heart as well as in age and appearance, he was often confused for an elder brother.

Brovie stood over six feet tall and was lean and hard with an eagle eye. Although he regarded shooting and fishing as 'the serious business of life', Vivienne recalled many years later: 'How many-sided Brovie was! Artistic, musical, philosophical; yet he would throw his whole soul into tying a fly and outwitting a trout. No one took his sport (or his golf) more to heart, slaving as if the world depended on his getting one more brace of ryper [willow grouse], or (in Africa) on bettering a trophy by a fraction of an inch. Painting excepted, he had never worked in his life, yet whatever he did—practising ski-turns or hunting the bongo—he gave himself to the last ounce, never sparing himself, rarely sparing me. With it all, what fun he was: witty, imaginative, full of charm, throwing over life an inward courtesy that shed a glow on everyday things.' Brovie's habit of smoking hand-rolled cigarettes through a long holder added a dash of continental elegance to his normally conservative attire: well-cut tweeds, silk ties and stiff white collars.

At Christmas 1909, when she was thirty years old, Florence died of cancer. Vivienne and Brovie were heartbroken. From then on, Brovie shared Vivienne's upbringing with his mother, 'Grandminon', and Florence's unmarried elder cousin, Alice Mary Blandford. Brovie,

Grandminon and Alice (whom Vivienne nicknamed 'Semi-lini') showered her with affection, but the strong influence they exerted as individuals failed to harmonise, so that Vivienne's life became a whirlpool of contradictions.

Brovie called her 'the dickybird', yet he treated her more like a son than a daughter, encouraging her to shoot and fish and climb. 'Since childhood,' Vivienne wrote, 'I had looked out through a man's eyes, felt more at home among men, preferred their companionship, and knew very little of women. . . . My youth had been that of an adventurous boy without a career to think of. With this strange upbringing I was yet (by the grace of God) fully feminine; I had plenty of maternal instinct, but I didn't bother about the domestic trifles which go to make up life.' As for Grandminon, on the other hand: 'In spite of twice embarking on the unquiet seas of matrimony, she was *au fond*—or so Brovie had maintained—a man-hater.' Alice Blandford alone, it seems, trod a middle path and remained a devoted, sweet-natured, sisterly friend whom Vivienne adored.

Somehow, Vivienne managed to adapt to the bewilderingly complicated jigsaw of her new life, whose strange pattern contained gaps only her imagination could fill. Brovie held her 'on a taut rein, jealous of [her] every move.' As an adolescent, her interest in young men was frowned upon. Instead of fighting back, however, Vivienne strove to please her father and for fifteen years assumed the difficult role of son, daughter and companion.

From the age of nine, she spent most of her summer holidays in the wilds of Upper Siredalen, Vest Agder, in south Norway, where Brovie leased 'a stretch of mountain', a trout river and two lakes, and built a substantial wooden house. Until the First World War, he employed a ghillie and a housekeeper.

Father and daughter's daily expeditions after ptarmigan, willow-grouse and reindeer were arduous but, for Vivienne, tremendously exciting. Gone were the days when Florence had dressed her in ribbons, a smock and an enormous straw hat which framed her tumbling soft brown curls. Now Brovie would relentlessly march his small jersey-clad daughter up and down steep mountainsides in tight-fitting boots, till her legs ached and she howled for mercy. Vivienne recalled: 'It was a toughening kind of life . . . he seldom waited, and I would even go so far as to lie down in the heather and sob with abandoned fury. I had to learn to get over such moments uncomforted.' Yet, she admitted, she never felt lonely nor wished for a friend of her own age.

Already she and Brovie were 'sworn companions'. Fortunately Vivienne was hardy, for the nearest doctor lived two days' journey from the hut. She wrote: 'I grew tough as a little Norwegian pony.' But still she missed Florence and sought the comfort of mother-earth, of nature 'which took the place of the mother I had adored and lost.'

Brovie entered easily into Vivienne's childhood fantasies and together they acted out the parts of her favourite storybook heroes, 'characters which to the end we completely lived in.' Vivienne always looked foward to the evenings, 'that cream of the day when after supper Dadboy would read aloud *The Wild Swans* and *The Little Mermaid* and later on *Bret Harte* and *Jock of the Bushveld* and *Treasure Island*.' Sometimes, when they wearied of playing the ship's captain and Murray, the first mate, they pretended to be Fritz and Pete, the 'Bärlies', a family of Swiss bears. The game perhaps originated with the bear which had figured in Berne's oldest-known civic seal, or the succession of live bears kept at the town's bear-pit, the *Bärengraben*, since 1513. The Bärlies' humorous antics—rather like the episodes of a miniature soap opera—inspired the Christmas and birthday cards which Vivienne drew and painted for Brovie, each with a few lines of verse, or a witty caption, written underneath. One of her birthday inscriptions read:

> A present from Father Neptune.
> To help a bare bear bare the plunge,
> He's sending him a tiny sponge.

The memory of these happy summers became Vivienne's refuge in later years. She wrote from Meru, in August 1923: 'The wind roaring in the thatch reminds us of Norway!' And again, in 1928, lying feverish and alone in her tent at Selengai: 'My mind floated away independently, now to England or the Alps, but more often back to the summer holidays of my childhood, in Norway.'

During the First World War, Brovie travelled and hunted for two years between 1914 and 1916 in north-eastern Rhodesia, and made a fine collection of trophy-heads which he presented to the Berne Museum. Meanwhile, Vivienne continued her education at boarding-school—St George's, Ascot—whose imprisoning atmosphere she found frustrating after months of freedom in the wilds. But as time progressed, life at St George's began to prove surprisingly instructive. An entry in her school diary, dated 1 June 1917, read: 'My first term of this after so much freedom and solitude made me to shun as far as possible my fellow beings—to get out of the turmoil when bedtime came was the recompense of the day—but I am no longer man-shy, and have less hankering after solitude. I have been wondering if the change is for better or worse? Of course it is for the better, in the sense that it is a weakness overcome . . .'

By mixing with other girls of her own age, Vivienne grew less self-opinionated and dogmatic. Yet she dreaded that too much forbearance, or a kind of 'mental dormancy', might swamp her carefully-nurtured individualism. 'If one ever had originality or freshness,' she complained, 'it very soon wears off . . .' The mood of despair was quickly banished. Self-pity soon gave way to renewed hope inspired by the maxims of her old favourites, Dickens and Stevenson. Vivienne consoled herself: 'One thing is certain, something will always turn up, and I am going to expect it as confidently as Mr Micawber. And Robert Louis says that "what a man truly wants, that will he get, or he will be changed in trying."'

From the moment Brovie returned from Rhodesia, his longing to hunt in Africa again eclipsed every other ambition. For the next seven years, he and Vivienne schemed and saved with this sole objective in view. Vivienne planned to 'study about birds and insects' and plunge into 'a course of domestic economy'. When she and Brovie visited Norway again in 1919, they looked after themselves. 'Besides doing the cooking and housework,' Vivienne wrote, 'I milked the cow, made butter and cheese, baked bread; and as to water, there were two pails to be filled at the lake and carried up a couple of hundred yards of steep path. I managed it all somehow without its interfering with the day's sport. And what fun it was! . . . when we washed up at the hut—I washing, Brovie drying— . . . we enlivened the task with the singing of duets till the roof shook.'

She went on: 'Those were the times of perfect companionship. . . . Living away from the world our days were unclouded. Then he would declare with deadly earnestness that I must marry, that he would never stand in my way. My spirits leapt at this change of heart. But the moment we came back all that was forgotten. The voyage out to Africa tried him sorely. . . . Brovie tortured in the flames, then turned life into hell for us both. It never seemed to occur to him that he fell in love a good deal oftener than I did. That, naturally, did not count.'

In the preface to Vivienne's third and last book, *Seeds that the Wind May Bring*, published in 1965 after her death, J. Alan White, her publisher, criticised Bernard de Watteville's too-exclusive and too-precious attachment to his daughter. It was a relationship, Mr White observed, which 'is more essential to the elder than to the younger; and however affectionate and warm-hearted it may be, it cannot be a substitute for the marriage of either.' And yet, thinking back, it seemed to Vivienne that Brovie's 'black depressions' and love-sick tantrums hardly mattered. On their last visit to Norway before leaving for East Africa, a blizzard had trapped them for a fortnight. The stores almost ran out and the cow lived on soup made from dish-water, thickened with flour and an occasional mouse! Vivienne and Brovie made light of the hardship; together they were invincible. Vivienne wrote: 'Even snowed up and short of food could be a joke so long as we were two to share it.'

The 1923–4 East African expedition was finally clinched when the Berne Natural History Museum's newly-appointed Curator approved Brovie's proposals for extending its collection of African mammals and agreed to underwrite the considerable expense of shipping them to Europe. After a month's voyage from England, Vivienne and Brovie reached Nairobi where they bought provisions for the journey. With the help of the Chief Game Warden, they engaged thirty porters, skinners and gunbearers, including Brovie's personal gunbearer, Kongoni, who had recently returned from a safari with Prince William of Sweden and the Swedish wildlife photographer, Oskar Olsson.

By then, Kenya Colony, as it was known, had already emerged from the raw pioneer era. Although vast tracts of country remained wild and largely unexplored, influential entrepreneurs and settlers, among them Lord Delamere and Karen Blixen, had opened up farming and development in the White Highlands. It was forty years since Joseph Thomson had made his first historic crossing of Masailand. The war-like Masai had been pacified and Kenya Colony's twenty-five-year-old capital, Nairobi, boasted multi-storey buildings, comfortable hotels and broad avenues lit by electricity. By then, motor cars had replaced wagons and rickshaws. In the streets, the de Wattevilles found police-men on traffic duty, up-country farmers and hunters, settlers' wives in topees and cool, white muslin dresses and khaki-uniformed askaris each wearing a smart red fez. On Nairobi's outskirts, imposing, stone-built Edwardian villas with lawns and sweeping driveways were screened by trees and neatly-clipped hedges. Little wonder that Martin Johnson felt proud to comment: 'Nairobi, in the heart of a black man's country, is a white man's town.'

Compared to the Johnsons' lavishly-outfitted 1924 Mount Marsabit expedition, which included 50,000 dollars-worth of photographic equipment, six specially-constructed hunting cars and seven tons of stores carried by 250 porters, Brovie's preparations for their foot safari to the Tana River appeared frugal and, even then, quaintly outdated. Brushing aside practical considerations, Vivienne wrote enthusiastically: 'For once, to be poor was to be free. We might argue that trekking was a good deal more romantic than travelling by motor car, or that though the experience of a professional White Hunter might ensure greater success, the whole salt of the adventure was to buy our own . . .'

Since the turn of the century, the Colony's healthy climate, teeming wildlife and relatively easy hunting conditions had attracted sportsmen in large numbers. In the early days, some enormous bags of big game had been recorded. Between 1907 and 1908, for example, clients of the famous safari-outfitters Newland, Tarleton & Company, shot almost 200 lion on the Athi Plains, close to Nairobi. Chasing lion on horseback became a popular sport, whose colourful devotees included Kenya Colony's first Game Warden, Arthur Blayney Percival. The 1920s were the heyday of Kenya's legendary safari guides: men like Philip Percival, J. A. Hunter, Pat Ayre and the Hon. Denys Finch-Hatton. The prestigious record books of Rowland Ward, the taxidermist, listed hundreds of trophies which they had helped rich visiting sportsmen to shoot. Even in those days, the professional hunter's services were expensive, though as yet they were not compulsory. But as it turned out, the de Wattevilles were to pay a far heavier price for the decision to go it alone.

In a letter to Semi (Aunt Alice) Blandford from Grindelwald dated 28 February 1923, Brovie had outlined his original plan for a six-month safari beginning in June and ending in December. In the event, six months barely covered its initial stages. Vivienne and he marched north, past Thika and Fort Hall, skirting the eastern slopes of Mount Kenya as far as the upper reaches of the Tana. From Meru, they crossed the Isiolo Plains to the Guaso Nyiro River and the Lorian Swamp—'a limitless expanse of grass and mud flats' blurred by mirages. After the Lorian Swamp, they veered south again and rejoined the Tana for a canoe voyage to Lamu and the coast. The safari's final stages, which occupied most of 1924, consisted of two months' hunting in the Aberdare Mountains, followed by a journey overland to Uganda, the Kivu volcanoes and the Congo borderland, finally trekking northward by way of the Semliki Valley to the White Nile.

As Brovie's eye got accustomed to the deceptive

equatorial sunlight, he made the first bags of impala, buffalo and lion, the deafening report of his .416 Rigby-Mauser 'blasting the stillness with the shock of a cannon.' The skinners, led by Mwanguno, 'a surly old fellow with the most ludicrous bow-legs', proved their worth by expertly fleshing out the skin of a black-maned lion. Vivienne was impressed, yet she shared Brovie's anxiety about preserving the tough hides of the larger species. Brovie's previous experience of field-taxidermy had been confined to Rhodesian antelope; and even the dextrous Mwanguno was uncertain as to how to flay the lion's nostrils. Much as Vivienne regretted killing these magnificent animals, the thrill of tracking and the finer points of skinning fascinated her. She described tracking as 'that glorious madness when your heart beats in your ears and you pant with fear and excitement, when you are terrifically frightened, and yet somehow detached and unafraid.'

Whereas Brovie thirsted for action, Vivienne's greatest pleasure lay in observing the birds, animals and landscape. Morning and evening possessed a special magic for her. She remembered how at dawn, beside the Tana, 'a bird twittered, a little wind stole over the veld, and a round hill, outlined in flame, marked the rising sun. Instantly the colourless grass ran gold, unfolding lilac shadows, and the larks went up drumming their wings in the bright sky.' Best of all, she loved the dusk when the camp fires burned 'like reassuring beacons to banish fear.' Then Brovie would roll cigarettes and command Vivienne, ' "Light up Murray, my son" '; and they would relive the day's adventures, soothed by the contents of 'the life-restoring blue teapot.'

At Maji Chumbe, a brackish waterhole on the Isiolo Plains, Brovie allowed Vivienne to assist in skinning a reticulated giraffe, whose hide proved to be even tougher than that of an elephant shot in the Meru Forest. A series of further adventures culminated in a long hunt for bongo and giant forest-hog in the Aberdares. Back at Nairobi in April 1924, Brovie streamlined the caravan and engaged a new gunbearer, Simba, who replaced Prince William's 'brave, wide-awake and splendid' Kongoni for the final trek across the Congo. They crossed Lake Victoria from Kisumu via Damba Island where Brovie shot four sitatunga, a semi-aquatic antelope with long spreading hooves, which the Nile explorer John Hanning Speke discovered in 1861.

The great lakelands of the eastern Congo, extolled by hunter and entomologist T. Alexander Barns in his book *An African Eldorado*, remained an unspoiled wonderland of big game, unlike the Athi Plains of Kenya. The Congo lion, compared to those found on the Tana, appeared quite undisturbed by gunfire. Brovie hunted them relentlessly. He shot twelve lion, five within the space of a week, besides waterbuck and buffalo. Vivienne's descriptions in *Out in the Blue* suggested he had thrown caution to the winds. A buffalo, charging 'like a tornado', nearly impaled him. Several wounded lion had to be finished off at dangerously close quarters, including a furiously angry lioness with a broken jaw.

All at once, everything began to go wrong. Hamisi, one of the porters, died after eating some rotten hippo meat; Kasaja, whose enchanting fiddle-tunes haunted Vivienne, narrowly escaped being trampled by a buffalo; and Brovie's gunbearer, Simba, who until then had proved staunch and reliable, left the safari after being butted in the midriff by a wounded kob-antelope.

On the Ruindi River, south east of Lake Edward, Vivienne was struck down by spirillum fever. On 30 September 1924, Brovie left her behind in camp and in the grilling heat went out after lion among the reed beds near the lakeshore. Vivienne lay tossing and turning on her camp-cot until several hours later when, to her horror, she saw Brovie staggering into camp, his clothes ripped to shreds and blood streaming from a mass of terrible bites and gashes. On 24 October, Vivienne wrote to Semi Blandford explaining what had happened:

Brovie wounded a lion and followed it into the thick cover of the reeds, and the lion waited for him and before he knew it had sprung out and pulled him down. It hardly scratched him, and made off at once, but B. fired and missed, and the lion, furious, came for him again and before he had time to reload had pulled him down and began tearing at him with its claws. B. managed to push him back far enough to give him a shot under the jaw, which found the brain and killed him instantly, and he fell across B's legs, the claws buried into the flesh. . . . [In *Out in the Blue*, she gave more detail: 'The claws had contracted in the last grip, so that B. had to tear them out one by one before he could get up.']

Knowing I was down with fever B. would not have me sent for, and in that state he *walked* for two hours back to camp under the torrid noonday sun. I won't go into too much detail, but only say that his arms and legs were absolutely lacerated, flesh and muscle to the bone, and that I managed to cut away all damaged tissue and apply antiseptics, which was all that we could do, and B. managed to sleep a good deal, and next day ate quite a lot, Brand's Essence, egg flip etc., and I thought if only I could keep him going and the wounds clean (because of course the terrible danger with lion mauling is septic poisoning) for six days, the doctor for whom I of course at once sent, would, if he came immediately, arrive. But at sunset the same evening (that is thirty hours after the mauling) B. suddenly died. I cannot tell you how unbelievably heroic he was. If it had to be, it is the death he would have chosen, brave and clean, and if it had to be, I thank God with all my soul that it happened out there in the wilds. If it had been in civilisation I do not know quite what would have happened to me, but in the wilds—ah! I cannot tell you what strength one draws from those great solitudes. . . .

Brovie had made Vivienne promise to preserve the lion-skin, 'the most glorious of all the lions he had shot.' While the porters hacked a grave from the metallic-hard earth, Vivienne 'worked on the lion skin without pausing, for it had begun to "slip", and it had to be saved—this lion of all lions. Yet it was merciful. It held me back from the tent where death hung in the air; where I could not choose but look upon that form dimly moulded through the blanket, the clasped hands rising in a mound upon the breast.'

As the men carried away Brovie's body to be buried, Vivienne, heartbroken, ill and exhausted, faced the lonely horizon and the even lonelier beginnings of a new life. She wrote: 'The mountains trembled in lilac mist, the cloudlets drifting in front of them like a flock of birds. Some topi lifted their heads to watch us. . . . Following in the wake of the little procession, I could only think over and over again: "But isn't it beautiful?"'

She assured Semi Blandford: 'I *had* to pull myself together, everything depended on me alone. I had to get the safari back, and 50 men depended on me to shoot them meat.' Vivienne accomplished this successfully, forcing herself to shoot waterbuck, bushbuck, buffalo and a white rhinoceros which completed the trophy collection, 'this work—*our* work—which B. had given his life for.' Although the tragedy had cast Vivienne adrift, in a sense it also liberated her. She wrote in *Seeds that the Wind May Bring*: 'The time I spent in the wilds after Brovie's death lifted me to an awareness of the spirit so intense that beside it ordinary existence faded to a shadow. Out there in the Congo desert my course was set for me. The title of the book I must write about it, *Out in the Blue*, dropped into my mind. For Brovie I must go back to Europe and write it. Then I was free, free to return to Africa . . . to track with single-pointed intent the spirit which called me.'

Speak to the Earth, the record of Vivienne's second African journey, made from 1928 to 1929, expresses her new-found independence and testifies most eloquently to her unshakable belief in Man's ability to live at peace with Nature. Yet Vivienne's superficial motive for this journey—elephant photography—disguised her true objective, the pursuit of solitude. 'Solitude meant the quest (however blundering and experimental) for God', which in turn meant the quest for self-awareness. Her search demanded the renunciation of material things. The chrysalis had to be discarded before the butterfly could take wing. 'Possessions dragged me back into the past . . .,' she wrote. 'Peace can be won only in exchange for the total surrender of personality. He that would find his life must first lose it.'

The journey which this book describes is itself in many respects an action-replay of Vivienne's past. The book, like the journey, divides naturally into two parts. The first tells how for five months, during 1928, she camped on the Kenya–Tanganyika border. At Selengai, she found herself surrounded by herds of wildebeeste and zebra; at Kidongoi, her camp was stalked by lion, reputed to be man-eaters; at Longido and Namanga, she wandered among elephant and rhino. The second part describes how Vivienne returned to Nairobi shortly before Christmas and almost immediately set out again for Mount Kenya, where she spent two months, latterly quite alone, at 10,000 feet in a tiny alpine hut.

Her months camping on the plains were filled with almost daily reminders of Brovie. Her followers included the old bow-legged Wakamba, Mwanguno and Muthungu, one of the Tana safari porters. The rifle which she kept loaded but never used reminded her of many dawn prowls with her father after game. Even if her attempts to bridge the gulf separating Man and Beast did not entirely succeed, we learn how Vivienne achieved something close to the fulfilment of her dream among the elephant of Namanga. In her preface to *Speak to the Earth*, Edith Wharton praises the 'elusive, wary phrases' which evoke the glorious mystery of Vivienne's rediscovered wilderness.

It was inevitable that her spiritual journey should lead her to the mountains. She climbed the Black Mountain, Ol Doinyo Orok, and after that, Longido, before she finally settled at her Mount Kenya retreat with her dog, Siki, and a box of classical gramophone records. Some of the most beautiful passages in this book can be found in the pages devoted to Mount Kenya. Vivienne's language is as crisp and light as the high mountain air, and its colourings are as subtle as the 'choppy cross-seas' of Mount Kenya's heather moors. Whether she is describing a bank of scarlet gladioli at Lake Michaelson, or darting swallows by the Nithi Falls, Vivienne's acute perceptions and her touching sensitivity recreate perfectly each individual atmosphere. We feel the sunshine's warmth and breathe the fresh mountain potpourri of grass and heather. The exquisite poetry and precision of Vivienne's images —'the rainbow-coloured distance', or the 'ashy silence' before dawn—are some of the loveliest, most moving things in all the literature of Africa.

The great mountain explorer, the late Eric Shipton, met Vivienne in January 1929 on his way to climb Mount Kenya with his friends, P. Wyn Harris and Gustav Sommerfelt. To Shipton, the 'big-game huntress' appeared an unworldly character, yet at the same time independent and capable. In his book, *Upon that Mountain* (1943), Shipton wrote: 'It seemed unkind to disturb her peace, but she welcomed us with charming hospitality, and gave us a dinner that would have done justice to any English home.'

There had been moments when Vivienne needed all the self-reliance she could muster: once, a raging heather-fire threatened to engulf the hut; on another occasion, racked by agonising toothache, she extracted a molar using a pair of carpenter's pliers! Yet, when the time came for her to bid the mountain farewell, Vivienne did so with a heavy heart. Her quest for enlightenment had sometimes been a lonely ordeal; nevertheless, she felt amply rewarded by the brief moments of beauty and 'its rare and fleeting visions.'

Vivienne began writing this book on the Mediterranean island of Port Cros, off the coast of Toulon, where she lived between 1929 and 1930. She was alone except for a prima donna manservant, Josef, a parrot and a donkey named after Robert Louis Stevenson's immortal, Modestine. Her last book, *Seeds that the Wind May Bring*, told the strange and often amusing story of that island year.

By March 1935, when *Speak to the Earth* was published, Vivienne's life had changed irrevocably. She had met 'Bunt', Captain George Gerard Goschen, the younger son of the Rt Hon. Sir Edward Goschen, Bt., whom she married on 23 July 1930 at Holy Cross Church, Binsted, in Hampshire. Bunt shared Vivienne's passion for music, literature and nature. Although Brovie had represented her ideal, to her relief, unlike Brovie, whose search for simplicity had ended 'in an ever thickening maze of complexity', Bunt '*was* simple . . . the pure in heart.' His oldest friend, Tommy Lascelles, assured Vivienne, 'he is one of the real sunshine-makers of this world. . . . He is, moreover, a very genuine musician.'

Even so, she resented the ties of marriage and consequent loss of freedom. She had turned down Bunt's proposals many times, and, panic-stricken, wrote telling him 'I was going back to my hut on Mount Kenya, or to Crete with Grandminon, or even to Tibet. Always the old hunted feeling, making me turn wildly to the atlas for a way of escape. . . . Like the Flying Dutchman I was doomed to wander the earth in everlasting banishment.'

Marriage, to cynical old Grandminon, was 'the longest word in the language', yet deep down Vivienne knew that in marriage lay her own true fulfilment. 'When Grandminon chided me for the perfection I looked for,' she wrote, 'I hedged at once. My requirements in a husband simply boiled down to three things: he must not snore or be jealous, and he must have a white chest. "But how will you find out first?" asked Grandminon, opening her blue eyes very wide and pretending to look scandalised.'

In photographs taken at this period, Bunt, 'the blond and blue-eyed stranger', looked remarkably like Brovie, especially his thick moustaches and angle of brow. Like Brovie, Bunt was too trusting and impractical. In 1933, the advice of an unscrupulous broker lost Bunt a large sum of money through the Stock Exchange. After that, the couple were entirely dependent upon Vivienne's capital. Between 1932 and 1934, they lived at Wild Acre, Farnham, in Surrey. After this house was sold, until 1950, when Vivienne inherited Semi Blandford's house at Hopesay, they lived with their children, Tana and David Bernard, at Coneybury, a rented Swedish timber cottage which Vivienne's friend, Becky (Lady Clarke), had built on the Clarke's estate at Ardingly, in Sussex.

According to Tana, by modern standards, Coneybury

'was not so very small but by (her parents') standards it was
the smallest house in the world even though (to begin with)
there was a cook and a governess!' Vivienne and Bunt 'lived
very simply and were very happy, and though neither of
them worked professionally, they were always busy, both
writing a lot in their separate "dens".' For two children, 'it
was a wonderful place to be brought up. . . .'

Tana's recollections continue: 'On Nanny's day off my
mother used to take us into the woods and always let us sit
on wet grass or roll about on dead leaves, of which Nanny
would have disapproved. Later, when we were about six or
seven, we were allowed to camp in the valley below and out
of sight of our house. The farmers, when they heard of this,
raised their hands in horror. My mother's reply was: "But
there aren't any bears in Sussex!". . . . During the War she
got for us an old hut from one of the disused quarries and
here we cooked, and played. . . . It was a wonderfully free,
untrammelled childhood. Above all she relayed to us the
beauty of nature, of art, of literature and of music.

'My mother possessed an imaginative generosity that is
still remembered by people so long after her death. I
remember a little parcel with a message saying "To the one
with the golden voice" or some such words. This was to the
woman at the telephone exchange . . . with whom my
mother had struck up a pleasant telephonic relationship. At
Christmas, having trudged out to our house which was
miles from anywhere, the postman would receive a special
present, a tot of rum and other little attentions to alleviate
his labour. I remember during the War, when tea was
rationed, we used to take little parcels of that precious
commodity, so prized amongst the farmers and country
people, to all sorts of most unlikely people. In her will she
made the dreams of some people come true, like the old
cook at a nearby farm who was left enough money for a

holiday in Switzerland. Fifty years after my mother had left
Port Cros . . . my brother went there for a holiday. She was
still remembered with pleasure for the unfailing attention
and imaginative help she gave to the islanders.'

Last summer, at Ardingly, a few days before her death,
Lady Clarke recalled her twenty-year-friendship with
Vivienne. An inscribed copy of *Speak to the Earth*, carefully
preserved in the original brown-and-beige dustjacket
designed by Beryl Ash, lay on a wickerwork table beside
her. Lady Clarke's affectionate memories were so vivid and
so natural that at any moment, it seemed, Vivienne might
have stepped indoors from the garden. Her recollections
evoked Vivienne's shy, soft speech, her quiet manner, her
grey-blue eyes and sun-bleached, bobbed brown hair.

She believed Vivienne's innate shyness had been masked
by a series of disguises: for example, the childhood games at
Upper Siredalen, when Vivienne and Brovie had pretended
to be sailors, or the anthropomorphic fantasies of later
years, when Vivienne imagined herself as a bird, a bongo,
or a bear.

Disguise had also reflected Vivienne's taste for occasionally bizarre, practical jokes, for which she was
invariably excused due to her immense fund of charm and
goodwill. Lady Clarke remembered a Women's Rural
Institute meeting held at Ardingly in 1936, when Vivienne
arrived wearing spectacles, baggy tweeds and brogues,
with one of her front teeth blacked out. Posing as the formidable 'Mrs Trebilcock', she harangued and thoroughly
disconcerted Lady Archer, Sir Ralph Clarke's cousin, who
had been invited to lecture on Uganda. Olive Archer
completely failed to recognise Vivienne, whom she knew
well and had met first in 1924, when Vivienne and Brovie
stayed with the Archers at Government House, Entebbe,
on their journey to the Congo.

In 1937, Vivienne and Bunt travelled across the United States with friends, and between 1936 and 1938, Vivienne once or twice visited Switzerland. After the Second World War, she and Bunt spent part of 1948 to 1949 in Majorca and Ibiza before moving to Shropshire. After Bunt's death in 1952, Vivienne returned to Coneybury, where eventually she fell ill. It was left to Tana to tell her the final diagnosis. When Vivienne heard that she had only a few weeks to live, she greeted the news 'not with despair, but, amazingly, with relief, and even a kind of exaltation. . . .' According to Tana, their conversation ran as follows:

Vivienne: 'Have I got cancer?'

Tana: 'Yes.'

Vivienne: 'But how wonderful! How exciting! Why didn't those long-faced doctors tell me instead of pretending I was going to get better?'

Quoting again from the Preface by J. Alan White: 'She saw no reason , she said, for deep grief; she was fifty-six and had had a satisfying life; the only difference between her situation and that of millions of others was that she knew her span of time was almost up, and this she considered preferable to not knowing. The few pain-free hours in the last two weeks of her life were devoted to clearing up her affairs. She was very anxious that upon her death her eyes should be given to the Eye Bank, and it is evidence of her courage that she could make this dispensation in the knowledge that the gift would take effect, not in the vague future, but within a matter of days. Among the other matters to which she attended at this time was the manuscript of a book, her third, which was not completely ready for publication.' The book to which Mr White referred was *Seeds that the Wind May Bring*.

Vivienne's daughter, like Lady Clarke and everyone else who visited her in hospital, was deeply moved by

Vivienne's courage. Despite a great deal of pain, she remained cheerful and kept a well-stocked drinks cupboard by her bed from which to entertain visitors. Vivienne died on 27 July 1957 and was buried beside Bunt in the graveyard at Hopesay. Her obituary in *The Times* paid tribute to her 'enthusiasm for wildlife' and the 'graphic power and craftsmanship' which had distinguished her writing. In the concluding paragraph of this book, she writes: 'Nature may be a cruel contradiction—life for ever warring against life—but Her ultimate message is the friendship of God. Secure in that friendship we cannot be afraid. Life is the glorious experiment, and Death the great adventure, when the mists shall at last lift long enough for us to see clearly.'

Vivienne de Watteville died as she had lived, a unique spirit and a courageous woman of magnificent, unselfish gifts, for whose loss the world is a poorer place. The moment of death, like Vivienne's return to the African wilds, held neither fear nor mystery for her. In her words: 'Now I was returning because I was under the spell . . . now I was going back in my own way.'

ACKNOWLEDGEMENT

I wish to thank Vivienne de Watteville's daughter, Tana (Mrs John Fletcher), for her generous permission to quote freely from her mother's books, and from the fascinating collection of previously unpublished letters and manuscripts which she most generously lent me. Her enthusiastic interest and helpful advice, together with these materials and many original photographs, enabled me to write this introduction.

I wish also to express my gratitude for the very useful reminiscences provided by the late Lady Clarke, which made an important contribution; and to thank Mrs A. G. L. Goschen, who guided my original enquiries.

I would like to thank the library staff of the Royal Geographical Society for their unfailing courtesy and valuable assistance; and finally, Ian McMorrin, who gave me *Speak to the Earth* some years ago.

ALEXANDER MAITLAND
February 1986

PUBLISHER'S NOTE

THE reader may wonder why none of the author's original photographs appear in this edition of the book. Unfortunately, the photographs themselves have been lost and those printed in the book are not of a sufficiently high quality for further reproduction.

In fact, those which appeared in the first edition were mostly connected with the second part of the book, for reasons which the author herself explained:

The elephant photography was done with a 16 mm. cinema, and the negatives, less than half the size of a postage stamp, cannot successfully be enlarged for reproduction.

Many of the results of the Reflex camera were lost in transit between Namanga and Nairobi (not, I am certain, through the fault of Karua, the Indian lorry driver).

Since photographs of African bush are all much alike, their absence is unimportant; far greater is the loss of the close-up portraits of the boys. If only the reader could have seen these: Mwanguno in profile with his round white cap, Mohamed carrying the detestable elephant gun; Jim, Asani, Abdi and the rest, the sight would have set them on the move for him through all these pages.

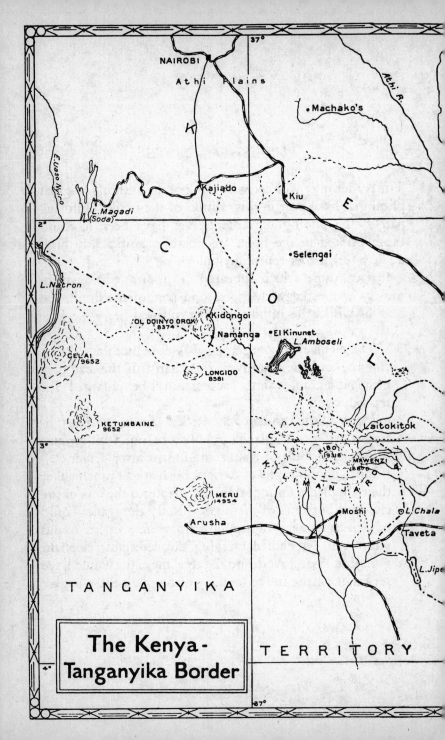

The Kenya-Tanganyika Border

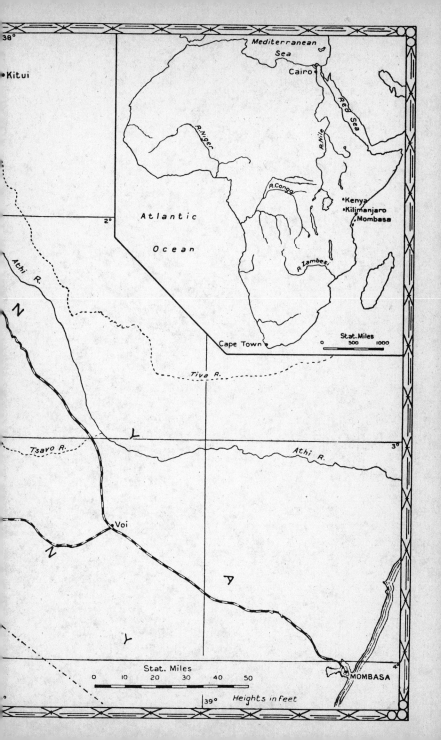

For thou shalt be in league with the stones of the field: and the beasts of the field shall be at peace with thee. . . . Or speak to the earth, and it shall teach thee.

JOB V, 23, and XII, 8

Part I

AMONG THE ELEPHANTS

Chapter I

IN WHICH I SET OUT

" AND so you propose to walk up to a wild African elephant and pat him ? " he asked.

With a gesture of disgust I threw my cigarette into the Red Sea. People nearly always jumped to conclusions of this kind when I tried to tell them about it ; but he had led me to expect something different, and I was disappointed. I wished I had merely said that I was going back to East Africa to photograph big game, and left it at that. Had I not been practising my cinema camera on the fleet of little boats filled with merchandise that launched out to the ship at Aden, I was convinced that nothing would have wrung from me the confession that I was going out into the wilds alone with a very special object ; but when he pointed out that a half-gauge cinema would not be much use on wild animals, and added that a telephoto lens was indispensable, I fell into the trap.

" The photographs are unimportant," I exclaimed ; " what I really want is to make friends with the animals ! "

Though I hoped that he might refrain from talking lightly about patting elephants, I was not unprepared for it. It seemed to be the accepted answer, not disdained by even my dearest friends, who were all unanimous in pouring cold water on my plan. Solitude was unwise, they said, and making friends with the animals sheer lunacy. But then, whatever you want to do, if it were only a bicycling tour, friends (though they do not wish to sound discouraging) just cannot help trying to put you off.

My chief (and only) supporter was the last person whom you might expect. My wildest schemes of travel and adventure always found a sympathetic hearing from my grandmother. *She* never poured cold water ; on the contrary, she added the most inflammable fuel to the flame, and at the end she would unfailingly catch my own enthusiasm and sigh :

" Ah, if only I were forty years younger, I'd go with you ! "

" Solitude ? Why, it's the finest thing in the world," she would declare ; " it's the only time we learn anything."

Possibly it never occurred to her that making friends with wild animals might be dangerous and improbable. Her faith in the project was boundless. She adored animals herself, and she thought it a beautiful idea.

" And, of course," she added, " I am sure that you will succeed if you really mean to."

I had a lurking suspicion that if I had suggested offering myself as food to a litter of starving lion cubs—like the story of Buddha and the tigress—my grandmother might have been equally persuaded that it was all for the best ; but that is neither here nor there, for it was her encouragement I wanted. She understood not only that Africa drew me back, but what it was about Africa that had awakened this longing which could neither be quenched nor silenced. Her sympathy was at once balm and incentive ; for to find but one other who has seen and felt as we have is assurance enough to brace us against a world of unbelief.

Before, I had gone out as a stranger, knowing nothing of what Africa held in store for me ; now, I was returning because I was under the spell ; for Africa had taught me that only in primitive vastnesses can one find oneself and grasp the meaning of the word Unity. This discovery was too precious to be brought out into the common day, or put into the clumsy sackcloth of words ; so that my outward pretext

4

for going back was of necessity that of making friends with the elephants.

Before, as I have already related, I had gone out with my father to make a collection of the fauna of East Africa for the Berne Museum. This had been his dream, which we had long shared and saved for. But my own private dream had always been to go into the wilds unarmed and, in some unforeseen way, to win the friendship of the beasts. I envied none as much as Androcles, who by so trifling an incident as meeting a lion with a thorn in his paw (coupled with his resource in pulling the thorn out) gained the lion's lifelong devotion.

And now I was going back in my own way.

With some pretence of secrecy, and the thrill of playing truant, I gradually collected together my equipment, and towards the end was put to shame for it by receiving all kinds of additional equipment (heaped—so it seemed to my guilty conscience—like coals of fire) from the very people who disapproved most. But no one took me seriously, and when I boasted that I had booked my passage they shrugged their shoulders, as much as to say that passages are easily cancelled. I hardly believed in it myself until I was actually aboard the familiar B.I. ship in Tilbury Dock, and with a heart beating with excitement I sniffed the smell of ships and heard again the winches squeak and groan above the open hatch.

I had a single deck cabin on the port side (I had learned by experience about the afternoon sun in the Red Sea) and while all the world was hurrying to and fro, sending messages, directing luggage, asking for letters or cocktails, and saying good-bye, I was busy settling in. Being by nature untidy, no phrase appealed to me more than the one about neat as a captain's cabin ; and I had taken enormous pains to design a travelling bookcase and other useful contraptions that in the inside of two minutes turned a cabin or a tent into home. People make themselves needlessly unhappy about leaving home, I thought, as I arranged my travelling clock, aneroid and compass with careful symmetry along the shelf. An armful of favourite books, a picture or two, and some rugs and chintzes for camouflaging luggage—and there you are. You take your home with you wherever you go. That is liberty in the truest sense.

Every one probably enjoys a long sea voyage a great deal more than he would have you believe. Nearly every passenger grumbles at that particular shipping line as soon as he comes aboard ; grumbles at the food, at the dullness of the other passengers and, above all, at the slowness of the ship which is robbing him of at least three more days of his hard-earned leave than the modern fast liner has any right to do. For me it was different. I loved every screw and rivet of the old *Mantola*, firstly because she was a ship at all, and secondly because she was taking me towards my heart's desire. I had no leave to worry about, no family ties or bread-winning problems to preoccupy me. My lot was the most enviable in the world. I was a free lance going out on an adventure of my own.

So it was with enchanted eyes that I revisited Port Said, looked across the rainbow-coloured desert as we glided down the Suez Canal, and fished all night for elusive luminous fish at Port Sudan. Being young and foolish, I even varied the programme by climbing the giddy iron ladder to the harbour lighthouse in pitch darkness, and making the astonished old Arab in charge show me the revolving red light. These musical comedy pictures of the East were to me as real as the Arabian Nights, and the bazaars full of gaudy carpets, jewels, silks and carvings (all made in Birmingham, my shipmates knowingly asserted) were to me as genuine as the treasures in Aladdin's cave.

And then Africa itself. To almost every one aboard she

was something to which one had unwillingly to return. Another term of office, another battle with the coffee crop (or any other crop) against locusts, disease and drought. Heat, dust, discomfort, fever, loneliness, hardship and exile— Africa stood for all these things. A heartless country to wrest a living from, and whatever you went out there to do, there was no easy way. You worked and worked to the last ounce of human endurance, and more often than not you fought a losing battle.

I, too, had found Africa implacable. The word called up endless marches through thorny deserts, and thirst and hardship ; and, like all the others, I was drawn back again as irresistibly as a needle to the magnet. Was it just because she made one endure so much, plucked one out of a too comfortable civilisation to fight elemental difficulties and dangers, and brought one close to vital issues of life and death ? Who can say ? Hunter, settler, Government official—all cursed her and all returned to her. And, in spite of everything, Africa is one of the strongest bonds in the world. Those who have left her will go miles to meet some one who has just come back from their own particular part. Heat, dust, mosquitoes —little things, prosaic things . . . they never survive in retrospect ; and what lingers in memory long afterward is that elusive something which all in a greater or a less degree are seeking, and of which, at rare moments in the solitary places, Africa accords a splendid never-to-be-forgotten glimpse.

We sailed into Kilindini Harbour, where palm trees waved along the shore as green and good to behold as an oasis, after nearly a month at sea. The water lay still and blue as a lagoon ; then the reflections broke before the ripple of our bow-wave, and our arrival called out a score of bright-coloured boats—canoe, sail, native craft of every kind—and the harbour was soon a scene of gay animation. Crowds of natives, shouting and expectant, lined the quay ; here and there an Indian (distinguishable by his Western clothes and pith helmet) pushed his way through the throng, and a handful of Europeans waited to meet their friends aboard. Hasty or prolonged farewells were said to month-old friendships ; all rushed for the gangway and promptly met their friends again in the Customs House.

This stretched for about half a mile, scorching under a roof of corrugated iron, and the process of identifying and collecting one's luggage was long and engrossing. The duty on cameras and gramophone records was exorbitant. I took pride in being honest in such matters, but it was a great mistake.

Even Customs cannot last for ever, and I kept reminding myself that this was beloved red African soil underfoot, and that the crowds of yelling, sweating natives, variously clad in long white *kanzus* or khaki shorts (with the shirt worn preferably outside) were all a part of the local colour.

The train (Nairobi-Kisumu-Entebbe) was just as full of gritty red dust and rather uncomfortable-looking black American cloth as tradition demanded ; but four years had sadly altered its habits, and it had become so outrageously modern as to have a restaurant car. The guard beamed. " We save six hours now, between here and Nairobi," he proudly informed me. But I would gladly have had the six extra hours and climbed down for meals at the sidings as we did in the leisurely old days. Then, you sat at a long table with your fellow-passengers (served by an army of feverishly hurrying Indian waiters) inside the station. There was far too much local colour here to be over-curious about what you were eating, and between mouthfuls you looked about you at real African savages, clothed in beads and blankets, and peering in through the doorway ; and beyond them to the palms or flat-topped Japanesy thorn trees etched black against the bright tropic moon. You had paw-paws for dessert, and perhaps a grenadilla or a custard apple, and you could buy more outside—if there were time left—picturesquely spread out on mats by a still more picturesque black tribesman. The train was never in a hurry in those days ; it whistled impatiently once or twice as a matter of form, and the un-initiated swallowed their coffee in agonised haste, but the train always waited. And then, when every one was safely aboard, and after many whistlings and snortings, and delighted yells from the onlookers, it would get under way again and steam off, shedding a trail of sparks and red-hot embers through the silvery night.

Those were the days of Romance with a big R, when the *Man-eaters of Tsavo* seemed recent history and even a train journey held the elements of adventure. The present restau-rant car saved time, of course, but there was nothing about it that was essentially different from any other restaurant car, except that the food was possibly a little worse. Also, it meant that you arrived at Nairobi inconveniently early next morning.

At sunrise the Athi Plains were covered with herds of zebra and wildebeest, and I alternately watched them, longing for the train to stop there in their midst, and impatiently looked at the time. We were nearing Nairobi and I was almost dancing with excitement. Would it be changed ? How soon should I be off on my trip ? Should I find any of our old boys ?[1] These unanswered questions kept racing through my mind. The train at last pulled in ; I let down the window and put my head out to call a porter.

And then, before I had quite taken in what was happening, twenty porters hurled themselves at the window shouting frantic greetings ; and I recognised Bokari, Jim, Asani, Mwanguno, and most of the old lot with their enchanting ugly black faces grinning in welcome from ear to ear. It was

[1] It will be understood that the word " boy " refers to native porter or servant, and it will not, therefore, be written with inverted commas.

over four years since I had seen them (when my father and I had gone on a two-year collecting trip in Kenya, Uganda and the Congo), and I could scarcely believe my eyes. It was touching enough that they should have remembered me—they had probably heard of my intended return from the Game Department—and the surprise of this welcome drove every word of Swahili out of my head.

I was standing in the midst of this excited gathering, shaking hands all round and saying Hurray ! and Jumbo ! indiscriminately, when one of the Government House A.D.C.s came up and, introducing himself, informed me (a little ironically, I thought) that he had come to meet me. I thanked him and felt suddenly like a small child caught scrapping with the village urchins.

As my boys swiftly piled the luggage into the car, I tried to explain about their being our old porters, and wasn't it splendid of them to meet the train ? Splendid or not, it left him cold, and he was probably thinking that had he only known how much I was going to be met, he need not have bothered to come to this horribly early train himself. He presently forgave me, however, and we were soon speeding through long avenues of blue gums—Nairobi's greatest (and perhaps only) beauty—which led up out of the town, past deep-verandahed bungalows, and gardens still wet with dew in the early sunshine.

After the heat of the Red Sea, the cramped quarters of the ship, and the grit and stickiness of the long train journey, the cool twilit spaciousness of Government House was like a dream. Governors' staffs may grow indifferent through long familiarity with Government houses, but I was only a visitor and the glamour always outlasted the visit. Against the torrid sky and the smell of dust, the tall white pillars with shadows of pure cobalt had a freshness that was almost alpine ; and in a country where grass is nearly always brown, the soft deeply green turf of the courtyard had something of the dreamy delight of Omar Khayyám. This feeling of unreality pleasantly pursued me every time I went up and down that which hardly exists anywhere else in the East—the wide European staircase. There was also the mediæval thrill of having luncheon (or even breakfast) with Their Majesties looking graciously down from their long gilt frames at either end of the room ; and beyond the cool shadows of the awning you had a glimpse of red cannas flaming in the glare of noonday. How much more poetical than butler and footmen were the velvet-footed Somalis, gorgeous in scarlet and gold ; and what a heroic climax to a dinner-party, when the port had gone round, and every one stood up for the solemn toast : The King.

The days sped by quickly enough, and the only thing that troubled me was my trip. It was England over again. Here I was, on the threshold and all ready to start off, and still no one could be made to look at it seriously. Whenever I mentioned it they laughed good-naturedly, and suggested a game of tennis or a ride on the Athi Plains, as though I were obsessed by an unfortunate idea that might be worked off by good hard exercise. What delayed matters most was the absence on safari of the head Game Warden. As soon as he returned I rushed round to see him. He was an old friend and I felt sure that he would help me. I wanted his permission to go into the Southern Masai Game Reserve down towards the Tanganyika border, for I had been told that it was by far the best place left, and full of game. Its special advantage was that it was unspoilt, for no shooting parties were allowed in. This much sought-after permission had already been refused even to photographers.

" And how do I know," demanded the Game Warden, turning on me, " that you won't shoot something in so-called self-defence ? Photographers are often the worst offenders."

I assured him that it would not happen.

" Besides," I went on, to strengthen my argument, " my whole idea is to make friends with the game."

" What ? " he almost shouted. " Make friends with the game ; go up and pat an . . . Tcha ! Preposterous ! They'll never let you go on such a fool's errand."

I tried to mend matters.

" Oh, well," I said soothingly, " not exactly make friends, you know ; it's just an attitude of mind ; don't want to shoot them, and all that."

Like all people who really know something about wild animals, he saw red over these childish theories. But he gave the permission and signed on the porters I needed ; and his parting words were : " If you're really going, come to lunch and we'll map out your trip."

I returned to Government House elated beyond measure, and the first person I ran into was the Private Secretary.

" All that means nothing," he assured me with undisguised relish, " and personally I shall do everything I can to dissuade the Governor from allowing you to go."

" In that case I might as well take the next ship home," I replied, gratifyingly crestfallen. I began to realise that to collect a handful of porters and go off on my own into the wilds was not going to be as easy as I had anticipated. It had happened to me before, through force of circumstance, that I had found myself alone in the middle of Africa ; and having done it once, I never imagined that I might find difficulties about starting out to do it again.

The staff now painstakingly explained to me the other point of view : that if anything happened to me it would be a dreadful nuisance, and all the wrong people would be sure to be blamed.

Argument was cut short, for it was time to dress for dinner. I went thoughtfully upstairs, and the first thing my eye fell upon was the barricade, imposing as the Great Wall of China, built up of neatly arranged chop-boxes, kit-bags, cameras and impedimenta that ran the width of my room. Every day I had scoured the town and the Indian bazaar for stores and lanterns, rope, knives, water-bottles, pots and pans, and all the exciting and indispensable things requisite for safari, and now everything was complete down to the last detail. The word to start might have been given at that moment, the loads could not have been made more ready.

By the time the gong went I had decided upon my plan of action. I would risk all on a single throw that evening. One must take the bull by the horns, I thought, mentally screwing myself up to the hazardous task. Anything, even a good plain No, would be better than this unbearable uncertainty. I felt that my only chance lay in talking to the Governor before my self-avowed antagonist the Private Secretary had a chance of doing so first.

A splendid opportunity presented itself later in the evening, and I jumped at it quickly. Everything hung on the next five minutes, and it was so desperately important that my throat went dry with anxiety and my mind was a sudden blank. Having taken the plunge, however, my stage fright left me. I felt almost impersonal about it, as though it were some one else's and not my own fate that was at stake. I was careful not to plead, and said little : merely how sorry I was to have caused so much bother, and that I was, of course, ready to give up the trip at once and return quietly to Europe.

His Excellency thought that that would be a great pity, and said, sympathetically, that he was sure that something could be arranged. Couldn't I take a white hunter, or join forces with another expedition ? No ? Well, anyway, it was not so serious as all that, and I was not to worry.

I glowed with gratitude ; and to make quite sure that the Private Secretary could not observe any fresh signs of elation,

I slipped up early to my room. Jim (my personal boy) was arranging the mosquito net when I opened the door, and on his way out he paused to ask, for perhaps the fiftieth time, that awkward and dreaded question :

" When are we going on safari, Memsahib ? "

This time I was looking forward to his question, for I could answer with something like truth :

" Probably the day after to-morrow ! "

After that, the battle was unaccountably won. Every one was helpful where before they had looked for spokes, and even the Private Secretary, considering everything, was remarkably gracious. I asked him, then, why he had tried to prevent my going.

" Oh, partly jealousy, I suppose," he answered lightly. " You see, I'd give anything to have your opportunity."

But no one could have made more generous amends, and the best friendships often begin unexpectedly and inauspiciously. He not only remembered to send me parcels of books, but surprise hampers would also arrive, out of which, in the midst of the thirsty desert, fresh fruit and vegetables, eggs and butter miraculously appeared.

And he did far more than this, for when, five months later, I returned from the Masai Game Reserve, he arranged for me the expedition that had always lain nearest my heart—the climb up Mount Kenya, of which I am going to tell later.

I had never remotely considered the possibility of this second trip, and when I set out for the plains I did not dream of the two months in an alpine hut high up on Kenya that were in store for me. It was well that I did not know, for knowing had made me impatient of the road ; and looking back over these two adventures, so different in setting, I cannot say that one was better than the other. Rather was one the fulfilment of the other ; the break was in the setting : and although the one was concerned almost entirely with elephants, and the other with mountains, the same unity of purpose ran through them, binding them together and leading them up to the final conclusion.

Now that the main issue was settled, I had only to choose where I should go. I telephoned to the Game Warden to ask if the luncheon invitation still held good.

" Come round to the office at once," was the answer. " Denys is here now, and no one can give you better advice about the Tanganyika border than he."

I dropped the receiver, jumped into a car (visitors, like the sleuths in the films, are always privileged in the matter of cars) and tore round to the Game Department.

Almost the best part of any trip is planning it out on paper and poring over maps. The maps were already spread out over the office table when I arrived, and both men were bending over them in attitudes of deepest absorption. It might be I who was going to carry out those plans, but they were at least going to have the fun of drawing them up. Time was no object. That gave them unusual scope, for most hunting parties wanted to cover as many miles of Africa in as short a time as was humanly possible. We were now in the middle of June, the rains would probably not start till well on in November, which gave them five whole months to dispose of as they wished. This grand slice of time appealed to them immensely, for the trouble is that scarcely any one can afford to spend five months sitting down in the wilds waiting for things to happen ; yet in any form of nature study (and especially photography), time is the one indispensable element.

The Game Warden said that I must start off with three weeks or so at Selengai, a water-hole about thirty miles from Kiu (down the line halfway to Mombasa), and he drew me a plan of it. Denys cut in with :

" What about Magadi ? She can't miss out that. Not

much game, but that soda lake is worth seeing—amazing colour effects." So they agreed between them to combine Selengai and Magadi, scoring in an extravagant zigzag across the map.

I reminded them as tactfully as I could that although time was no object money unfortunately was, and as the Masai tribe never have and never will carry loads, my only means of transport was to be an Indian lorry, which, next to the Imperial Airways, must be the most expensive form of travel ever devised. They brushed the argument aside as too trivial for consideration and took me firmly in hand.

" Now after Magadi," they continued—" here it is, only thirty miles from Kajiado, which is only sixty miles from Selengai, which is only about thirty miles from Kiu—after Magadi you will strike back south-east (another zig, I noted) to Ol Doinyo Orok, which is the Masai for black mountain. You ought to find elephant, and might do well to camp there for some weeks. Then across to Ambuseli—dry salt lake and favourite place for all kinds of game—then on to El Kinunet and up to Laitokitok on the slopes of Kilimanjaro. From there you can make your way down to the Rombo country and the head waters of the Tsavo. Here there is no road and you'll have to use porters (we can fix that up when the time comes). Then work down the Tsavo river—grand game country and still full of lions—till you reach Lake Chala. Curious place that : a crater lake, and the natives swear there's a monster in it, and a tree near by that drips water. Incidentally, one of the finest places in the country for birds. When you've had enough, you can march to Taveta and come back by rail to Nairobi."

I resented this tame ending.

" If I get as far as the slopes of Kilimanjaro," said I, asserting myself for the first time, " I shall try very hard to climb to the top before I book my ticket."

To this day (I must confess it at once) Lake Chala is only a mysterious name to me, Magadi shimmering in prismatic hues, only hearsay, and I have not climbed Kilimanjaro nor even reached its foothills. Other things happened instead. There were the man-eaters of Kidongoi, then the breakdown of the lorry; but more than all else there were the elephants of Namanga. There I had a unique chance to study elephants at close quarters, and though I admittedly never quite came to within patting range, it was a study so fascinating that I made my home among them until the rains drove me away.

At last the great day arrived. It happened that the Governor was moving down to Mombasa, and the staff went ahead to make preparations. I travelled down with them as far as Kiu. It was a pleasant journey and I felt sad at saying good-bye, even to the Private Secretary, who had at the last minute thrust into my hands a copy of Kinglake's *Eothen* (and was, as usual, as gruff as an old bear when I tried to thank him). By the time we reached Kiu, the red had died out of the sky and night swooped down over the great rolling plains. My kit was turned out onto the platform, and my six boys stood shivering beside it in the wind that invariably howls round all African sidings. The Indian station-master came up swinging a hurricane lantern. My friends gave him special injunctions that he was to look after me, and the train moved slowly out. They waved good-bye, and their last words were (inevitably):

"Take care of yourself and don't go patting too many strange lions and elephants!"—and next moment the train with its lights and big friendly noises was swallowed up in the darkness.

Kiu immediately became a black desert given over to the howling wind, howling native curs and the howling of the station-master's snivelling, yellow-coloured brats. I was to camp in the waiting-room for the night. It was draughty and dismal, with a creaking floor and a window that looked out on the station-master's backyard. Natives yelled raucously (and it seemed to me unnecessarily) to one another across the line, Jim began gloomily to unpack, and even the cook was depressed by the general state of things which I had made rather worse by temporarily mislaying the keys to all the chop-boxes. As for me, free at last, and (to adapt R. L. S.) :

> With the jolly heaven above
> And the road before me ;

there was no use denying it, my elation had vanished like a pricked bubble. Kiu of all places was never destined for the opening scene of a great adventure. I had longed and planned and counted the hours, and now I was fairly started I felt suddenly homesick and, ridiculous though it may sound, miserably lonely. Perhaps, after all, they had all been right and it was a fool's errand indeed.

I could afford to admit my folly and indulge in a little homesickness, for at the back of my mind I knew quite well that everything would be all right once I had shaken off the dust of Kiu and escaped from the sound of the high-pitched voices of too many Indians. I should not attempt to begin my diary to-night, it would not have the right ring ; and I turned in early. Except for the roaring and clanking of the passing goods trains, which sent a momentary barred light across the ceiling, nothing wakened me till sunrise, when even the backyard, with its heap of scrap-iron and garbage, looked almost lovely in the golden light ; and I was up quickly, eager to be gone.

But the promised lorry (ordered by letter in advance) had broken down. Indeed, she looked almost derelict, with a hole in her radiator the size of a soup-plate. The driver assured me she would be as right as a trivet in a month's time.

A month at Kiu! I suppressed a shudder and ran to every store in turn, till I finally discovered the owner of a box Ford. It would take two journeys to bring all the boys and equipment to Selengai, and the price, after prolonged bargaining, was £35. Outrageous, of course, but there was no alternative, and escape from Kiu seemed desirable on almost any terms ; so after a delay of not more than three hours (which, for the East, was looking lively) we started. It was a momentous journey over a practically non-existent track, charging madly down stream-beds, leaping holes and dodging round trees ; and it was well into the afternoon by the time we made the thirty-odd miles to Selengai. The driver was a man of his word, and without waiting for a rest or food he went back at once for the second load.

Thirty miles had done wonders to transform the landscape, and had brought me out of the illimitable bare wind-swept plains of Kiu ; and although it was still the country of plains, they were now softened by undulating thorn scrub and distant hills. At Selengai, the broad, dry river-bed forked round an island of elm-like trees near which was the water-hole and a tiny trickle over the dazzling white sand. I crossed over, and walking a furlong into the bush, I hunted for a site for camp. It was going to be my permanent camp for some time, and the choice of a site was therefore important. I found it, at last, where there was a wide, flat-topped thorn tree to shade the tent, and in front (facing south-east) the ground sloped gently down to an open glade. Beyond it, the trees by the river gracefully framed the distance, and at my back was rising ground sparsely wooded.

The boys set about cutting the grass and levelling the ground ; and when all was ready to give the word and they pulled on the ropes, the tent like a sail unfurled went up with a glad flapping of canvas, and my heart bounded for joy.

At last the dream had come true, and at sunset I slipped off over the rise to taste the reality in the immensity of the silence. Around me the plains ran out to the far mountains melting into the night, and above all, like an invisible presence, Kilimanjaro drew a faint gleam of snow under the first stars.

When I came back, the driver, who had by then arrived with the second load, was waiting to know when I wanted the lorry ordered from Kajiado. In the exuberance of the moment, I told him that I should not want it for at least a month; and as the tail-light vanished into the darkness I watched my last link with civilisation irrevocably snap.

My first camp fire was leaping up under the roof of the thorn tree, and out of the stillness beyond came the thousand-fold song of crickets. These things combined to touch a half-forgotten chord, to waken a response long dormant, and I felt suddenly happy, as if after years of wandering I had come home.

Chapter II

SELENGAI AND FEVER

AGAIN and again it called me. One note liquid as a bell repeated three times. It was the song of the hoopoe, and because it is so easy to remember, it brings back an African morning almost more than any other sound can do. After leaving Africa I had heard it again in Teneriffe, and had responded with an agony of longing; and then in the south of France it had called : " Come back a-gain, come back a-gain " with an insistence which I could only obey.

Now I *was* back, and his song, falling into my sleepy consciousness like pebbles dropped one by one into a pool, held fulfilment instead of an aching and incommunicable regret. I spun out the deep content of this first awakening under canvas, and lay listening to the doves crooning on and on with voices sweet and rough as the texture of honey. Presently I became conscious of the boys' droning talk somewhere far away, and the crackling logs. I opened my eyes to a fairyland of green. The early sun pierced the walls and the roof of the tent so that they shone with a luminous green light, across which the branches sent swaying patterns. My tree was the home of a colony of little birds, whose twitterings and flutterings were all about me as I sat up in bed and looked through the sharp eaves of the tent to the sun-filled glade shining with dew, and the flat-topped thorn trees green as enamel against the flawless blue sky. A wisp of smoke curled slowly upwards from my fire of over-night, softening the almost crude intensity of colour beyond; and as I jumped up and ran to the door I sniffed again the familiar, half-forgotten smell of dew and wood-smoke.

Month after month you may see morning come over the veld, yet its new-born freshness and beauty are things which you can never become wholly used to. You know what it will be like, yet every morning brings a new thrill of surprise and wonder.

Everything seemed full of surprise on that first day when anticipation and reality met at last ; and it was not only the big things, but the little details which I had forgotten that were so good to find again : things like having breakfast under the tree with cicadas shrilling through the stillness, and how good porridge tasted out of doors ; and never having to go indoors again, for even in my bath I could look up through the crack (where the bathroom joined on to the tent) and see the trees close above ; and in bed I could put out my hand and feel the earth warm and somehow inexplicably friendly beside the ground-sheet.

As I finished breakfast I saw a string of natives filing through the grass up the glade, led by a tall warrior-like figure holding a spear in his right hand and clothed in a flowing red blanket. After an impressive interval, Jim escorted him to me, introducing him as the Chief of Selengai, who had come with some of his followers to give me greeting. He was very friendly (luckily he understood a little Swahili, as at that time I had no Masai interpreter) and he had come laden with presents in true Eastern fashion. With a wave of the hand he ordered his subjects to set down the gourds of milk, adding a live chicken, and some eggs wrapped in banana leaves. The last and greatest of these offerings now struggled to escape his captors, and was nothing less than a young ram, black as ebony.

All this was most unexpected, for I had been told that the Masai were averse to supplying strangers with meat from their flocks, and the whole problem of a safari into the Game Reserve (where I was pledged to shoot nothing) was how to supply the boys with meat. I was completely at a loss to account for this welcome, when the Chief himself let me into the secret by saying that he had heard of my coming from Bwana Decki (the Chief Native Commissioner, and evidently much beloved), and that for any one recommended by Bwana Decki he was ready to throw wide the gates of his kingdom. The proper counter to this would have been an offering of silver, or a new hunting knife, or a couple of gaudy blankets and a plug or two of tobacco. But I had been much warned against giving presents of money, and told that even presents in kind were to be given only at parting, so that in the matter of gracious retaliation my hands were tied.[1] I racked my brain for some kind of return, and hit upon the expedient of offering to doctor any of his people who were ill during my stay at Selengai. He went off obviously pleased with the bargain, and I little suspected at the time that it would end by my having to turn the camp into a sort of field-hospital.

Although this was the first morning in the wilds and I was eager to explore the lie of the land, I had by now lost the cool hours and I decided to unpack and settle in comfortably.

This unpacking was not lightly to be passed over; it held the thrill of First Night after many rehearsals, for now all the things planned and chosen on dark foggy days in London came into their own. Blue and white plates and cups came out of their straw to reflect the African sky, and table-cloths had a starched freshness never to be regained in after days. Leather was yellow and untried, and even the theoretically useful objects soon to be discarded as useless clutter enjoyed short-lived honour with the rest. Later on, things would

[1] Since reading Thomson's *Through Masai Land,* where (in the year 1883) he was plundered of nearly all he possessed, I understood why the Government had made these rules for the protection of travellers.

become precious because they were battered through hard service in exciting places. There was, for instance, the old blue enamel teapot (dating from our safari in 1923) which I would not have exchanged for a piece from the Ming dynasty. The sight of its cheerful blue colour and steaming spout had put heart into us on many a long march and thirsty hunt from the Lorian Swamp to the Congo.

The bookcase was new and my own invention, and with all the inventor's pride I set it up and found (incredibly enough) that it worked. Its sliding lid fitted into a grooved batten at the back (like a photograph frame) so that however uneven the ground it stood firmly ; and its three rows of books were, to my mind, the making of the tent. The gramophone and records had venesta boxes lined with velt and, like the books, needed no unpacking.

Bringing music into the wilds was an experiment. It had seemed to me that out there music was the only thing one really missed. When I sat night after night alone over the camp fire, looking up from the living flames to the millions of stars shining stilly overhead, I was ever crushed by the sense of my own littleness, and struggled with miserable dumbness to express something in the consciousness that transcends mere words. On the wings of music it at last seemed possible to fly up across the silence and embrace eternity.

That evening, after a long debate over what it was to be, I chose Beethoven's Archduke trio in D minor. Played out there in the African night, the effect was extraordinary : that most beautiful of slow movements flowing out against a background of forest sounds, crickets, night birds, and the distant moaning of lions.

Next morning, I stole down to the water-hole through the dew, as the full moon set red as a melon behind the trees. Dawn was awaking, and in the half-light I made out the shadowy forms of some wildebeest drinking. It was too dark to photograph them, and I passed them by and followed the bank of the river. I had gone about a mile when I looked across to a lovely bend where the trees came down to the water's edge, and at that moment the sun rose and threw his level rays over a herd of impala feeding among the tree-trunks.

For a long time I sat and watched them as they picked their way through the flashing dew-drops, now feeding, now pausing to look round or to lick a golden flank ; and the two rams bent their heads to nibble the grass, so that the dark curve and points of their horns were drawn crisp against the pale stalks. All at once they rallied together startled, and the rams stamped their hooves and snorted in alarm ; and then discovering that it was only a monkey in a branch overhead, they placidly resumed their feeding ; and I had no shadow of doubt that the monkey was acting as sentry for them.

Mohamed, a Government askari (soldier), and Asani (who carried the cameras) had meanwhile sighted a large herd of wildebeest, and we stalked them unsuccessfully for miles over the bare plain. They are at all times difficult to approach, and now that they knew we were there nothing could allay their suspicions. At last, determined to be rid of us, they swished their tails over their backs (with that circular rhythmic action peculiar to wildebeest) and galloped over the skyline.

I stood up from my hiding-place behind a tuft of grass, and started back towards the river. The gladness of early morning was upon the world, bathing it in golden transparency. Plains, hills, trees and the rippling sere-grass were swimming in light, and far away the snow cap of Kilimanjaro shone in the blue sky, the only cloud in heaven.

Five ostriches lured me to a fresh stalk ; but they are wary birds, and if they cannot smell they have eyesight that more than makes up for it. I then came upon a herd of zebra, and creeping up to them with immense care I hoped to redeem the morning's failures. The wind blew true from them to me, and I had narrowed the distance between us to nearly twenty yards when, without warning, the whole herd stampeded. They streamed past me, and among the last was a very small foal. His stripes were only vaguely defined on his woolly coat, and he was closely followed by his mother who urged him forward and pushed him gently along with her muzzle.

When the thunder of their hooves had died away, I heard a Masai whistling shrilly through his teeth, and at the river I found him watering his cattle. It was he who had alarmed the zebra, and many a successful stalk was spoilt in this way, for the country was full of Masai herding their cattle. They have a very ingenious way of watering them, and instead of allowing the herds to come down to a pool where the first comers would foul it for the others, they build a long mud trough against the bank a foot or more above the ground, and run the water through it, so that all may drink clean water at once.

When I reached camp again I set the boys to making a "hide" in the river-bed below, and I spent the afternoon in it waiting for something to come down to drink. I lay concealed under a tunnel of branches at the edge of a shallow pool which still trickled from the water-hole, and while waiting for larger game I passed the time happily enough watching the birds.

The field-glasses used at a few yards range opened up an undreamed-of world of colour, enlarging the little pools in the sand to opal lakes that reflected the reeds like wands of emerald, and revealing the tiny birds (drab to common sight) to be most delicately marked, with beaks and eye-rings of bright orange. They and the sand-pipers were there always, and as evening approached they were joined by guinea-fowl, partridges, kivities and other birds who were so thirsty after the hot day that they drank within arm's length of me. Two Egyptian geese wading in the distance sent wide ripples across the sunset water, marabou storks walked meditatively along the bank, and the pearl-breasted doves flew down in pairs to drink. There was no sound but of the birds themselves. In a branch opposite, a little grey bird spread its wings for its mate; and with rapturous song they flew away above the tree-tops.

The heat and burden of the day was over, and through the stillness and the ineffably soft colours came the blessing of the day's end with all-embracing and universal love. It took me in so that I was no longer alone, and I understood in that moment how all things lived and breathed through its inspiration.

As dusk fell I crawled out of my ambush, and then I saw why it was that every animal had carefully avoided drinking near it, for silhouetted on the top of an ant-hill not a stone's throw away sat that wretch Mohamed, mounting guard.

Mohamed, from the start, had been a thorn in the flesh. I had never wanted him, and I hated the big elephant gun he carried on his shoulder whenever he clattered after me through the bush in his hobnail boots. But it was Government orders that he was to look after me, a task which he must have found equally uncongenial, for I often made it very difficult for him. I looked upon the rifle with particular loathing, for the whole point of this expedition was to go unarmed. A rifle in case of accidents, spoilt everything.[1] The authorities, however, could hardly be expected to see it in this light. They had laughed at me good-humouredly and told me not to be ridiculous. Either I bowed to the conditions, or the trip was cancelled.

As time went on, I could not help admitting, in spite of prejudice, that Mohamed was a lovable character with a quite extraordinary loyalty to his sense of duty. But he carried it

[1] I kept my little .318 loaded by my bed, but it never left the tent.

27

to extremes. His motto out hunting was to shadow me, which was trying enough, but when it came to giving me away to all the game of the district while I endured agonies of discomfort from mosquitoes and my cramped position in the hide, I protested in good earnest. Argument proved futile and undignified, for he always had his answer pat:

"The Bwana Governor said so"—which was irrefutable, and he was not to be browbeaten.

He was small and slight, with little wrists and the obstinacy of a woman. Although he called himself a Nubian he had not the Nubian's very dark skin or thick lips, but finely cut features that suggested Somali or Arab. The most striking thing about him (for it is rare with a native) was his moustache, a thin wisp that drooped sadly at the ends. Taken with his almond eyes, it gave him a rather Chinese look. His expression was sad and a trifle wistful, his appearance always excessively neat, for he wore with pride the khaki shorts and dark blue jersey and puttees of the King's African Rifles, with whom he had served for nearly twenty years. On his head was the hottest-looking brown Balaclava helmet (which I never saw him take off) and at the end of his spindle shanks the largest, clumsiest and noisiest pair of boots in the Army. I often caught myself thinking what a dreadful old maid he was, yet at times he could be extraordinarily disarming. He was either maddening or pathetic, and actuated, in either case, by loyalty to duty (however unpleasant) rather than any inborn love of adventure.

He was always quietly and efficiently at his post, and his duties began at six-thirty a.m., or before sunrise if I were going farther afield, when I would take a wide beat over the country on either side of the river. I generally came back at about ten for breakfast, after which I read or wrote or doctored the Masai till luncheon at one o'clock. Between the hours of ten-thirty and four photography is at a standstill; for pictures taken

between these times are never very satisfactory, partly because
so near the Equator there are no shadows except early and late.
I started out again at three o'clock, and either hid near a
favourite drinking-place or hunted until sunset.

Though mostly arid bush or bleached grassy plains, it was
lovely country (because, perhaps, it smelt and looked as I had
remembered it), and following down the river-bed, which
wound between low red cliffs, or cutting through belts of
acacia forest, and creeping about looking for game held an
ever growing fascination.

But photography, I found, was much more difficult than
shooting. An impala ram, with a pair of splendid curving
horns glimpsed through the bushes, would have given a perfect
shot but was quite impossible to photograph ; and after looking
in vain while the sun was shining, I would come upon herds of
zebra or wildebeest at dusk when it was too late. Then again,
the game was approachable only up-wind, which ruled out
any choice of lighting. Often sun and wind were in the same
quarter so that the sun shone directly on the lens. Sometimes
wind and lighting were exactly right, and you crept up at last
really close to your subject, to find that a bush partly obscured
it, or the grass was too high. A good picture could be spoilt
by a single grass-stalk waving across it unnoticed a few feet
from the camera.

On the whole, this month at Selengai was a failure. It ought
to have been the most productive part of the trip, for during
the dry season there is no other water in the vicinity. But the
rains had been unusually heavy, so that during my first fortnight there, the river still trickled over the sand from pool to
pool for several miles above and below camp. This meant
that the game was scattered, and it was a question of luck
whether, with so many pools to choose from, anything would
pick out the one where I was waiting. Day by day I watched
the trickle which fed this long chain of pools gradually dwindle

away till it left only a damp stain on the sand, and every day I noticed new herds of zebra and wildebeest drawing in towards Selengai. But just as conditions were nearing perfection, something happened which finally dashed my hopes. The drought brought vast herds of cattle. Over the plains they came lowing in slow-moving processions under a canopy of red dust. They came in from the east and from the south, even from as far away as the foot of Kilimanjaro, driven forward by their shouting and whistling owners, for the lesser water-holes had already dried up. Their coming disturbed the game, which grew so restless and wary that it became impossible to approach.

Curiously enough (with such opportunities for meat) there were very few lions, and none ever came near the camp; though hyenas howled round nightly and were unusually fearless.

One night I was woken up by a rattle of tins close to my ear and a sharp scuffle of claws inside the tent. I sat up and with trembling fingers lit the lantern, but nothing further happened and I fell asleep again. When I came in for breakfast next morning, after a prowl with the camera, Jim asked me what I had done with the milk. I said that I had not seen it, and told him of my night's adventure, whereupon he at once jumped to the conclusion that the hyena had stolen the milk. I thought it quite possible, but pointed out that no hyena could have walked away with the saucepan. But this was exactly what he had done. Mwanguno, who had gone to gather firewood, found the saucepan some way above the camp. It was sitting upright on the plain with its lid well jammed down, and the milk all intact inside it.

He came up with it, followed by the whole camp, to show me the sharp dents made in its side by the hyena's teeth. I laughingly pointed at Mwanguno's own teeth which were every bit as sharp, for he was a Wa-kamba and his teeth were filed to points like a saw. The boys seized on the inference with glee, and pretended to compare the dents in the saucepan with Mwanguno's fierce canines. Mwanguno enjoyed the joke as much as any one, for none took a chaffing better than he. He always had more than his share, but he could afford it, for he was a great character. Even when I signed him on, the Game Warden looked at him with an affectionate twinkle, and exclaimed :

" Hullo, here's that old devil Mwanguno again ! "—a sally which brought the house down. That was just it. He *was* an old devil, bone lazy and always grumbling, and yet you could not help being fond of him. He had absolutely no *raison d'être* on the present trip (he had been our chief skinner before) but he had come to the station to meet me with the rest, and the sight of him had called up old times. It was just sentiment, of course, but I had to take him on again. Had he looked different I might have reconsidered it ; but he still wore the same dirty white round hat (which looked like the lace paper put under cakes), and his dirty baggy white calico trousers, which had always vaguely reminded me of Israel Hands, still came only halfway down his ridiculous bow-legs.

His face is more difficult to describe, for he had two, like Jekyll and Hyde. When he was particularly annoying, his receding forehead, flat dilated nostrils and too long upper lip made him look like a surly ape. His arms seemed to hang down below his knees and his legs to become more than ever misshapen. And there were other times when you forgot all this and were suddenly struck by the beauty of his expression. He had a finely cut, sensitive mouth, and the dilated nostrils lent to his face a suggestion of suffering. He was an old man (though you can never tell how old a native is, since he does not know himself), and his eyes were sunken. For all that, they were very much alive, and could look anything you chose to read into them : intelligent, kindly, humorous, or sad. That funny round hat may have had something to do with it, but there were times when he looked as fine as one of the old Doges.

He had, of course, two distinct characters to match. When there was nothing to grumble at he grumbled with all his might, so that you expected he would raise a mutiny. But it was when things went seriously wrong that he proved the devotion which lay hidden somewhere under all that uncouth grumpiness. Then he would work uncomplainingly until he dropped. I could never forget how, when my father died from a lion's mauling, Mwanguno had slaved with me over that lion skin ; nor, later on, with what conscientiousness he had looked after the white rhino's hide. He was never one to give a word of praise. Even the bongo (secured after seven weeks of hard hunting) failed to thrill him as much as we had hoped ; so that when he praised my waterbuck, I never forgot it. It was not the praise (the horns were only an average pair) but the unexpected flash of intuition which prompted it that touched me ; for the waterbuck had been hunted in difficult circumstances, when I was alone on the Congo border and trying to complete my father's collection. After days of heart-breaking hunting I eventually brought back the head and skin, and old Mwanguno carefully counted all the rings on the horns, and declared that the waterbuck was an old beast and *makubwa sana* (very big).

A strong contrast to Mwanguno was my personal boy, Jim, also a Wa-kamba (though his teeth were not filed), and also on our former expedition, when he had been my father's personal boy. He was as silent as Mwanguno was garrulous, and put me in mind of the saying about still pools. No one ever knew his thoughts. Among my six boys he was the only tall one, and because of his slimness and the way he carried himself, you never forgot his height. The second thing that

struck you about him was his high, prominent cheek-bones.
They gave him a gipsy look. He was a perfect servant. His
decorum was as impeccable as his spotless, perfectly ironed
brown kanzu (a robe that fell to his feet) and his red fez. He
kept everything spotlessly clean and tidy ; he quickly learnt
my ways and anticipated my wants. He was even quick to
notice my love of silence. He rarely spoke unless I spoke to
him, and he moved noiselessly, like a panther. In a word, I
could find no fault with him. And yet, beneath the surface
of that perfect deference, I guessed a personality that was
vaguely antagonistic. He glided as silently as a shadow, and
he had a habit of appearing suddenly when I least expected
him. And although he seemed genuinely glad or sorry over
my good or bad days, his presence was as disquieting and
critical as my own conscience.

Jim had found me Karioki—a Wa-kikuyu and an admirable
cook. He could make baker's bread in an iron pot, and was
one of those rare and obliging cooks who never come for
orders or look vague about dinner when the larder is empty.
He had unflagging imagination, and however meagre his
resources he scorned repetition. The cook is (for obvious
reasons) a very important person, for, holding great prestige
among the boys, he can make or mar the expedition. Karioki
certainly made it. He was quick and always cheerful, overwhelmingly honest, and a good influence in the camp.

Fifthly, there was Muthungu (one of the porters on our
former trip) whom I took on again as kitchen-boy. He looked
every inch a scullion. He was small, his clothes were as per-
petually ragged as the professional beggar's, and he was neither
handsome nor clever. But he meant well, and he, too,
belonged to the past. He was a Wa-kamba and his teeth were
filed to such a degree that his amiable grin made you think of
a little Chinese dragon.

Sixth, and last, was Asani (who should have been described

first, for I liked him the best) and he shall have a page to himself in the next chapter.

The boys were still haranguing Mwanguno in front of my tent for biting the saucepan, when a native broke through the throng to say that he could lead me to a herd of giraffe "not very far off." The news thrilled me, for I had seen no giraffe at Selengai, but I mistrusted his allusion to "not very far." In Africa it invariably means two to three hours' brisk walk. It proved even more than that. I set off at one o'clock, the hottest hour of a sweltering hot day, tramped a good eight miles and never clapped eyes on any giraffe. To make matters worse, I lost the way back. I underestimated the détour I had made, and struck northward, when in reality the camp lay a couple of miles south. The guide had gone home long before. At last, by a lucky chance, Asani cut the motor track from Kiu, and we followed it back with all speed to reach camp before nightfall.

As I tramped along, dog-weary through failure (this was only one of many fruitless outings) and cursing the lameness which made walking a sudden torture, I wondered whether I had been wise to come back to all this, or whether I was not just one of the countless fools who try to recapture the past. Glorious though it all was, Selengai was proving a time of bitter probation, a place in mid-desert with past and future both equally beyond my reach. I had given up friends, civilisation, everything, for something that was undefinable. I had found it in the wilds before, indeed it was the initiation of those weeks in the Congo, when I had been quite alone, that had since made the pursuit of all else seem beside the mark ; it was in order to find my way deeper into that initiation that I had returned ; but now, to my anguished bewilderment, I could not find my way back to it.

During that blind search I felt often stranded and lonely to the point when I longed to run away from it all. But I had talked lightly of a five months' trip and, if only for pride's sake, I feared turning back even more than I feared loneliness. Five months is, after all, a trivial length of time ; yet five months alone with one's own thoughts, without a single human being with whom to exchange an idea, can be an eternity unless one can find the means of escape from oneself. Nature and solitude held out this means at every turn (so much more truly than ever civilisation could do, which for escape can offer only a temporary forgetfulness), but the price was a need of the spirit, and great vistas of loneliness that had to be traversed alone. One hankering look backwards lost everything.

And now, as I trudged homeward, the harshness of the day was forgotten under the melting colours of the evening. The tenderness that spread over earth and sky was like a sudden relenting of the indifference that surrounded me ; and as surely as though a hand had been laid upon my shoulder, I was made aware of a protecting watchfulness. To be compelled to plunge through a great deal alone was inevitable, for it is the only way of learning ; but in that moment came the assurance that I should never be left to my own mercy beyond what I could endure.

It was like a rainbow before a blacker storm. Darkness fell, and I was still a long way from camp. At the end of another hour I could scarcely crawl for the pain in my foot, and was near to tears, not so much for the pain, as for the day's utter defeat. At last a light pricked out, I broke through the trees and reached the tent.

But the crowning humiliation came after supper, when Jim said good-night and omitted to ask for orders for the following morning. It had always been tea at five-thirty if clear, breakfast at eight if cloudy. I was dreading the question, but he never asked it. Somehow or other the boys had divined that I was tired and out of spirits, and they were being sorry for me. That was hard to bear, for I had pride in matters of endurance. I had known well enough that I could no longer tackle the long treks, and I had imagined that photography was a game of endless patience and sitting beside water-holes. But in Africa (at any rate in the wilds) you must either sweat out your heart's blood in toil, or you must not go there.

I wished I had not brought the same boys. They saw through my bluff and expected something better. I felt the bitterness of the *prima donna* singing to an indulgent audience that tries to recapture through her faltering notes the beauty of a voice long past its prime. My spirit was eager : lameness and fatigue were as bitter as old age.

I sat by the fire without music, my mind filled with black rebellion. I suddenly hated Selengai with a blind unreasoning hatred that included its miles of dried-up grass full of ticks and despairingly empty of game, and all its desert and thorny places, and especially my own senseless decision to spend a month there.

Early next morning the hoopoe woke me, and stung with the remembrance of overnight I jumped out of bed and called for tea. The sky was golden, the earth velvet with dew, and the trunk of the thorn tree that sheltered me shone red as a larch in the first rays of the sunrise. The glory of it filled me again with joy and lifted me up. My faint-heartedness did not bear thinking of, and I blushed for shame.

I dressed quickly, for I wanted to set the boys to work on a new hide before the sun came into power. I led them to a bend in the river-bed below camp by a favourite drinking-pool, and after quartering over the sand I marked the site by the edge of the reeds.

The sappy green bushes were no good for the purpose, for they withered as soon as they were cut. The intractable thorn scrub was the only thing that could withstand the heat of the sun. It was stubborn to cut and brutal to handle—it took me hours to hew through the smallest branches—and I loved to watch how the boys, armed with their light axes (long, flat blades called pangas) chopped and handled the stuff. When I examined those pangas I found that they had practically no edge to them; in fact, the steel was so blunt and frilly that you could scarce have sawn through a piece of string with it. The boys rarely swung them from the shoulder or put out their full strength; it was a trick of the wrist, and the thorn branches fell like sugar-cane.

While the boys went inland to chop down branches, I cut armfuls of reeds by the water's edge and spread them over the floor of the hide. They were bright green as flags in a meadow and sparkling with dew. All round me the world had gone mad with colour. I had to stop and look at it upside-down to see it as it really was. The long shadows of purest lilac and cobalt fell across the golden sand, and the water was blue as turquoise so that the sky seemed almost green against it. All this, and the joy of work—primitive work like cutting rushes in the early sunshine—and all the birds singing, caught up my spirit on the wings of the morning, and I knew again how good it was to be alive.

I saw a giraffe that same day. A herd of zebra unfortunately gave him the alarm and he was unapproachable. Following down the river-bed, however, I twice came upon him unawares. The second time, I edged up close under cover of a tree between us, but he himself kept it between us to better purpose, and disappeared before I caught another glimpse of him. The last time I saw him he was cantering slowly down the broad avenue of the river-bed with that clumsy grace that seemed so unhurried yet carried him so swiftly into the distance. Then, where the river-bed turned at right angles, he stopped, and after gazing anxiously back he straddled and bent his neck to drink. He kept his eye on me, and as there was no hope of coming nearer, I sat down and watched him through the glasses as he lingered there dappled and dark above the golden sand, taller than the stems of the thorn trees that stood out red in the late sunshine. He straddled to the water again, then gathering himself up, he cantered silently round the bend and out of sight.

When I reached the place, I understood why he had stopped to drink in full view. The river had ceased some way back, and this was the last water-hole. I had followed down splashing my way through the shallow stream, when it abruptly vanished in the sand before my eyes. Even as I reached the spot, the natives up-river must have undammed one of their cattle troughs, for the stream began trickling slowly forward like the flow of the tide. The sand had a rime of white deposit over it, and the water tasted bitter and salt, though it was very good and sweet by the camp.

I was about to turn the bend as the giraffe had done, when I saw seven zebra coming towards me. Signing to the boys, who were some way behind, I slipped quickly into a hollow under the bank. Ambush was never more successful, for the leader passed quite close to me, very tired and thirsty, head drooping, eyes half shut, and languidly whisking his tail against the flies.

I waited for him to come parallel, and as I began to fire off the cinema, he heard it and caught sight of me. He stopped dead, spun round with his heels in the air and tore off at a mad gallop, the sand flying up in a cloud about him. Never have I seen such sudden fearful panic, and I was filled with contrition. Meanwhile, the others looked on at this extra-ordinary display without moving, asking as plain as words what was the matter. I exposed as much film as I wanted, for instead of galloping off, they only trotted a little way and turned round to look at me. I think that they were too thirsty to care. I then sent Asani on a beat inland, so as to come round and drive them in the rear, while I hid, hoping that they might pass me again ; but they were wiser than that, and I climbed out of the river-bed and left them in peace.

It was unwillingly that I gave up and turned for home. From this point I was exploring new country full of possibilities ; nothing is more engrossing than following down a dry river-bed, and I wanted to see round just one more bend before turning back. But as it was, I did not reach camp till after dark. Mohamed led badly, and while I had no difficulty in checking landmarks, he kept looking uncertainly at the river to get our bearings. We had taken to the high ground so as to cut out the loops of the river, and seeing that we were going far out of the straight line I pointed to the trees where I had first seen the giraffe, and striking a right angle I impatiently took the lead myself.

The inspiriting joy of leading lengthened my stride, a cool breeze blew about me, and the crimson banners of the sunset flamed over our heads.

But out of the tail of my eye I saw Mohamed lagging farther and farther in the rear. I thought that he might be nursing a grievance, which he well might, but it was very unlike him. And it was not that, after all, for when at length through the darkness I picked up the light of the camp fires, he divulged to me that he was going down with fever.

I was down with it myself next day, and nobody escaped. The mosquitoes were the fever-carrying *anopheles*; there were billions of them all day as well as all night, and in spite of our nets we had been bitten to death.

And so, for the next few days, the Masai clamoured for medicine in vain, the game drank in peace, and camp was unwontedly quiet.

Fever, like seasickness, is a thing you can never believe in until you fall a victim to it ; and then, while it lasts you feel that nothing can ever be the same again. Even the boys were miserably dispirited. They took their rations of quinine and aspirin, rolled themselves in their blankets, head and all, and lay in the full glare of the sun. For all ills the sun is the infallible doctor.

As for me, I lay in bed alternately shivering and shaking with cold (in spite of four blankets on a tropical day), or I was consumed with fire. My mind floated away independently, now to England or the Alps, but most often back to the summer holidays of my childhood, in Norway. After endless difficulty I found a favourite stretch of water and threw my fly where the current bore it neatly across to a boulder amidstream. The screech of the reel brought me to the surface with a start, always to resolve itself tantalizingly into the sibilant noises of the cicadas beyond the tent. Dimly I pieced together my present surroundings, and became conscious that my head was throbbing with pain. The four notes of the hoopoe now struck into my fevered brain with blows as loud and insistent as a hammer on an anvil. The anvil loomed up monstrously above me and each blow sent a fresh wave of pain surging through my head ; but toss and turn as I would, I could not escape it. Then, for no reason at all, a couplet I had read years ago (in Bret Harte, I think) began to haunt me :

" I sez to Maria, Maria sez I,
    Praise to the face is open disgrace ! "

It began as a perfectly rational statement. Then the cicadas took it up and repeated it in long, insinuating hoarse whispers ; the hoopoe syncopated it peremptorily, the frogs amplified it and tossed it to and fro like a rollicking tune. The doves took it and changed its rhythm, cooing it over and over in a senseless repetition till it became unbearably languorous and supplicating. The cicadas snatched it up again shrilly like three hundred saws rasping to and fro with an insane and nightmare emphasis till they seemed to be sawing deep down into my brain. The speed became terrific. Everything revolved on a huge wheel, sparks flew, and strange shapes ; there were sudden explosions, and queer noises like the squealing and grinding of dredgers, that made me jump with fright. Faster and faster it went. I panted and hurried to keep up, but my feet were far away and clogged with lead. Then I began falling, falling . . . till blessed oblivion closed over me.

Hours later I awoke. The eaves of the tent framed a pale pyramid of sky in which the stars shone faintly. The hoopoe had gone, and a delicious little breeze stirred through the dusk. Everything was normal, tangible and still, and, above all, infinitely quiet. It was over. I felt deeply refreshed and idiotically happy. Only one thing lacked to my content— a long, long drink. And then Jim appeared with a tray, and I caught sight of the blue teapot twinkling in the lantern light.

Chapter III

SELENGAI AND WILDEBEEST

AFTER this reminder of the hidden weapons of the tropics, every one made a quick recovery. I felt bodily as weak as a kitten, and mentally on the crest of the bluest foam-tipped wave. This was the way of fever and an atonement for its black depression.

I began to have some good days. Photography was greatly a matter of chance and of sticking to it long enough, and as time went on I came to know the beats of each individual herd, and where and when to find it.

I spent a whole afternoon close to some impala (of all antelopes the most graceful) and watched three rams leap over a fallen trunk the height of a five-barred gate. The shadows had already gathered, and it was only at the height of their spring that each one was caught for a fleeting second in the sun's last rays so that he shone like burnished gold, and the arc of his horns was thrown back as he sprang into the gloom beyond.

Once and once only did I manage to come near the wildebeest, and that was by a complete fluke.

I had been stalking some zebra who were drinking in the river-bed below me. I crawled very slowly on all fours through the grass, the sun full in my eyes, till I came out on top of a low red cliff. Inch by inch I dragged myself forward till my face was level with the edge and I could look over. At the first glance my heart jumped with excitement. Directly below me were about twenty wildebeest, so close that I could easily have dropped onto their backs. Beyond them, in full sunshine, were the zebra. The setting was as perfect as the heart of any photographer could desire, for the zebra were framed by the overhanging trees, reflected in the water and set off by a bend of the river-bed winding into the background. But the wildebeest stamping in the dust below me had no suspicion of my presence, and for nothing in the world would I risk the metallic click of the cinema. Any one, I thought, could photograph a herd of zebra ; but to come really close to a herd of wildebeest is a rare chance, and I could not waste it.

They were waiting their turn at the water, and standing together ceaselessly tossing their horns and swishing their tails, while the flies buzzed round them in a droning black cloud. The dust hung above them in a red mist against the sun, and their coats shone like silver or molten lead. They were the Kilimanjaro or white-bearded gnus, and their heavy forequarters were outlined by a white fringe of hair running down the throat, and a black mane on the neck. The sickle curve of their horns and their massive shoulders made them look more like little buffalo than like antelopes, and though their hindquarters sloped down and dwindled disproportionately, this was redeemed by their noble black tails sweeping below the hocks with long hair like horses. They grunted and blew, and their flanks heaved with heat and exasperation. In fact they behaved exactly like a herd of domestic cattle on a hot summer's day ; but just because they were wild, they were different and exciting. It was exciting to be close enough to smell them, to hear them breathe, to see them blink their dark and bluish eyes or lick their wet nostrils. They seemed so much more real like that than when I watched them through the field-glasses.

Yet the closer you come to wild animals the greater the feeling of frustration. The stalk is successful, the prize so near ; but whether as a hunter you kill it or as a photographer you take your picture of it, it has eluded you to the end. The trophy is dead, the picture is nothing. I belive that every one who has held the spoor through long hours of alternate hope and despair, be he never so keen a collector, feels before all else as I felt when I lay watching the wildebeest, that the real reward would be to go among them without their minding.

I have always hated circuses. As a child, the smell of bruised turf, dung, dust and grease-paint mingled together in the close twilight of a tent gave me a nasty sick feeling inside. I was sure that the clown joked and laughed with such forced uproariousness to hide a broken heart, and that behind that terribly dumb and patient look in the eyes of performing animals were unimagined depths of hopeless misery. But I was not strongminded enough to refuse to go, and I sat through the performance hugging the hope that at the end I should be taken round to see the animals properly, when I could stroke them. But I never was, except once, when I was allowed to pat the Smallest Horse in the World.

And now it seemed to me that life was like that : one was never taken behind the scenes afterwards. Here was I, in the very front row, almost able to touch those wildebeest ; yet one movement of mine would have made them buck down their heads, swish their long tails round and round over their backs, and stampede in terror. But I wriggled quietly away before they discovered me, and there was a grain of consolation to be drawn from that.

As I walked home, elated yet sorrowful, I thought how curious it is that the people who love animals most are often they that hunt them. There are maddening theorists in the world who will not admit of such a paradox. Yet who knows more of the ways of birds and beasts than the gamekeeper ? Who could write so sympathetically of fish as Izaak Walton, that keenest of fishermen ? And no one who has not followed the spoor of some particular animal for a whole day can quite appreciate how intimately you can come in touch with the mind and personality of that animal. He has left his thoughts traced upon the sand like an open book for you to read : here he trotted, here galloped in fresh alarm ; here he paused to look back, or walked, fed, drank or lay down. And as the hours go by, and again and again from those footprints you visualise the whole beast before you, you are so much of one mind with him that you think yourself into his character. We hunt what we love because we want to possess it. It may not be humane, but at least it is human. And no one who did not primarily love animals would spend his life in studying them, thinking about them, following them. That particular kind of theorist who loves animals so much that he leaves them entirely alone, has never felt the unquenchable craving to get near his subject.

Although it called for all too little of the fascinating art of spooring, I came to realise more and more how much closer in touch with Nature photography brought me than ever hunting had done. This was because I could observe quietly, and was not always on the prowl. The whole essence of the game was to watch animals as closely as possible without disturbing them, and to retreat before they had any idea that one was there. I soon acquired enough guile to elude Mohamed, and when I was back in time I used to slip off by myself at sundown to an ant-hill beyond sight and sound of camp.

One evening I was watching a covey of guinea-fowl scratching in the dust, when I looked up and saw a giraffe coming quietly towards me through the bushes. I held my breath, praying that he might come nearer, but an eddy of air must have brought him the smell of camp, for he changed his mind and moved out of sight.

It was these moments quite alone that really counted. The twilight would merge the thorn trees in flat, grey tones against the sky, grouping them with a quiet serenity that made me think of Corot ; and though the sun had gone, the earth was still warm to touch in the growing darkness. Night came down suddenly, with wings outspread, before I was aware of it, and the stars were lit. Tearing myself away from that immense, friendly silence that was already husky with the song of crickets and the endless rhythmic chorus of the frogs, I crept stealthily back to my tent, where the fire burned up companionably beneath the tree. I picked my way among the ropes (on the side farthest from camp) and slipped into my chair. It became a game to reach it undetected. Often I thought I had won, and then suppressed a jump as Jim quietly emerged from the shadows. If I were very late, I imagined a note of reproach in his voice when he announced that my bath was ready ; but he never gave me away.

One day a native came into camp with the news that there was an elephant positively not far off. I set out at once, though as I followed the guide across the blinding sand of the river-bed I anticipated (not without cause) a repetition of the first giraffe hunt. The sun scorched down from the zenith, the wind was shifty and the spoor already trodden out by the cattle. We wandered aimlessly for hours, when at last Asani picked up the elephant a mile away crossing the open beyond a belt of forest. I seized the camera and tore through the long grass in pursuit. The grass reached to my waist, and the next moment I fell headlong into a hidden ant-bear hole. Mohamed followed suit and, a little farther, Asani also disappeared with the Reflex camera, and our progress was anything but circumspect.

The wind was very uncertain, so that when I had nearly overhauled the elephant (he was still about seventy yards off) Mohamed implored me not to go too close. The elephant went ambling ahead, flapping his ears and now and then throwing up the dust into the air with his trunk, which the boys declared he was doing in order to test the wind. I could not cut him off (he was moving too fast for that and, as it was, we were running to keep up with him) and since I could immortalise nothing but his back view, I finally let him go.

It was Asani who had first spotted the elephant, a mere speck in the grass a mile away and against the sun at that. Although on our former trip he had been only a porter (later promoted to skinner) and now carried my cameras, he was a Wa-kamba, and therefore a born hunter.

From the first I had always liked Asani. He had good manners and was as gentle and willing as old Mwanguno was rough and surly. He was essentially good-natured and without guile—a straightforward, easy character with none of Jim's hidden depths—and if there were any trouble I could count upon Asani for having no finger in it. He was small but intensely wiry and, for all his slimness, I have seen him lift half a tree and throw it on my fire. One of his duties was to replenish my fire at night, which he did with Muthungu to help him. He was a clever spoorer, a first-rate skinner, and nimble in handing me the right camera at the right moment. Like Mwanguno, he wore exactly what he had worn four years ago : a khaki shirt with sleeves cut at the elbow, worn outside khaki trousers in exactly the same ragged state as then ; sandals made from old tyres (not boots, thank Heaven!) and a ragged white Balaclava worn rakishly on one side like a tam-o'-shanter. He had a broad face, wide-apart eyes, a smile unmarred by filed teeth, and when not otherwise occupied he invariably chewed a grass-stalk.

While hunting, we moved in single file—I leading, Mohamed behind me followed by Asani ; and, except for a whispered consultation over some fresh spoor or change of plan, we went as silently as possible. It is often when you least expect it that you come upon game, it generally sees you first, and on the veld the human voice has an uncanny power of travelling. But on the way home the rule of silence was tacitly broken and the boys walked as they pleased.

When I had given up the elephant, therefore, and set my face toward camp, we walked over the plain more or less in line ; and the boys were laughing over our many disappearances underground when we came to a green bush, dome-shaped and as large as a house. On looking at it more closely we found that it was reinforced by thorn branches all round, and hidden behind these was a little door scarce three feet high, stoutly made with interwoven branches and hinges of twisted bark. Feeling like Alice, I knelt down, pushed it open and looked inside. When my eyes grew accustomed to the subdued light, I made out a little room which was obviously meant for a kitchen, for the most important thing in it was a ring of blackened hearthstones.

Mohamed explained that it was used by the Masai in olden times as a secret place for eating meat, but that now the District Commissioner forbade the practice, for these orgies " made them very fierce." But farther on, we discovered another smuggler's den, outside which a whole tree was burning (its roots reaching down in fiery pillars three or four feet deep into the earth) which pointed to there being a few outlaws left.

The Masai look to their flocks and herds for food, drink and clothing, nor did I ever see signs of cultivation round their huts. Once the most warlike tribe, they are still very independent, proud of their warriors and not always easy to manage ; but they seemed to be happy and self-supporting, with few and simple wants. Until a few years ago, money with all its problems had never come into their lives. They did not understand it or want it. The Government soon recognised, however, that enormous resources to the country lay latent in these herds of native cattle (much more immune from the many diseases that wrought havoc among imported stock), and the Masai received all possible stimulus to enterprise and competition.

Dairies and schools under Government supervision sprang up all over the country, opening to them every facility for bettering and increasing their herds, selling their produce and growing rich. But according to his own needs the Masai accounted himself very well off as he was. He had never learnt to wish for the things that money could give him, and he did not see any reason for increasing his cattle beyond his needs. Scientific breeding, hygiene and the methods of modern stock-farming were anathema to him. He could not be roused to the spirit of competition because the vision of power and pleasures that riches could realise for him had as yet struck no root in his imagination. Now the call of progress has dragged him from his simple paradise, and he has learnt to set store by those very things which all our religion and all our philosophy teach us to hold worthless.

The Masai who came to me for medical advice were distinctly of the old order, and I could not help wishing that a few principles of hygiene had come to benefit them. The filth in which they lived was not to be imagined, nor how the flies swarmed upon their wounds. How they ever survived infancy was a miracle to me, for they used to bring tiny babies almost dying of bronchitis and leave them to wait their turn in front of the tent, naked in the cold wind, unwashed, with caked eyes upon which the flies settled in scores unheeded. One baby I took especial interest in was left to the care of a *blind* mother. I bathed him, rubbed his chest with camphorated oil, bandaged him in cotton-wool and wrapped him in a blanket. He was only two months old, and his mother, unable to nurse him, came every day for Horlick's Malted Milk.

The ordinary complaints of the grown-ups could generally be dismissed with quinine or Epsom salts, and for sores and the frequent cases of toe-nails torn out, lysol, iodine and Germolene did wonders. But there were sometimes cases which needed expert care, and then I came up against a difficulty.

I realised this for the first time when a man came to be treated for snake-bite. His finger was septic and enormously swollen (he had already suffered from it for three weeks) and I gave him what first aid I could by soaking the finger in hot water and strong disinfectant for an hour every day, and inserting crystals of permanganate of potash in the wound. At the end of the third day I could bear the responsibility no longer, and told him he must go to the hospital. I believed (quite erroneously) that there was one at Kajiado, sixty miles away, and I arranged with the chief to have him carried there. But the mere mention of the word " hospital " terrified him so thoroughly that he ran away and I never saw him again.

The scourge of flies was, of course, due to the cattle. The Masai never seemed to mind them. On the contrary, they appreciated them for, as one old man explained to me, " where there are flies there are cattle," and they were looked upon as a good omen. Luckily for me I could always escape into my meat-safe of green mosquito netting, an invaluable contraption slung from the ridge-pole, which covered my table and chair. But for this net, life at Selengai would have been nearly intolerable, for the flies swarmed in thousands and it needed all Jim's ingenuity to hand in my food without letting in a cloud of flies at the same time. Once under the net, I could read and write in perfect comfort, and laugh at my tormentors hopefully conning over the meshes for a weak spot.

My library, besides old favourites, consisted mostly of the kind of books that get put off being read for want of time to settle down to them. Out there, amid oceans of silence, there was no reason why I should not delve into history and philosophy, poetry and astronomy to my heart's content. It had seemed a splendid idea in theory, the opportunity of a lifetime ; and Plato and Shakespeare, Plutarch's *Lives* and many other works were all there to hand. But in practice, time was still as precious in the wilds as anywhere else, and I soon discovered that " Nature's mystic book " open round me demanded all, and a great deal more, than my fullest attention. Literature was a relaxation and a change of ideas ; and the first book I turned to was one that had just appeared (I am writing of 1928) which a friend had picked up for me at the Nairobi bookstall : Philip Gibbs's *Day After To-morrow*.

I naturally belonged to the school that rebelled against the cry of progress when it meant linking up the world and making it smaller, and opening up Africa with too many motorcars and aeroplanes. Of course, there was no going back. Progress had to be accepted with a good grace, and one could only move with it. And besides, I was far from being independent of its advantages. I had only to glance round to notice that the lining of my tent was made in China, that my butter came from New Zealand and my fish from Stavanger, my cameras from America and my equipment from many parts of Europe. I was quite content without a wireless, the weekly papers or—up to a point—letters. But the book shook me. Perhaps my desire for tranquillity was not wisdom but merely the stubborn survival of a need no longer felt.

Yet, when next morning I walked through the quiet caressing beauty of the dawn, I felt again that the aims of solitude were justifiable, and that no one coming into contact with the serenity of the spirit could help receiving something precious to take back and give again. But it was finding that contact that was so hard. In my diary I wrote :

To come into harmony needs persevering concentration. It does not wait for you with open arms. You must desire it ardently enough to cut yourself off from all outward support, and give yourself up in love and humility. You must lose yourself in the whole to regain yourself without self-centredness. So long as you look back, you must remain estranged, afraid, poor and angry. But once you desire only this unity, then the protecting harmony wraps you round, and all fear is gone. You are immeasurably strong, free and simplified, not because you are you, but because " Thou art That." Waking or sleeping, you have your whole being in that wonderful universal spirit which I can only describe by the word " love," a love you are made aware of continually, a love so great and abiding that you can pour yourself out in thoughts of love upon the whole world.

Solitude peeled off many outer skins, and I became deeply impressed by all I read. The *Day After To-morrow* disturbed and troubled me. Yet out here, I wrote in fine exaltation, so far away from it all, those unanswerable riddles of the conflict of nations seem almost simple. All that welter of mankind fighting, struggling, backbiting, planning, robbing each for himself and all under a cloud where none can see proportion or perspective because none can step clear of the crowd and see beyond.... From this distance it is like reading the history of some past race, and the solution seems to lie not so much in a new set of rules to meet new conditions, as in some big thought which might come like a thunderbolt to arrest this frightful blind speed, and bring people back again to the idea of charity.

I felt strongly (though impracticably) that if the members of the League of Nations could be transported to the middle of Africa, and were each given twenty square miles of uninhabited bush to himself, with the proviso of not making a speech for a whole month, they would be able to ponder these questions with the proper detachment. It is possible that they might not altogether enjoy it ; and although the Eastern delegates would settle down happily enough to contemplate the Infinite (or their navels), it is conceivable that some of the more highly strung among the Latins might go mad. The measure is perhaps extreme, but I believe that they would all be grateful for a little respite (even if in a modified form) from that ever more powerful slave-driver—Time.

Looking up from my book, I would see the herds of cattle being driven up from the water and browsing through the glade on their way inland to pasture. They were small and humped, mostly black and white or tawny, and some carried magnificently sweeping horns. But I watched them anxiously as they pushed and jostled and bellowed, and the dust rose under their stamping feet, while the herdsmen whistled through their teeth, and the dogs yapped in and out ; for a little partridge had her nest somewhere in the grass they trampled. Every evening on my way home from hunting, I used to pass by that way to see how she was getting on, till she became so tame that she would eat the crumbs I brought her while sitting on the nest. One evening I could not help exclaiming in wonder to find that the nest had still escaped, though the cattle had trampled there all day ; but Mohamed answered, with naïve simplicity :

" For every creature, God is there " (*killa kitu, Mungo iko*).

And one day the four chicks hatched out, and before I left they were big enough to look after themselves.

Although I had looked forward to reaching new country, when the morning came to leave Selengai it was a wrench to go. Leaving the thorn tree that had so long sheltered me was like saying good-bye to a friend. Its trunk was gnarled with age, and when I looked up I could see countless nests like little tufts of hay swaying beneath its shadow. And whether it warded off the heat of noonday or held the Southern Cross like a jewel in the black filigree of its branches, it was always a friendly presence full of wisdom and understanding. Sometimes the moonbeams fell through and played softly among the embers ; the song of crickets and the oft-repeated note of a little owl wove themselves into the silver texture of the silence. Long after camp was still, and the sleepy moon-shine had cast its spell over the glade, I would sit between the roots of the tree and, forgetful of time, drink in the infinite beauty of the night.

When everything was packed up and stowed into the lorry (which after the Ford seemed as splendidly capacious as a pantechnicon) it was already past nine o'clock in the morning, and we wasted further valuable time driving through the herds of cattle that kicked up such a cloud of dust that we were unable to see, and were obliged to pull up to a standstill until it cleared.

And then, just as I thought that we were away, the Selengai huts and Indian store hove in sight, and Karua, the Indian driver, told me he must go in and buy petrol. He might have done this on his way to camp some hours before ; however, it was too late to point this out to him, and I was waiting as philosophically as I was able in the front seat of the lorry already grilling under its tin roof, when a wonderful thing happened. A very bedraggled little Irish terrier pushed her way through the crowd of natives and jumped on the running-board to make friends. To my questions they said that she had belonged to a white man and now to nobody at all, so I just picked her up and took her with me. She had probably had a hard time and seemed quite overcome by this turn of fortune ; as for me, I was overjoyed beyond words, for I had longed for a dog and had tried in vain to find one in Nairobi before I started.

This coincidence was more than I could keep to myself. and impulsively I appealed to Jim. He seemed to take it very much as a matter of course, declaring that "God just gave her !" (*Mungo na nipa, tuh*).

Karua at length reappeared from the dark recesses of the store, mounted into the driver's seat and, once out on the open plateau, he trod manfully on the accelerator till we rattled along the overgrown and scarcely visible track at very fair speed.

It was when we had to cross river-beds that our troubles began. We would crawl down the steep slope, nose first, bracing ourselves so as not to fall through the windscreen, at which critical moment the engine invariably stopped, and the ever faithful John (Karua's A.D.C.) was called out to come and burrow away the sand and crank up. With a jerk the lorry would start off again, this time full steam ahead to get up speed enough to assail the opposite bank. We nearly always *almost* reached the top, but just short of it the lorry would begin to slip, and suddenly give up the ghost in a sickening rush backwards. Karua, in spite of all past experience, had boundless faith, and would never give up till he had made at least three ineffectual charges. Then there was nothing for it but to unload, carry everything to the top and load up again. This took time, for we had to be fitted in like a mosaic : at the back six boys with all the camp equipment, cooking-pots, two live hens, lanterns, ropes, axes, and John with his spare tyres and petrol tins ; in front, myself (next to Karua) with the cameras, records, gramophone, rifles and field-glasses, and the dog on my lap. One thing I never could understand was why the lorry could not be sensibly watered during these forced landings in the river-bed, where there was water to hand. The steam hissed out of her most of the way, but it was not till we had left a river by half a mile that Karua would stop, get out, examine the lorry thoughtfully, and upon a sudden inspiration call John to go back for a tin of water.

In the afternoon, near the end of a glorious hog's back, we had a puncture. I thought this an excellent excuse to get out and have luncheon. But the sun went down upon the mending of that puncture, and in that waterless spot we had perforce to spend the night. It was a fine place, all the same, with a tremendous view, a starry sky, and the Great Bear heading down into the north.

It is no use denying that Karua was dreadfully improvident, with his worthless spare tyres and inadequate repairing outfit, but the way in which he slaved over that puncture made it quite impossible to be angry with him. By nightfall he had all four wheels off (I never quite knew why) and the whole contents of his tool box scattered over the ground. At regular intervals throughout the night came the mournful sigh of the expiring tube (each time this happened, the dog barked) and I realised between waking and dreaming that he and John were still indefatigably at work.

Incredibly enough, sunrise found the lorry with all its wheels on again, and all of them properly inflated. We started off with extreme caution, our hearts in our mouths with the crackling of every twig; but the tyres held and we made Kajiado, our destination, by midday without further mis-adventure.

On the way, I saw silhouetted against the sky what looked like an ant-hill with a post sticking out of it. The nearer we drew the more I was puzzled, till I saw that it was a giraffe lying down. We drove up close to him before he roused himself to the effort of getting up, and as I had been told on good authority that giraffes never lie down I thought that there must be something very wrong with him. But a little farther on I saw a herd of fifteen, and three of them were also lying down.

So long as we kept inside the lorry (and they did not get our wind) they did not mind how near we came; in fact, Karua, always ready to oblige, left the track altogether and drove the lorry, perilously rocking over the bumpy ground, into the very midst of them. It was certainly the nearest I was ever likely to come to patting a giraffe; and I was forced to the sad conclusion that although there is no romance in photographing wild animals from a car, there is also no comparison in the results. However long I stalked them on foot, and however hard I worked, I should never be able to come so near them. Cars roused only their curiosity and, as yet, were unconnected in their minds with danger.

I now spent a few days at Kajiado with the District Commissioner and his wife, and as he did not think much was to be gained by going down to the Magadi soda lake, I pushed straight on another forty-five miles to Kidongoi and the Black Mountain.

Chapter IV

KIDONGOI AND THE MAN-EATERS

OL DOINYO OROK[1]—the Black Mountain—throws out its southern buttresses to the Tanganyika border ; it was a stronghold during the War, and my camp at Kidongoi was moated on two sides by the trenches of 1918. Barbed wire still lay about in forlorn and rusty tangles, and on top of a little hill I found the remains of the K.A.R. camp. Except for this scar running down its side, the mountain was thickly wooded, and half encircled the camp like a horseshoe. A stream cut its way down through the rocky ground, and below me the acacia forest stretched out to the horizon of jagged blue hills.

The forty-five miles from Kajiado (in spite of a fair road and no breakdown) had taken more than six hours, and I had tramped up and down for the rest of the afternoon hunting for a site for camp.

I could not make up my mind. The forest was stifling, the high ground sloped up without any shady trees ; between the two lay the road and, what was worse, the Masai cattle track, which meant a fresh plague of flies. Finally, I picked out the old trenches through the gloaming, and chose a couple of scraggy thorn trees—poor substitutes for the spreading roof at Selengai—but the ground beneath them was at least flat enough to pitch the tent on.

[1] " Ol Doinyo Orok, 8,374 feet, is an isolated mass, forty miles in circumference, which rises more than 4,000 feet above the surrounding plain and is situated on the southern boundaries of the Reserve. . . ."—G. R. Sandford in *An Administrative and Political History of the Masai Reserve*.

Trekking by lorry held none of that good healthy fatigue of a long march. It was no doubt a quick way of swallowing up the miles, but having done nothing to earn them but sit passively enduring the heat and the grit, one had none of the satisfaction, either. I believe it had the same effect on the boys, and by the end we were all tired and on edge. There had not been time all day to stop for food, and no one had eaten since breakfast, eleven hours before. Once camp was pitched, the fires were soon blazing up through the blue night air, and the boys laughing and chattering again as they cooked their evening meal.

I had finished supper, and with the inner man restored and the petty annoyances of the day forgotten, I listened to Brahms's Fourth Symphony. The full moon lifted above the horizon, wrapping the veld in a honey-coloured haze, and the silence of the desert once more enfolded me. The night was so beautiful that I could not leave it, and with Siki (my dog) curled up asleep in my lap, I sat thinking of the past five days I had spent at Kajiado. A dash of civilisation had been utterly delightful, and it had sent me back into the wilds with an added zest. Selengai, with its fleeting visions and sudden bitter despairs, hardly counted, I thought, and the trip would really begin from now.

After a month's solitude, meeting people again was extraordinarily alarming, and yet I was pent up with theories that I was dying to pour into the ears of the first person who would listen. I understood, then, why people who live alone are often such intense talkers. It has got to come out somehow. With me the torrent was astonishingly confused and my discoveries, disappointingly enough, awoke very little echo. Indeed, they fell so flat that I began to lose faith in them.

But now that I was back again, the wide vision returned like an unruffled sheet of water reflecting the sky. Everything again seemed simplified, and it is undoubtedly these stretches of solitude that renew in one a feeling of serenity and strength. There, I firmly believed, lay the way to internal poise and unity; and having once securely found it, I should be able ever afterward to set myself aside, and with undivided calm and a kind of huge affection, work for an objective harmony with power not imagined but real. In solitude it was possible to stand back and see clearly what to aim for. It was a splendid idea so far as it went; but I had still to learn that nothing so delicate as poise is ever securely found—that, indeed, all life is spent in finding it. And it is given to very few to find and know themselves so truly that they can reach out beyond themselves to eternal freedom.

I had not meant to stay five days at Kajiado, and when I arrived there, begrimed with dust from the lorry and shy of imposing myself on the District Commissioner's hospitality, I had intended pitching my tent somewhere beyond the garden and starting off again next morning. But his wife, with her fifteen months old son, welcomed me on the verandah steps (the D.C. was away on safari) and declared she had been expecting me and that my room was all ready, so that within a few minutes my twenty-five preposterous loads lay scattered over the verandah. Her face lit up as her eye, running over the tumbled heap, picked out the gramophone, and we played the Symphonies till past midnight. My going next day was postponed because I " must meet Hugo," and the next for the same reason; after which the lorry grew impatient and snorted off on business of its own, and I watched it go without a pang. I was thoroughly enjoying myself.

On the following day Colonel W (acting D.C. in Hugo's absence) dropped in for a sundowner, and by degrees I learned about his farm, which had been the apple of his eye, and how year after year the rains had failed till he lost everything. He had eventually been forced to abandon the farm altogether, and had taken on the job of schooling the Masai and managing their dairies. He was working hard at these uncongenial tasks, endeavouring thereby to pay off the debts on his farm.

The story was typical of half the men who went out to settle in East Africa after the War. The country was written up in such glowing terms that people put their all into these uncertain El Dorados, and in so many cases lost it. One heard of such things often, but when you actually met some one to whom it had happened, it ceased to be abstract and you could not help wishing you were the kind of millionaire who might go about the world not subscribing to good causes so much as setting people on their feet again who sweat blood at their jobs, yet fail because circumstances really go against them.

After a month faced with only elemental difficulties, I rebelled the more to think how vital a part money plays in all our lives and how, out there, so relatively small a sum as a few hundred pounds might in many cases have changed the fortunes of an estate. And a little of it could even on occasion be turned into things like pâté de foie gras, langouste, champignons and smoked salmon, which to those trying to economise in the outposts of Empire was as exciting as exploring the traditional shipwreck. I had hitherto felt slightly ashamed of owning these Fortnum & Mason luxuries—I had brought them out to make up for the times when we had been reduced to painfully short rations—but broaching them in solitary state seemed as reprehensible as drinking champagne alone, and I had not had the heart to open any of them. But they came into their own at Kajiado, and I felt not only justified but proud of my forethought.

Colonel W's fight to save his farm stirred my admiration, yet I admired my hostess still more. She also was fighting the inglorious battle of economy and, having no nurse, she was looking after that young tyrant Christopher single-handed which (with only native servants) included doing all his washing as well. When I realised for the first time the full significance of this " looking after," the maternal longings that fitfully assailed me were nearly permanently quelled.

The W's were at that time the only other people in the station. Mrs. W struck me as being a rare friend in exile, for she grappled with adversity smilingly and was one of those unselfish people who, in the face of disaster itself, would somehow contrive to run things to time and make you feel that everything was safe and normal. But even she was sometimes away on safari with her husband, whereas Mildred, unable to leave her child, had no break from the monotony of that lonely life. This was the hardship and loneliness of the wilds shorn of the grand moments, and she could never have even the shortest holiday to go out and study the animals or to escape into the stillness. Not that she really hankered after these things. She had lived all her life in an English cathedral town, sheltered and surrounded by friendly people and occupations, and by a stroke of fate she found herself in one of the most arid bits of Africa, miles and miles from anywhere, and cast suddenly and absolutely on her own resources. And she made a tremendous success of it. Whatever her secret loneliness or misgivings she hid them bravely out of sight. Her house was always charming, and even after Christopher's wants had all been satisfied, she had enthusiasm left over to work at the Brahms Intermezzi.

I was soon persuaded that the secret of her happiness could lie only in the depth of her love. There was no other possible explanation ; and I took the moral deeply to heart. Love that endures through marriage is something which must be quite unmistakable and sent from Heaven. Being poor, enduring hardship, all is bearable where love is. And if people could only believe in the amount of good they put into the world simply by being happy. . . . I could not forget the afternoon when setting off to tea with the W's we suddenly heard the toot of a well-known car. All the cares of life—and there had been plenty of them to talk of and try to philosophise over—vanished, as, with an unsuspectedly glad little cry of "There's Hugo," Mildred with the pram and Christopher disappeared in a cloud of dust, and I was left standing there. Of course there was no tea-party for her, and I went alone, inventing excuses on the way.

Having heard a great deal about Hugo during the past three days, I struggled between tact in staying away and a very natural curiosity to get back as soon as possible to be introduced to him. Mildred greeted me bright-eyed and more absurdly young than ever, and Christopher was delivering himself of those peculiar gurgling sounds known as crowing. The whole house had sprung to life, and in its completely happy atmosphere I found myself in some inexplicable way to be included.

The idea of my starting off next day was instantly dismissed. They argued that since I had waited all this time I could easily stay a little longer. So I again talked Karua round, and stayed.

Time passed very pleasantly. Hugo, when he was not in his office working out some abstruse native problem, was obliged to listen to a great deal of music ; and we also discussed his article for *Blackwood's*, which led to his reading a more frivolous skit on the Indian station-master. And we played golf on the little nine-hole course which was justly his pride, for he had planned and made it himself. It was remarkably pretty, and demanded very precise golf ; if you left the fairway your ball was exposed to the hazards of the African jungle, and might become embedded in an ant-hill several feet high, or lose itself for ever in the long grass or down a wart-hog's tunnel.

There were also the police sports, and the high jumping gave me the only opportunity I ever had of using my slow-motion camera.

Lastly, there was the arrival of the mail. We motored to the station to fetch it and I actually had a glimpse of our station-master himself. There were letters from home, but the real excitement was Mildred's frock from England. It was Hugo's surprise, and I had been burdened with the secret since breakfast-time. We dashed back so that she could try it on at once, Hugo unpacking it while I amused Christopher. It was a lovely frock, and it had arrived just in time for her to wear at the Government House ball which was to be given for the Prince of Wales.

And so, armed with fresh maps and plans and a basket of juicy paw-paws, I again boarded the lorry. Hugo had also provided me with the two things I had most wanted at Selengai : a Masai interpreter and a riding mule. And at the last moment Mrs. W slipped into my hands a wonderful home-made cake which I surreptitiously nibbled during the eleven hours' fast above mentioned. African hospitality is the most whole-hearted in the world, and leaving Kajiado for my self-imposed solitude made me feel homesick over again.

News of my doctoring had travelled all too fast, and early next morning half a score of Masai women came flapping up in their cow-hide robes to be treated for their various ailments.

Their heads were shaved and they were covered with heavy iron bangles from the wrists up, leaving a gap for the elbow-joint, and from ankles to knees. They also wore them about their necks in ever-widening rings that stood out all round like wide unpractical collars, and they had ear-rings to match. None of these rings would come off, in fact they must have been forged on before the wearer was full grown, for they sometimes bit into the flesh as a strand of wire will grow into the tree trunks that press against it. It was impossible to dress any sores that broke out under these fetters, and the torture those poor women must have endured did not bear thinking of.

All the while these medical operations were going forward, a group of young El Moran (warriors) stood leaning on their spears and looking on. Their dress consisted of ornaments, belt and a loin cloth, and sometimes a hide cloak caught up on one shoulder ; and they were plastered all over with grease and clay that had a rancid, rather unpleasant smell. Their hair, mixed with red clay, was parted across the top of the head from ear to ear, and carefully rolled in strings which resembled bunches of worm-casts. The front part was divided into three short pigtails which fell forward over their faces, and the back was intricately dressed in a long pigtail bound with beaded leather thongs or plaited straw. They were fine-looking specimens of a once splendid race, and there was nothing whatever the matter with them. But they wanted a taste of this medicine they had heard so much about, so I gave them a generous stirrup-cup of Epsom salts all round (for their faith would have been shattered had it not tasted nasty) and they grimacingly took themselves off.

I was itching to climb above camp and explore the mountain, but it was already late by the time I shut up shop, and taking Mohamed and Asani I zigzagged up the first steep spur in the scorching heat of afternoon. At the top I looked into a wide grassy basin beyond which more grassy summits rose up. Resolving to make an early start and climb these at the first opportunity, I now bore left handed, circling high above the camp.

I was skirting below an outjut of rock when I surprised a pair of reedbuck, who quickly bounded out of sight. They were so slaty blue that I thought they must be Chanler's variety, which is much more localised than the reddish Bohor reedbuck, and found farther north.

The narrow path ran across the face of the mountain, past

milky jade euphorbia trees pointing up their fingers against the ocean of blue sunlit distance, and then headed down to the stream. I parted the curtain of creepers and found myself in the twilight of towering leafy trees, while at my feet the water flowed dreaming from pool to pool with soft music among the boulders.

I tried to follow it down to camp but it was too much overgrown ; so I crossed to the other side, and Asani drew his knife and hacked out a way along old elephant paths till we came to another stream which bubbled out of the rocks under a bank of golden convolvulus. At the same instant, I caught sight of a pair of bushbuck, but Siki saw them first and was after them like a streak, madly giving tongue. Her yapping came back fainter and fainter as she chased them up the mountain, and I whistled in vain.

There was not time to wait and talk to her seriously about it (I had already given her several beatings for chasing, and small as she was she had nearly frightened the life out of some giraffe on the way from Kajiado) for though camp was directly below us, we could not force our way down to it. Ledges of rock cut us off, and the cruel camel thorns forced us to descend in wide tacks. I was, moreover, half blinded by a grass seed the size of a grain of barley which had struck me in the eye with such force that I had literally to pull it out. It was a frantic race against the daylight, and had darkness overtaken us in that maze of thorns, we should never have escaped from its clutches. As it was, we were glad enough to have the light of the fires to guide us back.

I had fallen asleep that night when Siki woke me by a paroxysm of angry barking. She always barked at hyenas, and as she made sleep impossible, the only remedy was to get up and scare the hyena away.

I ran out of the tent shouting and waving my arms. The moon had not yet risen, but as I ran towards the faint glow of the embers, I suddenly pulled up in my stride before a huge shadowy beast standing stock-still looking at me. In a flash I realised what he was. But I dared not turn my back on him and make for the tent, he was too close to me—so close that had I put out my hand I could have laid it upon his back. There was nothing for it but to bluff. My voice came hoarsely as I yelled out more furiously than ever :

" Grrr, you beastly hyena you ! " (it helped me to pretend he was only that) and I made a rush, stamping as though to drive him away. For one endless moment he hesitated. Then he bounded sideways into the darkness with the deep-throated snarl of a lion.

I made a flying leap for the tent and my rifle (kept loaded by my bed for such emergencies), and my hands were trembling so that I could hardly unsafe it. I stumbled into my chair panting with fear, and sat with the rifle at the ready and my heart drumming in my ears.

Half an hour went by and nothing happened. Siki had stopped barking and was curled up beside me fast asleep. As my pulses quietened I went over the adventure. I had acted on instinct quicker than thought, yet several consecutive ideas had flashed across my mind. My father had drilled into me that if you run away you are done, and never to let an animal guess that you are frightened. I had often wondered how much I should remember of that in a real emergency, and I felt intensely grateful to that dormant wisdom (or instinct) which in moments of stress seizes the reins and leaps to the right decision. I realised in the light of after events (presently related) that I had had a miraculous escape, and that I owed my life to that absurd piece of bluff—really the same bluff put up by any animal closely cornered—for had I faltered for more than a fraction of a second, or tried to run away, the lion would undoubtedly have sprung on me.

I thought with a shiver of the ghastly but true story of the couple who spent their honeymoon in the wilds. The man, writing in front of the tent by lamplight, had fallen asleep with his head in his arms when a lion crept up, quietly sank his teeth into his skull, and crunched. The man made no further sound, and the lion was about to carry him off when the woman awoke, saw what was happening, and with a reckless and pathetic courage struck blow after blow in the lion's face with no other weapon than an umbrella, till she succeeded in driving him off.

My tent was pitched a good eighty yards from the rest of the camp, and sleeping as I was without a mosquito net (oddly enough, a mosquito net is often a safeguard), and the tent door wide open, I reflected how easily I might have shared that unfortunate man's fate had not Siki barked.

Reaction overtook me in an irresistible desire to sleep, and I finally screwed up enough courage to go back to bed, though not before I had lit the lantern, shut the front of the tent and conscientiously tied up every fastening. But Siki, far from reassured, kept getting up to sniff through the crack, her back bristling ; and she barked on and off until daybreak.

In the morning the boys made a tremendous fuss over her (Mohammedans will not usually touch a dog) for they said : " Siki saved the camp last night ! " No one realised this more heartily than I did, and Siki, who was almost permanently in disgrace for chasing or stealing, made the most of being the spoilt and petted heroine who could do no wrong for at least one whole day. After she had given the alarm, the boys had kept watch ; and they told me that three lions, all so thin that you could have counted their ribs, had prowled round the tents till it was broad daylight. The track of their pug-marks lay round the tents under the guy ropes.

After breakfast, the Chief arrived with some of his wise old men robed in hides or blankets, their heads shaved, and their ears weighed down with metal ornaments till the lobes dragged upon their shoulders. They wanted an audience, so I called Kabechi (my new Masai interpreter) to come and translate into Swahili while they, squatting in a ring in front of my tent, accepted tobacco or took snuff according to their habit, and settled themselves down comfortably to tell me a very long story.

Unelaborated, it was that the lions were well-known man-eaters who had haunted Kidongoi for weeks, that every one lived in daily dread of them, and that they had already killed and carried off three men. The Chief wound up with true eloquence and the statement that God had sent me to deliver his people, and he earnestly begged me to do it with all expediency.

There was something uncanny about these lions, for they never grunted or made the least sound. They prowled silently as ghosts. Fires, the common safeguard against wild beasts, held no terrors for them ; so that once the sun was down one never knew but that they might be lurking among the shadows at one's very elbow. All feeling of security had gone ; panic was in the air. Every bush began to look suspiciously like a lion's head ; the fall of a twig, the least rustle in the grass put one's heart into one's mouth. It was easy to believe that every Masai who laid himself down to sleep was obsessed by the thought that it might be his turn next.

That night I felt uneasy over Jim venturing from the kitchen fire across the darkness to my tent with supper, and I made Muthungu follow him closely with the lantern. Nor did I leave the tent as usual to walk up the hill under the stars before turning in. Lucky for me, I thought, that I hadn't known more about that lion on the previous night. Now I hugged the fire and those few yards of canvas rather as a child in the dark puts his head under the bed-clothes, and nothing could have dragged me out.

When the chief and his councillors had withdrawn, Mohamed and I held a consultation of war. Reserve or no Reserve, if the lions returned and gave us the opportunity, we determined to fire a volley and do our best to draw blood.

That same day a cow very opportunely died near camp, thus providing a bait, and we dragged her up to the foot of a thorn tree. It was essential to lay her in a strategic position, up-wind of camp and hidden from it, which I could also approach unseen, and which would be lighted by the first rays of the sunrise. Thus I might have every chance of getting a photograph before we discharged our weapons.

It would have been better to have sat up all night in a hide close by, but there was not time to make the kind of barricade which (though I should have been awake and armed to the teeth) Mohamed obstinately thought I ought to have. I had, therefore, to content myself with marking out an exact line of approach, and we secured the carcass to the tree with trench wire, and covered it up with the wickedest thorn branches we could find to make it safe from twenty hungry lions.

No one saw or heard anything of the lions that night, and at dawn I set off for the kill, inwardly cursing Mohamed's hobnail boots as he stumped along behind me. Bent double, with the camera ready, I crept round the brow and cautiously drew myself up.

The heap of branches appeared exactly as we had left it, and there was no sign of a lion. I walked up to it and found not a trace of the carcass. Nothing remained but the lengths of wire. Thus I lost a golden opportunity, for I was unable to procure another bait. The Masai, eager though they were to be rid of the gruesome menace, and to avenge their brothers, were by no means long-headed enough to sacrifice even a sheep in the cause.

But I could not find it in my heart to begrudge those lions

their reward : it had been so magnificently done. We had placed all the branches (each the size of a young tree) with their stems to the centre so that the thorns faced outwards in every direction like Winkelried's spears. Had I not seen with my own eyes how the branches had been carefully pulled aside I should never have believed it possible, for as Mohamed had said when ramming in the last wait-a-bit (thorns) :

" No beast on earth could come near the meat—only men ! " When I thought of all the kills I had seen successfully protected in this way and with half as much care, I began to think that, after all, there was something in Mohamed's craze for building me a hide like a fortress.

Next day, accompanied by Mohamed, Asani and Muthungu (who carried provisions and our water supply) I started off before sunrise to climb the mountain.

The rocks and long grass forced me to keep to the native paths which ran disconcertingly up and down the steep valleys that cut athwart my traverse, so that every hard-won climb was lost in a fresh descent, and it took us five hours to reach the summit.

High above on the hillside, Asani pointed out an eland, and I toiled up through the jungle of grass to photograph him. I came up just below him, and catching sight of the tips of his horns above the grass I set the camera, crawled on hands and knees a little nearer, and suddenly stood up. There were barely a dozen yards between us, and I snapped him as he threw up his head before galloping away. I thought that eland (who live in the plains) were possibly unknown at such a height, but higher still, I saw about twenty more. This was near the top by a stream that filled a basin of rock under a group of palms (the first I had seen in the Reserve) and we had drunk there and were crossing over, when a rhino with a tiny calf (he looked scarcely bigger than a little pig) trotted off into the undergrowth. I also found a great deal of fresh buffalo spoor.

The summit, which Thomson describes as being six thousand feet high and fine pasturage for the Masai cattle, held a disappointment in store, for when at last I reached it, I discovered that the real summit lay to the south, a good day's march away. The one I had reached, a bare grassy top, was the highest point of the north-western end, and the beginning of the long forest-clad ridge running the length of the mountain. It was not the arid acacia forest of the plain but luscious and tropical ; and after a halt for some food and rest—it was then nearly midday—I followed a game track which dived straight into it.

It was wonderful forest with its tall silver trees shimmering in the gloom with the effect of moonlight, its walls of creeper impenetrable but for the game paths, and hung with sprays of golden convolvulus ; its spires of rock and occasional visions of the plains below lying in a rainbow mist of heat and cloud shadows. One could have wandered through it for ever. Some of it reminded me of Meru Forest on the slopes of Mount Kenya, and the tree trunks bore the same muddy marks above my head where the elephants had rubbed themselves ; some of it was like the bamboo forest of the Aberdare mountains, and again I found the carpets of little pink flowers (*Impatiens*), and the tangled creepers where you might have seen a forest-hog or even a bongo.

Silently in the unbroken silence, we moved through the shifting pattern ; while the sun-filled glades and the trees trailing festoons of moss, or like tall pillars sending up arches of silver under the leafy roof, formed endless pictures before my enchanted eyes. The forest was always friendly, and to walk in it quietly hour after hour was to become a part of its own mind and spirit. As I touched the trees in passing I felt as though each one gave me his individual blessing.

I was padding softly along the path, when it dived downward into some dark shiny-leaved bushes, and I found myself on the edge of a cliff. Some two hundred feet below me the ridge still ran upward to the summit which now shone redly in the westering sun. It was later than I had dreamed, and we were cut off. Mohamed, with a doleful shake of the head, declared that we were lost, and began to cast about for another path. Knowing roughly our position in relation to camp, I told him (with wholly fictitious confidence) that I knew the way ; and doubling back on my tracks I plunged straight down the mountain-side.

The mingled joy and terror of being half lost with nightfall close upon me and the chance of running into buffalo at any moment, awoke a kind of sixth sense, and I dashed ahead with a sure instinct choosing this path in intuitive preference to that, and resolutely shutting my ears to Mohamed's counsels. Finding presently that I had left the boys out of earshot, I stopped to wait. Their woolly caps had been torn from their heads a dozen times by the thick undergrowth, Mohamed's nailed boots slipped where my rubber soles clung like a cat, and the rifle was a further impediment. I was free, for my hat was tucked into my belt and I had no rifle to hinder me. I was sitting on a fallen trunk when a djin of the forest whispered in my ear :

" Supposing you could be changed into anything you liked for seven minutes, what would you choose ? "

My heart thumped for joy.

" Oh please, a *bongo* ! "

" Nothing simpler," he said, waving his wand over me, and at the same instant I sprang away into the thick foliage, leaping the fallen trees, doubling through the tunnels of greenstuff with my horns laid back along my striped and chestnut flanks, and cantering down the steepness with effortless and wingèd speed. The boys crashing their way behind me were now my pursuers, but the forest was more than ever my friend : its language was my own and my kinship with it was now complete. Every smell struck my nostril with its particular message, a hundred sounds men cannot hear I could interpret (Mohamed, for example, could never have detected those velvet footfalls of a leopard stalking her prey ; and, a little farther on, the faintest snap of a twig as a bush-buck leapt away unseen) and through the maze of jungle all paths were revealed to me.

All too soon I broke cover into the open, the spell slipped irrevocably from me, and I was my ordinary self again, panting and limping prosaically along a native path.

I had come out directly above the deserted Masai huts which I had passed on my way up, in the early morning. They were about four feet high, well made, with a framework like a lobster-pot, covered with grass and overlaid with cow-dung, which is not only warm but (so the boys told me) raintight. Inside, I found hearthstones, a sleeping-place, and a corner railed off for the live stock.

By this time the boys caught up, and, finding the path, we slithered and ran steeply downhill to camp through the gathering dusk.

I was wakened in the night by a terrific detonation, followed by a deep vibrating snarl. This continued for about an hour, sometimes near, sometimes far off, now like a groan, a kind of gasping sigh, now rising to a roar. I pictured a lion trying to make off with a broken shoulder, and wished it were light enough and I courageous enough to go out and give him a finishing shot. But I fell asleep again instead, to be woken as suddenly by Siki's sharp bark and the rush of a lion past the tent. I sat up with the rifle across my knees. But after such a climb, sleep soon lulled fear.

Jim brought my tea next morning with a face of impressive gloom, and announced that he had not slept a wink all night.

I remarked that such a calamity need not prevent his saying good-morning, whereupon his tragic expression melted into a large grin and he told me the whole story.

No wonder he had not slept, for the lions had come prowling so close round the tents that none dared venture out to make up the fires. The boys had sat up waiting, their hearts in their mouths—Mohamed in the doorway with the rifle at full cock—but although they could hear the lions padding up and down, it was pitch dark and they could see nothing. At last Mohamed's chance came as a beast paused between him and the smouldering embers. He fired, and it fell without a sound ; and when I went to look I found a lioness lying where she had fallen, about eight feet from his tent.

The groans which I had heard were made by her mate bewailing her, and it was he who had rushed past my tent, having hovered round till dawn. And yet, Jim said, he would come back that night to eat her. Nothing would make me believe that, yet, I reflected, sorrow and hunger are both natural emotions, and there is nothing sentimental in Nature.

As to my theories about being able to make friends with the animals, I did not, of course, count man-eaters. They were lean and hungry and had been entirely single-minded in their desire to eat one of us. But I was forced to realise that going out with all the love and fearlessness in the world would not win the beasts over from acting according to their nature. I might as reasonably sit before the rising tide with an unconquerable faith that it would not drown me, as go up to an elephant or a rhino and expect them not to trample me to death ; and only once in the ages has any one been so lucky as to find a lion with a thorn in his paw. Apart from man-eaters or single rogue animals, which are perversions through circumstances, the strongest instinct in all animals and even in snakes, is to *escape* from man, and if they are cornered, or surprised at close quarters, they will attack through fear.

So that to overcome my own fear was less than half the battle if I could not find the means of allaying theirs. Nothing would ever persuade me that it was impossible, but my difficulty (having promised not to take undue risks) was to stake all on the supreme test.

On the other hand, if the beasts had made a study of me, they would have been far more puzzled.

They might have watched a native bring me a hen and fling her down in the scorching sun with her legs tied, and then have seen me rebuke him furiously for such cruelty, release her, give her food and water, and then (unfathomable inconsistency) finally have her roasted for dinner. Or they might have realised that I had come into their wilds with the vow to kill nothing, not even a guinea-fowl, yet wondered why I pronounced the death sentence, in cold blood, on a bullock. They might have approved of my feeding the birds, or giving the wild bees sugar on my fingers ; and then seeing me sometimes kill the much-hated flies, and at others rescue them from drowning, they would probably have come to the conclusion that I was some extraordinary kind of animal with no real motive at all. One puzzles over trying to reconcile things in Nature, but how simple they are beside human nature.

The death of the lioness lifted the sinister cloud that had hung over the camp, and the sun shone with a more friendly benevolence. Every one had felt the strain of that silent and deadly menace. The boys had had no heart for the usual talk and laughter round their fires at nightfall, and the feeling of foreboding had kept them all strangely quiet.

Their spirits now rose to the heights of jubilation, and they prepared for a tremendous lion-dance. They collected bunches of herbs, whitened their faces with ashes and capered round the body of the lioness, singing a grand improvisation and beating out the rhythm with their feet. The Masai were ready enough to join in the fun, and were all in high glee. They were quite reassured, and declared that the remaining two lions would never return. I stayed on another week to make certain, but neither heard nor saw any sign of them ; and to my immense satisfaction, Jim's prophecy about the lion returning to eat his mate was not fulfilled. Although the carcass was devoured on the following night, the spoor round it was made by hyenas.

The lioness was in poor condition, but I took her skin. As I sat under the shade of a thorn tree with Mwanguno and Asani, the skin spread out between us, and I heard again the ring of the knives on the whetstone and the boys' droning talk, I felt anew (in spite of all my theories) the thrill of the taxidermist in handling the beautiful, supple skin, and the joy of working on the delicate tissues : cutting with the blade of a small penknife to divide the skin between the eyelids, the outer and inner lips, paring away the cartilage inside the nose, and turning the ears. The fangs were stumpy and yellow, and although a small beast she was probably very old, which perhaps accounted for her having turned man-eater. I had no preservative with me and was obliged to cure the skin with salt and ashes, but as it was the property of the Game Department and it made no difference to them if it were pegged out to dry (which cannot be done with a museum specimen) the substitute answered well enough.

As we were only three (Muthungu was too inexperienced to count) the work took us the best part of the day. I chuckled inwardly to see how much old Mwanguno was enjoying himself. After having been chief skinner—one of the most important members on our former collecting trip— he had found carrying firewood and water for the camp very tame and unworthy occupations. Now, as I looked up, I saw him sitting on his hunkers in the old style, holding forth in his grumbling monologue to Asani, Muthungu and

Kabechi, and a couple of very old and wrinkled Masai who could not have understood one word, but who nodded all the same. Every now and then he would interrupt himself to take a pinch of snuff, tossing the box across to Asani afterward. Asani took his snuff with a discreet and gentlemanly reticence which Mwanguno probably scorned as disgustingly genteel. When he (Mwanguno) took snuff, there was no mistake about it and he did it in the grand manner, with a mighty clearing of the throat, a generous spit (perfectly aimed and timed) followed by more wet snuffly noises as he flattened his nose on the back of his hand ; and so to resume work.

It was not till now that I realised how often I had seen Mwanguno go through this ritual. There was a touch of bravado about it, perhaps, but I noticed that Kabechi was impressed, and I considered that the end justified the means. For, in those early days at least, I could never abide Kabechi. He was young, patronising, and dreadfully pleased with himself. There was no doubt about his good looks. He had the profile of Nefertiti, and little ears that lay flat against his small, perfectly shaped head. He wore his hair long (my boys always shaved their heads just as the hair began to grow becomingly) and affected a couple of feathers stuck in it. He sacrificed utility to appearance without a pang, and trailed a kind of robe of royal blue lined with crimson which I thought could not have existed outside Clarkson's. He certainly manipulated it very ably, flinging it over one shoulder preparatory to action with a gesture that made me think of How Horatius Kept the Bridge. As an interpreter he was a failure, for he infinitely preferred his own version to anything the treating parties might wish to say, and the sound of his own voice was honey to him.

Although we were now left in peace, Kidongoi proved to the last a vaguely hostile place.

There was one good thing to be said for it : there were no mosquitoes. But there were other things. Jim soon made the discovery that every chop-box that had not been placed on the ground-sheet was practically eaten through from underneath by white ants ; and then there were those big black ants whose smell was so horrid that not the strongest bath essence could dispel it from the tent. And there were, of course, millions and millions of flies. But all these were minor evils compared to the mosquitoes of Selengai, and one other thing I checked up in favour of Kidongoi was the presence of the bush-cuckoos. Theirs is the sweetest, most lingering song of the veld. One of them pipes a hesitating falling chromatic, each note liquid as a drop of water, and the other takes it from the bottom note of the octave and comes up, so that their voices meet in the middle and cross and come back again. Even the memory of it evokes a picture of the wilds so poignant and filled with regret that you can smell the brittle grass and the cooling dust. For they sang during that time of day when the shadows overflowed in pools of lilac, and the plains ran out to the edge of the world in rippling gold under the almost lilac sky of evening.

I made the most of the bush-cuckoos, for fortune dropped to a low ebb.

The weather turned bitterly cold with an east wind that blew everything over and brought the dust flying into the tent, and I went down with the worst bout of fever I had known. The wind howled dismally through the rigging of bare branches, the ridge-pole groaned and whined, and the canvas flapped and yawed and thundered like a ship in the wind's eye. But the particular discomfort of that icy wind was that when drenched with fever I did not dare expose myself to it ; so that I dreamed endlessly of clean, smooth sheets, but could never get up to change them.

Some of the boys went down with fever, also, and even Siki sat huddled and disconsolate.

It was three days before I was up again, by which time the lioness skin showed signs of "slipping," and the familiar smell haunted me.[1] I dragged myself out to go and work at it, vainly hoping I might pass unobserved.

But the Masai had eyes like vultures, and in a moment a stream of them appeared from nowhere to be doctored. Their ills had accumulated during those three days, and there were endless cases of sore eyes and coughs and colds. I felt weak and giddy, and the stench of these people was more than usually overpowering. But just then there was a stir in the crowd, and a young boy was brought in on a litter with an ugly, gaping wound in the thigh where he had been gored by a bull from his own herd. Then there came a man with a septic arm from a lion's mauling *five years* before. Next was a man with a wound exposing three inches of shin-bone.

Jim brought relays of hot water and stayed to help me. Seeing that I was by now very faint, he tried to make them say thank-you by way of encouragement when I had done with them. To most of them this idea was too completely novel to be treated seriously, and ministering to them made me think of that great saying of Marcus Aurelius : " For what more dost thou want when thou hast done a man a service ? Art thou not content that thou hast done something conformable to thy nature, and dost thou seek to be paid for it ? Just as if the eye demanded a recompense for seeing, or the feet for walking."

That was a grand and inspiriting way of looking at it, but in my weaker moments I loved a little gratitude. And when half an army of Masai arrived with provisions in the shape of

---

[1] " Slipping " is caused by decomposition which sets in between the outer and inner skin, when the hair slips off.

live and raucously bleating goats, and ingenuously announced their intention of taking up permanent residence in my camp so as to be conveniently handy for daily treatment, I more than ever welcomed the arrival of Karua with the lorry, and I packed up with all speed, eager for a change of scene.

Chapter V

OL DOINYO OROK. TREASURE TROVE. INTOLERANT RHINO

NAMANGA was only eleven miles farther along the road, but the place charmed me directly I saw it. The Black Mountain still threw out its protecting buttresses in a half-circle, the ground sloped down to the river hidden among the trees, and these framed a view of Longido, a fine, sharp-edged mountain seventeen miles away which culminated at its nearer end in a rocky tower.

The day had not begun well. Every one felt wretched with fever and at cross-purposes. The loads were packed haphazard, and our progress was delayed a dozen times by one or other of them falling out of the lorry. By the time I had fixed on a spot for camp, the atmosphere was tense with exasperation.

There is nothing like fever to take the joy out of life and to make you feel suddenly forlorn and lonely ; and that lovely view, so remote and impersonal, weighed down upon my spirit. I turned my back to it and looked up, instead, to my own friendly mountain, and the words : " I will lift mine eyes unto the hills " came to my mind so comfortingly that I decided to pitch the tent with the doorway opening onto the hillside. This meant levelling the ground, which sloped the other way ; and the boys set to work half-heartedly, every one grumbling at every one else, when I looked up and saw—ambling quietly past—an elephant.

Our troubles were instantly forgotten as I grabbed the cinema camera to follow him.

All at once he spun round with a big snorting noise and began to come towards me. He made a splendid picture, if only there had not been so many bushes in the way, and he was just breaking clear of these when there was a deafening explosion at my elbow. He swerved aside, crashed into cover and was gone, and I realised, with horror, that Mohamed had loosed off the rifle. I turned on him wringing my hands in dismay, telling him I should be turned out of the Game Reserve for such a thing, and that he was on no account to fire unless the elephant were actually upon us.

As a matter of fact, the elephant was still a good twenty yards off; he was not charging but merely coming to investigate, and I knew that I could safely go on pressing the button for another second or so when Mohamed fired.

Kabechi, girding up his cloak, sprang to the nearest hill-top and sighted the elephant about two miles off and going at full speed. I held the spoor for over an hour to reassure myself that there was no blood trail, and that he had not been hit. I thanked Providence that Mohamed was a bad shot, whereupon Mohamed was, of course, up in arms for his marksmanship, and swore that he had not missed.

If the reader happens to be unacquainted with the wild African elephant, he may think of him as a large but entirely friendly beast whom he has looked upon with affection since his nursery days and generally connected with howdahs and childish treats. In this case he may wonder (not unnaturally) why on earth there was all this pother about taking the amiable creature's photograph. In justice to Mohamed, I must therefore make it quite clear from the start that the African elephant (unlike his Indian cousin) is one of the most dangerous of wild animals. He is much larger and probably far less intelligent than the Indian elephant, and until very recent years he was believed to be untameable. There are many differences between them, including their molar teeth and flexibility of the trunk ; but the most striking difference is between the size of the ears and the shape of the skull. The Indian elephant has small ears and a noble forehead that rises in two distinct bosses. The African elephant, on the other hand, has practically no forehead at all, and his ears are so immense that when he spreads them out he at once becomes twice as big. They are his trusty weapons of defence, and it is his acute sense of hearing that makes him so difficult to approach. Like all wild animals, he is very sensitive to smell. If he is suspicious, he will feel about for the wind with his trunk, twisting it slowly this way and that and raising it like a periscope above his head. Against these two great assets he has one disadvantage : he may hear you and smell you, but beyond twenty or twenty-five yards it is fairly certain that he cannot see you. This, at close quarters, may often be very comforting knowledge, for (so long as the wind blows true) however threatening he may appear, you know that you are safe so long as you stand perfectly still.

As soon as camp was pitched, I rode out on Marouf (the brown mule that had now arrived from Kajiado) to look for game. First I saw a troop of baboons who scampered off chattering madly for the trees, then a herd of impala and a giraffe, and later I came upon a herd of zebra. By a little subterfuge I managed to draw quite close to them. Telling the men to hold straight on, I turned Marouf's head and trotted towards the zebra, hiding myself as much as possible by lying forward in the saddle and keeping my head down behind his neck. The zebra were so much intrigued by this odd kind of animal approaching them that they forgot their caution. Those on the edge of the herd pawed the ground and snorted with mingled fear and curiosity. Even when I straightened up to photograph them they could not make me out, and though somewhat alarmed, for a minute or two they held their ground.

This was my first ride on Marouf, and he displayed great intelligence. The syce had evidently ridden him unsparingly from Kajiado, for he had bad girth galls. I found that the girth was hard as metal and slimed thick with hair and blood (a native syce has maddeningly little imagination in these matters) and it needed soaking for twenty-four hours, and greasing. Germolene soon healed the sores, and in the meantime I rode him without a girth. It speaks volumes for his kindly disposition that with such an advantage he never tried to throw me. His companion was very different, and had never in her life submitted to being saddled at all. Her use was not at first apparent, but it is a popular belief in Africa (and elsewhere, too, for all I know) that a mule must have a companion, and that he will never willingly go alone. But Marouf obviously did not think much of her, and he was quite ready to break through tradition; so that by tacit consent she was often left behind. She had a soured and negative disposition. I finally gave up trying to win her affection, and I did not even think of a name for her.

Next day one of my patients, after swallowing his cough mixture, said that he could guide me to the elephants. As he had not yet broken his fast and I was eager to start at once, I gave him a leg of a precious newly-slain goat, and afterward regretted not having given it to another and far more spirited guide whom I picked up on the way.

This was Lembogi. Where he came from or what his history was I never knew, but he cheerfully threw in his lot with mine, adopted the camp like a long-lost brother and was ready to act as guide in any adventure. Time was to prove him a born guide, and he had a love of adventure that was after my own heart. His face was pock-marked and he wore a little pointed beard. These two distinguishing features reminded me of the Batwa (half-pigmy) tribe of the volcano district on the Uganda-Congo border. His clothes can be described with one stroke of the pen, for with the exception of an engaging veld hat and a ragged square of calico (worn for some obscure reason on the left shoulder) he had none.

The elephants were in the swamp, about ten minutes' walk from camp (the swamp stretched parallel with the road for about three miles, but was divided from it by a belt of forest). From an ant-hill I could just see the tops of their backs above the rushes. Lembogi was explaining that we could not go nearer as the water was chest-deep, and that they rarely left the swamp in the daytime, when some of them did actually move out and disappear into the forest. The cover was very thick and the wind blew in circles, a peculiarity it had under the mountain, and with that old hen Mohamed any close-up work was out of the question.

Presently a herd of twenty-five elephants with three or four small calves streamed across an opening in full view. They fed and dusted themselves as they went, giving me a unique chance for a picture, but Mohamed was so full of fears (elephants when they have their young ones with them are admittedly dangerous) that he thought our ant-hill fifty yards away was too near. With my half-gauge cinema camera, which had no telephoto lens, nothing over fifteen or twenty yards was worth having, and I began to rebel in earnest against these wasted opportunities.

The fact was—and Jim told me about it that evening in a sudden unwonted disburdening of his thoughts—Mohamed was an askari (soldier) and had never been on a hunting trip in his life. One had only to try to shut one's ears to his pounding through the bush in his hobnail boots to realise that his vocation was that of the warrior and never the hunter. I was certain that he would face an enemy battalion unflinchingly, but of elephants he stood in positive dread, and although he failed only through his excessive zeal in the discharge of his responsibilities, I now gave him up as incurable.

He would have liked to paint DANGER in big red letters on every tree, and this carping spirit of prudence very naturally spurred me to a contrary recklessness. I wanted to argue with him, to laugh him out of it, and because my Swahili would not carry me so far and there was no one there to talk to, I turned it over the more in my own mind. I carried it much farther than elephant hunting. Life itself, I thought, is glorious only when you live it dangerously, accepting the challenge with glad faith, risking all, giving all with both hands, ready to " greet the unseen with a cheer." Nothing is securely your own, neither life, love, money nor possessions, unless you are prepared at any moment to give them up. For as soon as you want to keep anything possessively and safe from all risk of losing it, you have lost it already, and freedom of spirit also. The husk may remain, but the living truth is dead. " Give and it shall be given unto you." You have only to look back over the War, or at the countless experiments made in the name of science, or the pioneering of all kinds continually going forward the world over, to know that this is the root of all belief.

But the bright eyes of danger had little appeal for Mohamed. I gave up trying to reason with him, and instead wrote an urgent appeal to the Game Department to send me Kongoni (my father's old gun-bearer) or a good substitute, and I begged that he might be provided with rubber soles.

With the letter safely dispatched by Karua (who now and then plied between his store at Namanga, a couple of miles farther on, and Kajiado at rail-head) I felt that something had been done towards a change for the better. Mohamed's shortcomings at once seemed easier to bear with. In order to avoid further cause for friction, I decided to leave the elephants alone for the time being and to have another try for the summit of Ol Doinyo Orok. I therefore sent for Lembogi, to talk it over with him.

Even though I was now about twelve miles nearer the summit than I had been when I looked across to it over the length of the mountain from the north above Kidongoi, I foresaw that it would still be a longish climb, and that luck would have to be on my side if I were to accomplish it and reach camp again in the day. Judge of my surprise, therefore, when Lembogi told me with a confident grin that he could take me to the summit in four hours, and show me a little crater lake into the bargain.

The African's notions of time are notoriously unreliable, and I was determined, whatever happened, to make an early start; so I told Lembogi to come round at five-thirty on the following morning. Jim had orders to call me before daybreak if the sky were clear, and although lowering black clouds shut out all the stars, and the mountain was hidden in thick mist, he arrived punctually at five o'clock with the lantern. I went out to con the sky, and decided that it was not the day for the climb. When the clouds lay so thickly upon the mountain they often did not lift till noon or later.

I was lying in bed luxuriating in the thought of not getting up so early after all, when I heard the familiar sound of munching just outside, and I was lazily wondering why Marouf had been brought round at such an hour when I saw two rhino go by, cropping the bushes as they went. It was still too dark to photograph them, but I could not let such an opportunity go, and I took the camera and slipped out after them. They soon melted away in the grey dawn —it is incredible how such enormous beasts can literally vanish—and I was following hard on the direction they had taken when I looked round to find the ever-watchful Mohamed behind me. There was an unmistakable note of reproach in his good-morning. I had stolen a march on him for once, and although I brazened it out, I felt more than a little foolish for being caught chasing rhino through half a mile of thorn scrub in my dressing-gown and slippers.

The day remained overcast, and after breakfast I took Mohamed and Asani and struck up the hillside to do a little exploring. It was fearful country, rough, impenetrable and fascinating. I saw some fresh leopard spoor, and picked up a perfect snake skin which had been so carefully shed that, although eight feet long, it was practically intact. Throughout the trip I only once saw a snake. He uncoiled himself at the foot of a tree in the forest and slipped into a hole underground. He was about five feet long and darkish in colour, possibly a small python.

We battled through a jungle of thorns and came back with knees torn and clothes in tatters.

It was still only midday, and as the two most alluring occupations—the elephants and the mountain—were ruled out, I decided to walk into Tanganyika.

One cannot live on a boundary without sooner or later wanting to be on the other side of it, and Lembogi had wonderful tales of a dry stream-bed there where, he assured me, I should see far more game than on our own side. It turned out to be a barren desert, and hunt as I would I could find nothing but a meagre pair of dik-dik during the whole of the afternoon.

The boundary between Kenya and Tanganyika Territory ran like a broad band cut through the bush, taking in the lower slopes of Ol Doinyo Orok, and where the bush gave way to open ground there were stone piles four feet high, shaped like beehives. There is always a tinge of romance about crossing any frontier, a kind of psychological moment like reaching the rainbow's end; and this border-line out in the wilds, with never a soul to guard it, might seem utterly meaningless, yet I felt as impressed as though it had cried aloud with ten thousand voices. From out there I was able to see the summit of Ol Doinyo Orok : a bare shoulder of granite, rather bleak and forbidding, rising out of the forest.[1]   Pathless jungle protected it on all sides, and it seemed to me more than ever impossible that any one could reach it and return in the day.

I reined in Marouf and called Lembogi. Telling Kabechi to translate into Swahili, I pointed to the summit and asked again whether that was really the summit to which Lembogi proposed to lead me in the space of four hours.

Naturally no native interpreter asks a plain question like that and gives you a matter-of-fact answer ; and while the lengthy discussion went forward I had ample opportunity for watching these two together.

They were both Masai, and there the likeness ended. In character they were poles apart. Kabechi with all his robes and sophistication and his condescending air—it was plain that he thought my trip to the mountain a fool's errand—and Lembogi, naked and ingenuous, with his honest eyes puckered in the effort to concentrate on the matter in hand. They were both raw savages, unable to read or write, and so far without contact with civilisation. But these human traits were so intrinsically human that they were there long before the building up of any civilisation. Kabechi was there in the dim ages, playing his little rôle before the pyramids were built, in Greece, in Rome, right down to present times where he struts in every walk of life. He was not bad, in fact he could be disarmingly simple and kindly on the rare occasions when he forgot to think about the impression he was making. But his was a superficial nature. Secretly he was unsure of himself. He was always out to impress you and (like his Western counterpart) he chose the most super-

[1] The term " granite " is used to denote the undifferentiated series of gneisses and schists of Pre-Cambrian age of which Ol Doinyo Orok and Longido are composed.

ficial means of doing it. I can picture him in quite different circumstances, when he would have made you feel in some subtle way that your clothes were just wrong for the occasion and your conversation sadly commonplace.

Lembogi, on the other hand, never aimed at being anything but Lembogi. He was utterly without self-consciousness. Contrary to what one might expect, this is as rare a virtue in the savage as elsewhere. He is very like a child, with all a child's endearing qualities ; but few children can resist showing off. Even for this quality alone, Lembogi stood out from his fellows. He was at once younger and infinitely more mature than they, and there was something of that big patience and tolerance in him that was like Nature herself.

" At last," I thought as I sat looking down at him from the saddle, " at last I have found a guide who is *keen*. Let Kabechi sneer if he likes, Lembogi will somehow get me to the top of Ol Doinyo Orok."

I was waiting for Lembogi to say so himself, but his answer was unexpected and shattering. After a preliminary spit, he laughed a big, resounding laugh, clicked his tongue and snapped his fingers over this enormous joke. It was as though I had suggested a trip to the moon. No one, he declared in eloquent pantomime, had ever braved that jungle or reached the summit. He was ready and willing to lead me anywhere else I fancied, anywhere in the world except to the top of the Black Mountain.

This was undeniably a blow ; but by a superhuman effort I checked my impulse to argue with him—there might be some superstition or taboo mysteriously connected with the Black Mountain, and argument might ruin my cause altogether. It was only many years later that I learned that the Masai believe the forests on the mountain to be inhabited by the spirits of the dead. So I decided to bide my time, and without appearing over-keen on the real summit, I compromised for his four-hour summit and crater lake instead. I impressed upon him the advantages of an early start and told him to be ready before sunrise next morning.

But the mountain was still against me. Next morning was again cloudy and dark; the day afterwards I went down with fever, and nearly a week elapsed before everything conspired favourably for the climb.

At last the day came. I was ready to start in good time, the stars were still bright overhead, when it was discovered that Lembogi had not arrived. But I knew the direction if not the path, and I set off at once, for anything was better than losing the first cool hours.

The shortest climb in this country of great plains brought its reward, and soon the land began to stretch out below me under the golden mists of the sunrise, and at my back, Longido, with his head wrapped in cloud, rose ever higher as I climbed. It was steep going among rocks hidden in the long grass, and a couple of hours later I was glad enough to hear Kabechi and Lembogi hailing me from below. To make sure of not missing them I had left Mohamed and Asani behind at intervals to wait for them, and now I found that I had climbed too high and had altogether missed the path. I cut down to it and joined the men, and it presently led us out of some trees onto a rolling down where cattle were feeding, and two stone stockades, where formerly machine-guns had kept watch over the frontier, rose up against Longido and the morning sky.

Here I picked up a second guide—an old man clothed in a blanket, wearing iron ear-rings and his head close-shaved. He knew these jungle paths, Lembogi told me, better than any one in the country. He had evidently expected me, and came at once, without delaying to search for snuff or look to his goats; and after another short climb we plunged into the forest.

The way flattened out, the trees spread their foliage between us and the sun, and there was breathing space in which to look about among the flitting shadows and dappled trunks, and against green and darker green to see the interlacing patterns of silver in the silvery twilight. We were on the way to Lembogi's crater lake, and well I understood, following through what was becoming ever denser forest, how impossible had been that quest without the old guide.

At length we crawled down a steep tunnel of undergrowth, heard running water, and came out into a clearing by a group of palms where the water overflowed from a pool and ran over broad slabs of rock. It was interesting enough to see the Namanga at its source, and a gorgeous blue dragonfly darted and hovered in the sunshine ; but it was scarcely worth a hard three-hour climb. Yet this was indeed our goal, this the water we had come to see, and there was apparently no real crater lake or summit in store. This mean trickle was the Rubicon that none had ever crossed.

The situation was intolerable, the hour not yet ten o'clock, and beyond the stream the whole of that wild, untrodden forest with its deep shadows and tossing sunlight stood daring and beckoning me.

If the men were obdurate, so was I. I determined not to surrender without making a spirited fight, and I sat down and metaphorically squared my elbows for it. First of all, why not go a *little* way into the forest to look for elephant ? That set them off and Mohamed, as you may imagine, warmed to his subject. To go into the forest was impossible ; we were bound to get lost. Besides, he went on, there were things he could not explain, it would cross our luck. Once, long ago, ten El Moran were said to have gone into it, and not one had returned to tell the tale. It was dangerous : no one had ever wanted to do such a thing before. There I caught him up, for if every one could come and go, what would I care whether

I went or not ? The more he argued and put forth his solemn, cautious warnings (the others squatting round nodding their approval, chewing straws in indecision and spitting into the water) the more obstinate I grew, and I felt the light of battle kindle within me. If before I was half bluffing and not really so set upon the forest as I appeared, now I was absolutely determined that we should go into it, if only for a few yards.

We started. " No path " was ever their argument, but the elephant paths were every bit as good as what I had seen of native ones. This one led into thick gloom ; again and again I passed fresh elephant droppings, some of it faintly steaming in the twilight, and the flies rose up in clouds, buzzing in my face as, bent double, I shouldered my way beneath the branches. Presently I came out into a small clearing. As I straightened up, my eye fell upon a green mound in the midst, covered with rank vegetation and held together in the snake-like embrace of lianas.

What with the tales of tragedy, mysterious disappearances, and hinted taboo still ringing in my ears, I hardly knew what I expected to find beneath that sinister pile confronting me. A lonely shaft of sunlight fell through the gloom, piercing it like an arrow. The boys behind me peered at the mound with scared and superstitious faces, and spoke together in theatrically hoarse whispers. The atmosphere of suspense and undefined fear was now so overpowering that if any one had said boo, I should have jumped a yard into the air.

It was ridiculous to be impressed by these old wives' tales ; besides, I wanted to see what was under that living green mausoleum. With a voice that was meant to sound matter of fact, but which even in my own ears had a hollow ring, I said :

" Come on, let's see what it is "—and stepping forward I unceremoniously kicked a rotten branch. It fell inwards, leaving a gap behind it through which we now made out nothing more eerie than the whitened bones of an elephant. Hunting round under the débris of branches, moss and leaves, we found the tusks.

This discovery convinced me more than all their talk that the natives had really never set foot beyond the stream. The Government offers an attractive bonus for picked-up ivory, and the natives would never have overlooked it.

Although the tusks were very small, weighing scarcely more than twenty pounds apiece, they miraculously succeeded in putting cheer into every one. The ramble began to take on the air of a treasure hunt, and all were now eager to press forward. All, that is, excepting Mohamed, who was loath to let slip the chance of pointing the moral:

"Now that we have found ivory we can go back well content."

"Not so," said I; "this is a good omen, let us push on."

I was not entirely free of superstition myself, but I worked on other lines. I knew nothing of taboo, and though I would not for the world have offended the gods of the forest, or the fairies either, I felt that the spirit of the forest was something greater than these. It was in this spirit that I believed. So long as I could feel myself not an intruder but a part of it, and that it accepted me, I was safe. There was nothing hostile about the gloom or the listening silence; the trees were always friendly. And I cherished that line of the poet's: Nature never did betray the heart that loved her.

So I started forward again, and all went well till the old guide, who was following behind me, suddenly sat down plump in the middle of the track and held his head in his hands. We should be lost, he wailed; and now, just as I had begun to feel that we had shaken off these fears and were warming to the adventure, they would have me abandon it at the threshold. I turned on them with a torrent of sarcasm.

All right, let them turn back if they were no better than a pack of dogs to come cringing after me. Good heavens! was not this their own country, and had not God put eyes in their heads? That tree there with the twisted trunk, that patch of red foliage on the opposite ridge: would they not know these landmarks when they saw them again? Besides, Asani had an axe, let Asani blaze the trail. Saying which, I turned my back upon them and strode on. Little did I expect from this outburst, but, to my surprise, they followed without a word.

Asani was a quiet, stout-hearted little fellow, and though he had taken no active part in the altercation, I knew that he was with me. He was glad that we were not to give up, and he now heralded our way through the oppressive stillness with the cheerful ring of his axe as he notched our course.

Then, suddenly, toiling upwards through trees and creepers, I came out onto an open crest, and there before me, lifting its head above the forest, was the bare, grey summit. It might have been three hours away and it might have been thirty: all depended upon what lay between those intervening ridges suffocating under the tangled green barriers of forest. But to the eye it looked attainable, and the more I looked, the more it lured me on. It was no use discussing the possibilities with the men, and I took a high hand.

" The mountain is near enough," I said, " we'll follow the crest," but I dared not meet Mohamed's eye, nor did I glance at him.

Sometimes one guide led, sometimes the other, and when they flagged, or cast about, I struck ahead. But all at once it was borne in upon me that their resistance and also that of the jungle itself had both given out at the same time. Finding that I was not to be put off they had now cheerfully accepted the position, and put their interest in what lay ahead. As for the jungle, we had left the worst of it behind, and the ridge brought us out into the daylight clear above it. Following one ridge to the next, with occasional drops into the forest, we climbed a straight and broad path which was hemmed in on either side by dense hedges of greenery.

It was paved all the way with the droppings of rhino, buffalo and elephant. I was ahead and walking along with my eyes bent on the spoor, when I came to a grey boulder lying across the path. I was in the act of walking round it when it suddenly heaved itself up beside me with the terrifying snort of a rhino. I recoiled and leapt backwards, while the rhino (who was presumably facing the other way) tore off in the opposite direction. This is only conjecture ; for the instant the boulder sprang to life, I did not wait for a second glance but turned and bolted, colliding with the man behind me, who also turned and ran for his life shouting " Faru! faru! " (rhino) and in the twinkling of an eye we had scattered like chaff.

The rhino had disappeared, and the forest gradually settled back into silence. One by one, with hearts still beating with fright, we stole out of our several retreats and back to the path.

I suppose that the boys were now worked up to the adventure, or that they had hopes of finding more ivory, for none of them thought of using this as a pretext for going home before worse befell. Still out of breath, they laughed over the scare as each contributed some detail to our comically expeditious flight. But as I started off again, now a trifle daunted and very much on the alert, I began to think that losing the way was a minor evil compared with nearly falling over a sleeping rhino. I was trespassing in a sanctuary where no human being (according to the natives) had ever set foot before, and I could not tell but what there might be plenty more rhino ahead. The forest was ominously silent, and everything pointed to its being unusually full of big and possibly dangerous game. If any of them took it into their heads to charge, and casualties resulted, the blame would be mine for exposing my men to undue risk. It was an unpleasant thought, and responsibility began to sit so heavily upon my shoulders that I almost wished that I had given in to the boys an hour back, and left the forest alone.

The rhino, very naturally, had been annoyed at having his sleep so rudely disturbed ; and since the path was the only place where a rhino could bask in the sun, the path was obviously a dangerous one to walk, and other sleeping rhino, (or buffalo) might be less good-natured.

I was debating within myself whether I was at all justified in going on, when sure enough I detected another grey cumbersome shape above the grass-stalks ahead. It was only a few yards off, but I trained the glasses on it to make certain, and they showed up clearly the grey corrugations of a rhino's hide. I retreated on tiptoe and held a consultation with the boys. A détour was made impossible by the thickness of the jungle on either hand, but Lembogi, always the resourceful one of the party, said that if we retired to safety down-wind, he would climb a tree, wake the rhino by throwing sticks at him, and try to drive him away.

The reader may well wonder why I did not seize this golden opportunity myself, and (with the wind blowing so true) nothing would have been easier than to have crept up to the sleeping rhino and scratched him behind his ears. He might have loved it (and introduced me to the whole forest as a reward) but on the other hand if he hadn't, my chances for experiment would have been for ever curtailed. This would always be the difficulty, for when chances came I did not dare.

So Lembogi threw sticks and bits of caked mud at him till he awoke, and with many surprised and indignant snorts he took himself off, and we continued on our way.

Each time I hoped that we were on the final crest I would come to another disheartening drop. Mohamed urged me afresh to turn back, saying we should be benighted. I minded very little if we were, for it would hurt none of us ; we had matches and could make a fire. The more work I put into that climb, the less I could relinquish it. It is one thing to come home dead-beat but successful, and quite another to be defeated after all ; not only that, but I could never get the boys to face it again, and even I was not over-keen on a third venture.

Finally, it was the boys themselves who pointed to the summit and said that it was not very far.

Enviously I admired the way they could climb. As for me, I had put all my energies into the lead when it had been necessary, and now, under the burning midday sun beating fiercely down between thunderclouds, I was badly spent ; my knees trembled as I panted up through the reeling boulders. We rested a little, and Asani pointed (as I thought) into a tree-top at " a bird that makes a noise like a motor-car." I scanned the tree vainly for some strange kind of hooting vulture, when I heard the unmistakable throb of an engine, and picked up a black speck in the sky. I looked at it with profound disgust. Artistically, dramatically, from every point of view, its appearance was ill-timed, not to say tactless. Just as I was blazing the unknown trail, to find I was being actually looked down upon was sheer anticlimax. The fact that the aeroplane was ten miles off was only very mildly consoling. " But at least," I thought, " he can't land on the summit " ; and I pushed on.

At last I climbed above the forest zone, passing beneath the last outposts—stunted trees ragged with beard-moss in whose chequered shade lay a carpet of tiny peas (a kind of vetch with a leaf like wood sorrel, probably the *Parechetus communis*) whose blossoms were a lovely transparent blue. Above them flitted miniature blue butterflies, as though the petals themselves had taken wing.

Heath and boulders rose up against the flying clouds and

deep blue sky. I waded through billowing masses of white flowering shrubs, and beyond, all the ground was decked gold and blue and purple with flowers. There must have been fifty different kinds (possibly far more) and one I have never seen anywhere before or since clung to the rock in profusion like a blue mist. It had velvet purplish leaves and clusters of little powdery blue flowers like down, with a sprinkling of golden stamens.

This part of the mountain was a paradise of wild flowers. The Alps in the full glory of springtide could not have unfolded anything more tender or more vivid ; indeed, the intensity of those burning blues and golds nodding in the hot scented air against the almost sapphire sky and the shimmering pillars of cloud produced an effect that was peculiarly Alpine. I lingered there, willy-nilly, promising myself that I would return another day when I should have plenty of time. How often one bribes oneself with these false promises to return to something specially entrancing glimpsed on the road to something else !

The top, when at last I reached it was, after all, not really the top, and beyond a dipping saddle another granite head still frowned down upon me.

But meanwhile, below me the south side disclosed a grassy depression girt about by the two summits and bare granite screes ; and amid that desolation the grass stretched so green and rural that you had looked there for shepherds with their flocks. Instead of which, on the far side of a quaking bog, I saw—grey among the grey slabs—two rhino.

Leaving Lembogi, Kabechi and the old guide behind, I took Asani with the cameras and ran down the slope, crossed the bog and climbed up the far side. Mohamed was to follow at a short distance, on account of the clatter of his boots on the rocks. I drew to within forty yards of the rhino, yet they still looked like a couple of grey boulders as they browsed off an isolated patch of sere grass. The bleached stalks bowing before the wind alone gave a flicker of life to that adamantine expanse of stone.

The wind had risen to a tearing gale, and nosing straight into it I approached the rhino somewhat downhill. There was no chance of this steady blow jumping round to betray me, and it was strong enough to carry away any sound of my footsteps. Precaution was therefore unnecessary, and I walked boldly up to them. Just how close I was, it is hard to say ; but I felt that I could have flipped a pebble at them, and I noted subconsciously that the eye of the one nearest me was not dark brown as I had imagined it, but the colour of sherry.

And the experience has left me in some doubt whether a rhino has such poor sight as is commonly believed. Perhaps they heard the clicking of the cinema camera. This may have given the nearer one my direction, and then my coat or the brim of my hat flapping in the wind possibly caught his eye. At any rate, his ears pricked up, his champing jaws were held in suspense, and that little pale eye was very definitely focused straight upon me.

He lifted his head, trying to catch the wind. It told him nothing, but he now came deliberately towards me, nose to the ground and horn foremost, full of suspicion. I pressed the button and tried to keep a steady hand. This was not easy ; for a rhino seen through the finder of a small cinema camera looks remote, and it is only when you take the camera down to make sure, that you are horribly startled to see how near he really is. In the finder I saw his tail go up, and knew that he was on the point of charging. Though it was the impression of a fraction of a second, it was unforgettable. He was standing squarely upon a flat boulder that raised him like a pedestal, and he seemed to tower up rugged and clear-cut as a monument against the flying clouds.

Such a chance could never possibly occur again, and the

magnificence of that picture for the moment blinded me to all else. I had done better to bolt then, while he was still hesitating. I read the danger signal, yet in a kind of trance of excitement I still held the camera against my forehead. Then Mohamed fired a shot over the rhino's head to scare him, and I turned and fled for my very life.

The rhino was only momentarily taken aback. Before I had time to skip out of his sight he had made up his mind to charge me. The angry thunder of his snort, mingled with a screech like an engine blowing off steam, lent me wings. When I dared throw a glance over my shoulder I saw that both rhino were bearing down upon me with frightening speed. The boys had had a start of me, and as I raced after them across the vistas of stone bare as asphalt without a blade of cover anywhere, conviction swept over me that this time the game was up.

Though I ran and ran as I had never run in my life before, and my heart pounded in my ears and my lungs stiffened with the pain of drawing breath, time went suddenly into slow motion. Each step was weighted with lead ; I wanted to fly over the ground and, as in some horrid nightmare, I felt as though I were scarcely moving.

The rhino were swiftly gaining upon me ; their furious snorts overtook me on the wings of the gale. The boys, on the other hand, had disappeared as though the earth had swallowed them. I made one more desperate spurt and then, as I realised the utter futility of it, a fold in the hillside opened to receive me also. I tumbled headlong down a little cliff and landed on a ledge of heather.

The rhino would never face this drop even if they looked over and saw me. I glanced up apprehensively, but there was no sign of them.

In this sheltered place there was not a sound, and even the wind had dropped. With a thankful heart I stretched myself face downward on the heather, and panted as though I could never get a complete lungful of air again, while waves of crimson and orange rushed and throbbed before my eyes.

The boys climbed up to me (they had landed farther down) and seeing Mohamed's lugubrious expression of disapproval I quickly put my word in first.

"That," said I, "is the best picture I have ever taken!" And though unable at once to control my trembling fingers, I turned my attention to the intricate business of changing the film. Asani, taking his cue from me, stoutly declared he had never seen anything like the way the rhino had stood out on that rock; and the three Masai, who had witnessed the whole thing from the other side of the bog, now joined us and gave their version. Even at the time, I had been dimly aware that they were yelling with excitement as though they were cheering the winner of the Grand National. It must have been worth watching, and the pity was that there had not been a second photographer.

During their graphic recounting of what had happened, even Mohamed began to unbend and smile. Congratulations rained down upon his modest head, as well they ought, for his well-timed shot had undoubtedly saved my life.

As I was busy with the camera and listened to their talk, I too began quietly to enjoy myself. There is nothing like an escape to give you the feeling of exhilaration. The pleasant glow of it was stealing over me when I made a crushing discovery. In changing the film I found that I had overshot the end by fully six feet. This meant that the rhino's mad rush and the dramatic moment when he had stood silhouetted against the sky, were recorded on nothing but blind, red paper. The disappointment was bitter, so bitter that there were no words for it. The boys still talked of the marvellous picture, and I had not the heart to undeceive them.

I put the camera back in its case, and ran down the steep slope to the head of the bog where the ground was flat and we could rest in comfort.

It was now after three o'clock and we had been on the go for eleven hours. A rest and food had been well earned by all ; but by this time I was past food and only consumed by thirst, so I sat down in the reeds with a tin of peaches. It had been one of Jim's last-minute inspirations, and to this day I cannot eat tinned peaches without evoking a picture of frowning summits, and rhino, and the crude green of the bog against the scudding grey clouds. Nor, of course, have I ever quite recaptured the flavour of those heaven-sent peaches.

I was deriving not a little consolation from them when Mohamed came up to ask if I was ready to start for home. What with my recent adventure with the rhino, the lure of the summit had temporarily slipped into the background. Mohamed now recalled it and I jumped to my feet, for the hour was late :

" We must reach the top first," I told him decisively, and I strode off up the long grass slope at a speed which I knew that I could not possibly keep up. Mohamed had no choice but to follow. I heard him grumbling away disconsolately about it being so late and that surely we had seen enough. The three Masai did not even make a pretence of following, but openly sat down to wait for me. Asani alone came with a good grace. Perhaps he shared my curiosity to see the summit.

My course wavered deplorably as I zigzagged up the steep side with knees that were now like water. I was ready to own myself dead-beat, but that the boys (who climbed as easily as chamois) could be tired was a thing which I could not consider seriously. Yet I could not help reflecting how tremendous is the power of mind over matter, or I would rather say imagination over mere physical strength. Having just recovered from a sharp attack of fever, I was in no condition for the climb, but the idea of reaching the summit meant so much to me that I was incapable of giving it up. Lacking this incentive the boys felt only the fatigue, and to my amazement they all said that they were too tired to go on. Even Mohamed pleaded this excuse. I could not believe my ears : Mohamed, late of the K.A.R., and I had actually tired him out.

I reached the summit in about twenty minutes. Again beyond it was yet another dipping saddle rising up to a shoulder of rock. *Was* it higher ? There was little to choose, a matter of a few feet either way, and I longed to make a last dash to be quite sure. But this was the moment to be generous, and I kept my doubts to myself. At least we were on the middle and most peak-like summit, marked 8,374 ft. on the map.

It was four o'clock, later than I cared to think about, and there was not a moment to lose. The sun was hidden by a dark curtain of cloud, Longido loomed out through the murky pall, and the wind whirled about us, moaning dismally among the rocks. We hastily built a cairn, and took one last look round at that unforgettable view and that curious black mountain with its vista of hills and valleys forty miles in circumference, moulded in gentle contours beneath the unvarying mantle of forest, and culminating at the point on which we stood.

Then I turned and ran down the descent. The climb achieved, I now shared the common thought which was to escape from all that forest before nightfall.

It was laborious enough, then, to have to follow the game track conscientiously up and down every knoll instead of cutting round ; but the moment you left this middle line which ran up and down the crests like a seam, you met jungle as impenetrable as a mesh, and dark withal, and short cuts were too risky. Retracing our steps was not without its difficulties, and Lembogi alone had the true instinct for direction. I followed close upon his heels and, except for the unavoidable climbs, we kept up a steady trot the whole way. The others wrangled among themselves over the right course, dropping ever farther into the rear, and I shouted many a " hyah ! hyah ! " over my shoulder, for nothing mattered save racing the daylight.

At last we came to the place where I had blundered on the rhino early in the morning ; and Lembogi was carrying straight ahead over a fallen tree when I remembered that we had come upon it at right angles, and I swerved to the left. Lembogi shook his head, but I was sure, and Kabechi, catching up at that moment, bore me out. Farther down, where it was thick going, the tree on the opposite ridge with the red foliage caught my eye through a gap ; and several landmarks met me like friends just when I needed them most, for we were all casting about for our bearings, and it was I who had gibed at the boys on the way up for having no eye for landmarks. In the forest again, there were some anxious moments till by luck I hit on one of Asani's blazed trees, and all was well. I may have been sure of my ground here, but higher up I was nowhere in the running with Lembogi, who was a born guide.

We picked up our ivory, reached the water again and I called a halt ; for we were by now all parched with thirst.

Two more hours saw us home. They were a very painful two hours stumbling through the darkness among loose stones hidden under the grass, and we all arrived limping into camp. Poor Mohamed had fallen and hurt his hip and could scarcely walk. I was filled with remorse, for it was my fault for having made him take the nails out of his boots weeks before, so that they made less noise ; consequently he had hardly been able to stand on the slippery grass slopes. It was as cruel as drawing a beast's claws and turning him loose to fend for himself; and Mohamed had that same uncomplaining patience of the dumb animal which always touched me.

It was good to be sitting safe in camp again, better than a bivouac somewhere in that lovely, frightening forest; and when I looked up to the mountain standing so silent against the stars, I did not feel the glow of victory, but rather an intense gratitude. Conquering a peak is, I think, only a phrase, and no one ever meant it. For the mountain itself has so much to do with it, and can at any moment turn you back with even so small an accident as a sprained ankle, if it wished. And on this particular climb, the mountain and the forest and all the beasts whose sanctuary I had invaded had (except possibly the two rhino) been very forbearing, and I was grateful to them.

I soared on the crest of such high elation that despite having been strenuously on the go for sixteen hours, and still weak from malaria, I could stoop to nothing so prosaic as physical fatigue.

Long before I had dreamt of Africa, mountaineering had enthralled me. This climb up Ol Doinyo Orok, through tropical jungle with its own peculiar difficulties, held also its own fascination and spurred me with the old keenness. Stirring the fire till the flames shot up their forked tongues into the night, I played the Fifth Symphony; and on its irresistible tide, ambition rode untrammelled to the summits of the very giants themselves, and again I turned my thoughts to Kilimanjaro and Mount Kenya.

Chapter VI

FRIENDLY LIONS AND ELEPHANTS.
KILIMANJARO

THE climb had earned every one a day's rest. I persuaded
Mohamed for once to remain in camp (he was still very lame),
and collecting hook and line and a lump of raw meat I slipped
off by myself to the stream.

It ran down the mountain-side a few minutes' walk from
camp, first tumbling in cascades among the rocks and then,
when it met the plain, flowing unbroken from pool to pool
in the shade of huge banyan trees. I jumped from one stone
to another in mid-stream, and sitting close to the water,
dropped my bait through the dimpled surface. It drifted
down onto the floor, where the current rolled it over and over
with invisible fingers till the commotion sent up a little cloud
of sand whirling above it. Then from out of the shadows
came the barbel, nosing up into the current. They swam
slowly, undulating their long brown tails like seaweed. Now
they circled above the bait, seeming to feel for it with their
curious, mobile whiskers, dilating their gills rapidly and back-
watering to keep level. I moved the bait forward in little
jerks, tempting them, and they followed it shyly nibbling.
But whether I drew it across the current, or let it work down
of itself, or lie on the bottom, they would never pouch it
whole-heartedly. They came and looked at it, were a moment
eager, and then turned and darted away.

They varied from seven inches to a foot in length, and looked
to me exactly like the fish we used to catch off the Land's End,
which the Cornish fishermen called whistlers. They, too, never

pouched the bait, but hung on for an instant with their teeth, and in that instant you had to whip them out of the water.

The bait was pounded crab (shell and all) which you wound onto the hook with wool. The wool served a double purpose, for not only did it soak up the mushed crab, but the whistlers caught their teeth in it. This bait was called a " smear," and the whistlers were believed to be blind and to hunt only by smell.[1]

As I watched these fish in the little Namanga river, with their purplish brown bodies gracefully swaying in the current, and their four trailing whiskers as sensitive as snail's feelers, they recalled many a forgotten summer's day when we used to climb down the rocks an hour or so before the turn of the tide to catch whistlers, and it occurred to me to try the same method here. Catching them was more than mere sport : they were excellent eating, and though not quite so firm and delicate as the whistlers (which were nearly as good as trout) they had fine white flesh, unspoilt, like that of most African fish, by hundreds of bones. There were plenty of little crabs in the stream, indeed they continually fouled my hook, and I ran back to camp for some wool. But those African whistlers would have nothing to say to my " smear " ; they were not even interested.

I had been intent on fishing, and had become so much used to the sound of the river that I no longer heard it. Now I drew up my hook, and lying under the bank among the roots of the giant silver trees, I let the music of running water " creep in my ears." It sang with many voices, blending, dividing and modulating two distinct little phrases ; now whispering, and bubbling in liquid undertone, now pouring

[1] I found the whistler mentioned in an old book on sea-fish (in the Marob Library at Penzance) printed in 1775, in which he is classed with the five bearded cod. The account added that the Cornishmen whistled for this fish when they wanted to catch him and called out the mysterious words : " Bod, bod vean ! "

out the overtones round and clear as chimes. Now the breeze brought it quickening into the major key, and presently it died away softly into the minor. It was insinuating as sleep, and it completely shut out the world beyond its banks. " Past, future, all is illusion," it sang, " even Time itself. I am the present, and the present is eternal."

Dreamily I watched the water slipping towards me through the luminous green twilight of shadow, to be roused with a start of joy by a kingfisher skimming over the surface with jewelled wing incredibly blue.

Overhead, the sun found out the chinks in the broad, fat leaves, and splashed down fountains of quivering light. Mists of gold swam into it, shining against the dark forest, as a cloud of gossamer-winged insects rose and fell above the glassy green reflections ; and watching them I became aware of their drowsy hum above the purling of the stream. Sometimes a big opal-white butterfly sailed through the dazzling columns of light and fluttered into the shadows beyond. Tiny, bright green birds flitted above, and now and then a flash of scarlet ; while far away above the spell of the river a dove cooed on and on like the voice of Eternity. The little blue monkeys swung themselves down and dropped noiselessly to the ground. I called to them in their own chattering tongue till curiosity got the better of their fears, and they dodged nearer and nearer behind the trunks and sat gravely watching me, or scampered off again in pretended alarm.

It was dusk when I reached camp, and Jim, pointing to the rifle inside my tent, reproached me for forgetting to take it with me.

I had, of course, never thought of taking it. To go armed would be to go admittedly on the defensive and half expecting some kind of antagonism. Either you are outside Nature, going into the forest armed and hostile, or you lay down your weapons and walk gently into what is as truly your own as any creature's. There are no half measures. If you go in the spirit of absolute trust—not taking a rifle just in case, but desiring above all things to be accepted—then I think, indeed I know out of experience, Nature takes you to herself with an infinite sweet tenderness, giving you her protection all the time. Because you belong wholly, there is nothing to fear. If it were not so, if you remained alien, you would be crushed by her might and solitude as an ant is crushed beneath your heel.

A great surprise was awaiting me. Indeed, Asani had gone to look for me at the river to tell me about it (I had seen the tracks of his rubber soles close to where I had been fishing, and wondered at them), but he had narrowly escaped being charged by a rhino and had fled back to camp without finding me. This explained Jim's concern at my being without the rifle.

The surprise was Abdi.[1] He was a sturdy, grizzled old Nubian gun-bearer with the ugliness and charm of a bull-terrier, and beaming with smiles. He now presented himself, saluting smartly, and handed me a letter from the Game Warden, who wrote that Kongoni had been signed on for another safari just two hours before my letter had come in.

But I liked Abdi on sight. He was outwardly so unlike Mohamed, standing well over six foot and broad in proportion, whereas Mohamed, it will be remembered, was small and slightly built, that I felt sure that his attitude towards elephants must be correspondingly different. His recommendations were excellent ; he had been to Rhodesia, Uganda, the Sudan and Congo, knew all the places that I did, and was an experienced hunter. It was all too good to be true, and I blessed the Game Warden from the bottom of my heart.

[1] Though it is unlikely that he will read this, I owe him an apology for changing his name to Abdi. My only excuse is that his real name, Asmani, might be too easily confused with Asani.

Dear old Mohamed took it in very good part. I saw him into the car which had brought Abdi, and he took his leave without a shadow. Discipline—nineteen years of it—may have killed his own spontaneous initiative, but his fidelity to his sense of duty was touching, and I shall always associate him with the words " faithful unto death." He had the quality of gentleness also, nor could I forget his saying about the partridge whose nest lay in such peril at Selengai : " For every creature, God is there."

There were other surprises in store, for Abdi had brought my mail and a magnificent basket of fruit and vegetables and fresh eggs and butter, sent from Government House. There had been no butter for three weeks, and Karioki (the cook) was as excited as a small boy over this windfall, and eager to try his skill at once on every dish that could possibly need butter, including toffee.

Karioki's honesty always amazed me. My knowledge of native cooks had hitherto been limited to our tall, fierce-looking Somali on the Uasso Nyiro, who used to come to the tent door almost every morning with the one unvarying demand, fired at me like a threat :

" Marrowfat ! "

He would have made short work of the stores had I given him the chance, and once, in revenge for my stinting the marrowfat (a tin was supposed to last for cooking for a week) he fried the croûtons for the soup in lion fat.

But Karioki confirmed my faith in the saying about Trust men and they become trustworthy, and I never locked up the stores. It was a fine thing to be free of the atmosphere of suspicion ; and Nature itself ever taught me to allow a generous margin in all things both concrete and abstract without suffering from the feeling of resentment. I locked up nothing except money, and as Jim knew the inventory of my possessions, he was responsible for them. I felt that he was quite entitled to a pinch of my tobacco now and again (I rolled my own cigarettes) and, unlike a maid, he resisted the lure of my face creams.

Co-ordination inspired a stronger discipline than ever mere strength could enforce, for there was nothing the boys prized more than to be given a little responsibility. And, like children, they loved and respected (nay, much preferred) a firm hand, so long as justice went with it.

Abdi's first night at Namanga gave him a foretaste of its possibilities; for a rhino charged through the men's camp, and he had to fire a shot to drive him away, and then a leopard climbed into the tree overhead and stole their meat.

The rocks were full of leopards, and they were so fearless that I often heard them grunting in the middle of the day. I had a hunt for the thief next morning, unsuccessful, of course, but Siki was very restless and I believed that the leopard was lying up close by camp. There is nothing that a leopard likes better to eat than a dog, and I took to tying Siki to my bed at night for fear she might run out and be caught.

Benbow and good feeding had transformed her from the poor little ragamuffin I had picked up at Selengai, and she began to be quite puppyish and playful. Her disobedience was incurable, but I adored her pluck. She took a beating without a sound and never sulked afterward or lost her spirit, but would trot along as jauntily as ever with her tail well up, though I could detect a sheepish look in her eye. It was no good my thinking that I had found a second Jock of the Bushveld. Siki was too independent for real deep devotion, her wandering life had taught her too well to shift for herself, and (unlike most European dogs) she had come to like the company of natives, and spent far too much time round the kitchen. For all that, I loved her companionship; nor could I have pitched my tent so far away that the boys could make as much noise as they liked, while I enjoyed complete peace, had

Siki not been there to guard me. Besides, I thought optimistically, she might yet model herself on Jock as time went on.

I came in from the leopard hunt at midday, aching and shivering with the first symptoms of malaria, when Colonel W of Kajiado dropped in on his way south and read me a lecture on the subject. He prescribed thirty grains of quinine daily in liquid form, and added that one should never let fever reach the point of ague, but should take ten grains of aspirin and ten grains of quinine with a tot of neat brandy at the first symptoms. He warned me that I might go on as I was doing for a time (I had been going down with fever more or less regularly every third or fourth day) but that constant attacks might end in blackwater, or go to the brain, when one inevitably died.

This sounded funereal but extremely useful, and even though drastic doses of quinine are said to ruin the complexion, I saw that it was better to be yellow than to be dead.

It was all very depressing. Even the sky frowned, and a cold wind blew. I was half-heartedly writing up my diary when the sun broke through the clouds and the cowherd came to announce two elephants.

This was better than quinine. I called Abdi, and set off in high spirits across the swamp and entered the forest. As I was moving quietly among the trees I was arrested in midstride by a sudden angry burst of snarling, and I leapt back as a lion sprang up literally from under my feet. Like a yellow streak he bounded out of sight into some thick, green bushes. They fringed the swamp, and among them the cowherd, armed with nothing but his spear, at once proceeded to follow him. The search was vain, and the cowherd, pointing out the direction of the elephants, said he must go back and guard his cattle, for the lion had evidently been lying in wait for them.

I now felt keener to follow up the lion, but he had obviously cleared, whereas, in spite of the noise, the elephants were close by and quietly feeding. Testing the wind to be sure that it blew from them to me, I picked my way carefully among the trees, advancing on tiptoe among the brittle twigs till I came out into a glade, and there, not twenty-five yards off, stood the two elephants.

Abdi, following close behind me, had as yet made no sign, and I looked back to see how he was taking it. His face, so far from registering either horror or disapproval, was beaming with enjoyment, and he had that tense, alert look of a terrier straining at the leash.

"Wind's all right," he whispered. "You can go *much* nearer."

Trembling with excitement, I crept up another ten yards. Still there was no restraining hand, no warning hissed in my ear. I hardly knew what to make of it. Oddly enough this absence of leading-strings awoke my own inherent caution. I hesitated, then reluctantly took a few more steps forward. Still Abdi said nothing. This was getting beyond a joke. He had probably been told in camp that his success depended on his willingness to walk right up to elephants. I on my side felt that my reputation hung upon doing so, and as neither of us could give in, the deadlock was every moment driving me into their very legs.

"He thinks I'm funking it," I thought. This was true enough, but anything was better than that he should think so. If Abdi once got that idea into his head I was done, for you must never let a native suspect that you are not brave.

All this had taken about ten minutes, and the elephants were still quite unconscious of anything unusual in the wind. In fact, they were giving me a splendid and possibly unique opportunity, and I noticed that lying halfway between me and them was a fallen tree trunk. I now forgot all about Abdi and what he was thinking, in my eagerness to reach it.

Only once before had I been within ten yards of an elephant, and the photograph had given me a nice frontispiece.[1] But at ten yards, the value of a steady purchase for the camera is incalculable. Painstakingly as a chameleon, I put one foot cautiously in front of the other, and although the tree trunk proved to be considerably nearer the elephants than I had expected, it nevertheless gave me a sense of protection as I crept towards it over the bare ground.

At last I crouched behind it. Kneeling down, I rested the camera against it and looked up at the elephants. They had finished their meal and stood quietly side by side under a tree facing me, and one of them toyed reflectively with a bunch of green-stuff in his trunk. I hesitated to film them, for they were in a beatific after-dinner mood, a little drowsy and at peace with the whole of creation. Measuring the distance between me and the nearest elephant, I put it at seven yards, so that at the slightest sound or movement they were bound both to hear and see me, and their peace of mind would, in a moment, be shattered.

The lens was only three feet from the ground, so that I was obliged to tilt the camera up at them. Even for the baby cinema I was, for once, near enough. I panted with excitement, my hand trembled like a leaf, and but for the support of the tree trunk I should have been incapable of holding the camera steady. As soon as I began pressing the button, the elephants heard the tell-tale click of the motor and felt that something was wrong. They stiffened to attention and stood looking down at me with their enormous ears spread out. It was true that at any moment they might become dangerous, but just then I was struck only by their extraordinary lovableness. The way they stood there, puzzled and uneasy, blinking their eyes in a kind of huge, dumb patience, filled me with an insane longing to run up to them and try to explain.

[1] *Out in the Blue.*

But they could not long bear with that suspicious metallic noise, and the nearest one suddenly sailed out towards me. Then, and only then, did Abdi dart in and touch me on the shoulder, signing to me to retreat. I needed no warning, and scuttled back while the elephant reached the tree trunk which I had been using as a rest; and with this slight barrier between us he stood shifting his weight from one foot to the other and angrily shaking his head. He then walked away, but still seeing me out of the corner of his eye he turned and made a rush, again pulling up short of the fallen trunk.

We slipped back among the trees and waited. Having got rid of me he was soon pacified, and I saw him rejoin his companion and begin feeding. I turned homeward, trying to console myself that I had not, at any rate, made him very angry.

Abdi had proved himself one in a thousand. Mohamed, had he seen me kneeling before those elephants, would have had fifty fits. The film was as good as I could ever hope for. And yet, as I walked through the golden evening, I felt no elation, but rather an infinite sadness. The film, after all, was not an end in itself; it was merely a pretext for going up to the elephants. Any one with a good telephoto lens could take far more effective photographs with half as much risk. Could I have resisted such an opportunity of using the cinema, I might have sat and watched the elephants without disturbing them. But the original problem of making friends with them had really no solution, and this was the lasting regret.

I pondered it sadly, and when I reached camp again, I slipped off and climbed up among the rocks to a favourite place high above the camp where there was an ant-hill and a silver tree. I loved this place that no one knew, and often kept tryst there; for what I craved for (having come so far to seek it) was to make friends with all that world about me, to come near to its spirit. Alone in the listening silence and the beauty of that solitude, I sometimes came near to the fringes of it. Lying with my heart pressed against the red earth and my forehead upon the stones was not physical nearness only ; for as I lay there thinking how I, too, was composed of that same earth I touched and loved, and of the same elements that go to make the rocks and trees and stars as well as the birds and beasts, I felt myself merged into this deep love and unity with the earth, and found that it was at the same time unity with the spirit. The grey and silver thorn tree, soft-coloured in the dusk as the light on doves' wings, gathered me beneath its shadows ; and over all, like a healing stream, lay the spell of absolute and perfect quietness.

Night fell, and the breeze swept away every cloud before a heaven full of stars shining down in crystal purity. They filled the hills with music, with a beauty that surrounded and lifted me up. Composing my spirit to the uttermost stillness, I hearkened to the rhythm eternally throbbing through the universe. Time ceased to be ; and Akhnaton, four thousand years ago pouring out his soul before God, gave me words that were as living now :

" I breathe the sweet breath that comes forth from Thy mouth, I behold Thy beauty every day. It is my desire that I may hear Thy sweet voice, even the North Wind, that my limbs may be rejuvenated with life through love of Thee. Give me Thy hands, holding Thy spirit, that I may receive it and live by it. Call Thou upon my name unto eternity, and it shall never fail."

Before I was up next morning, I looked out and saw an elephant standing under the tree near the tent. He seemed to be in no hurry and was quietly browsing among the branches, and I quickly slipped into my dressing-gown and got the camera ready.

I walked up to him thinking that he must be the tamest elephant in history, when the wind jumped round and my reception was far from friendly. He was a lone bull of immense size and had a pair of thick, curving tusks such as I had never before seen.

Abdi joined me and urged me to extreme caution, for he had no liking for lone bulls, and this particular one was not in a mood to be trifled with. Though to me he was a strange elephant, he was probably an old resident, and (like all old residents) he was filled with a just indignation at finding that in his absence one of his favourite pastures had been appropriated. My daring to go up and annoy him with an infernal clicking machine was adding insult to injury, and he strode off into some bushes above the camp. I tentatively followed him, but he twice swung round with his head lifted in anger and his ears spread wide. He showed very plainly that he wanted to be left to himself, and that if I continued to disturb him, on my own head be it. I understood perfectly, and was daunted and went home.

It is psychologically an interesting point whether fear is due to one's own mood at the time, or to intuition. I had often been nearer to an elephant when he was coming much more determinedly towards me, and yet felt not half so fearful as I did now. Or take mountaineering, which also presents the same shadowy boundary between what is fearless and what is inanely reckless. There are days when you feel safe in the most hazardous circumstances, and others when a trivial snow slope or a bit of an overhang can fill you with apprehension.

While taking a beat round the swamp later in the day, I accidentally came upon him again, and a heron rose at my approach and flapped screeching over his head. He evidently read this as a danger signal, and without hesitation he turned and came for me, trumpeting shrilly and ploughing his way through the high swamp grass. Although I was safely perched on the top of an ant-hill fifty yards away, I did not wait for him, but turned tail and with all possible celerity put the length of the swamp between us. Abdi was right about lone bulls, and for the future we gave him a wide berth.

Time had slipped by so fast at Namanga that the days had already lengthened into weeks, and I saw, perforce, that if the programme were to be carried out before the rains, it was high time to push on. As a first step I sent off Marouf in charge of the syce ; for it would take him three days to cover what the lorry (barring accidents) could do in one, and I believed that Marouf would be safer if he preceded me than if I left him to follow after.

Now that I was on the eve of leaving the elephants, I remembered that I had pledged myself to try an experiment with a dummy.

This was a pet theory of a friend of mine who had spent the greater part of his life elephant hunting ; but he had had no opportunity of trying it himself. His idea was to place a dummy before a rather testy elephant and jog it into motion by means of a string. He thought that the elephant would not be particular about what he charged so long as he could rend something, and that he would not notice the deception. It might give me an opportunity of photographing a real charge, and in the interest of science (that all too convenient cloak for seemingly wanton experiments) it would be interesting to see if the elephant would kneel on his victim.

After breakfast next morning, I therefore set to work on a framework of sticks, padding it with grass and dressing it up in flowing lengths of trade calico. I made the face also of calico, with a nice grass wig and the features drawn in with iodine.

Though evolved by such crude means, when the finishing

touches were added she undoubtedly had a certain charm. The boys were delighted with her and begged to be allowed to come and look on. Jim himself, grave and dignified, immaculate in his brown kanzu, permitted himself an indulgent smile, though he could, of course, take no part in such childish amusements. The penalty for this superior aloofness was that he remained in sole charge of the camp. Even Karioki took the afternoon off, and Mwanguno, Muthungu, Lembogi, Kabechi and the cowherd (who had dashed after the lion armed with nothing but his spear), all lined up for the start. Seeing we were such a large party, I took Abdi and Asani and went ahead, telling the rest for safety's sake to follow at a hundred yards.

As we were walking along, I noticed that Abdi carried in his hand with evident pleasure and self-consciousness one of my discarded tins of talcum powder from which, turning the tin upside-down, he proceeded to shake out a cloud of ashes. This, he explained, was a far subtler way of testing the direction of the wind than throwing up a pinch of dust or holding up a wet finger, and with this dependable gauge we could safely go near the elephants. It was no doubt a great satisfaction to have found a use for this neatly perforated top, though Abdi later discarded it in favour of an ordinary bottle.

I made for the swamp and, working along the edge of it, had reached the tail-end and almost given up hope of finding the elephants, when Abdi sighted four of them feeding in an open stretch which ran like a meadow beside the tall reeds.

They were feeding with their backs to us, and I told Asani to creep up with the dummy, whilst I stood ready with the camera. But although Asani was ever willing and ready to oblige, audacity was not among his gifts, and as the elephants now began to amble forward, his timorous and reluctant steps failed to keep up with them. Once the elephants reached the end of the meadow they would disappear into the forest, and seeing that the opportunity was quickly slipping by I impatiently seized the dummy and ran forward as fast as I could go. Abdi trotted behind me, vigorously shaking out his tin of ashes on the wind, and was on tenter-hooks lest it should play us false, for the ashes floated out this way and that, and the wind was full of mischief.

The dummy was fixed to a long stick which was to be driven into the ground; but now, as I ran up behind the elephants to plant it, I found the ground so brick-hard that I could not ram it in deep enough, and the dummy tottered and fell at the first tweak of the string. Again and again I tried for a more strategic position, and ran up behind the elephants as near as I dared. Each time, as the calico fluttered in the breeze, one or other of them wheeled about, took one look at the dummy, and quickening his pace walked away in positive disgust.

My chance came when one elephant divided from the rest and stood in a patch of forest where the ground was moist.

As I crept up with the dummy, I saw him facing me through the branches. At the same moment he got a puff of my wind and charged. But at the sight of the dummy in his path he stopped short, and swaying his head suspiciously up and down he reluctantly turned back. He repeated this twice more, each time making a determined charge and each time stopping short of the dummy. She was now firmly planted, and danced bravely before him; but although her antics were wildly spectacular they entirely failed to draw his attention, which was not upon her at all, but wholly focused on *me*.

Seeing that the entertainment had fallen flat, the cowherd now took it upon himself to create a diversion by running in and out with the *sang-froid* of a professional matador, and literally daring the elephant. Things might have become serious but luckily the elephant made off, and we lost track of him.

I now thoroughly detested the sight of the dummy. Science had gained nothing through her efforts, and I felt like a traitor towards the elephants. The most successful part of the outing was when with much ceremony we burned her like a witch at the stake.

After that, we set out for home, Lembogi leading the way. His eye, ever on the alert, presently fell upon a dark green shrub growing at the side of the track, and whipping out his knife he lopped off a handful of small, straight branches. Whittling them into sticks a foot in length, he discoursed to me as he went along on the merits of this shrub, which he called arak. Its wood was so fibrous, he explained, that after a little chewing it became like bristle, and every native used it for cleaning his teeth.

I sometimes thought that if he could have read the classics, Lembogi's hero would undoubtedly have been the father in the *Swiss Family Robinson*. He had a way of finding strange uses for the most innocent-looking plants. I was once laid up with a sore throat so alarming that I felt positive I had jaundice, and even then Lembogi was not behindhand with the remedy. It grew everywhere in the grass, and was none other than a particularly offensive kind of burr. It was the bane of dogs and mules and stuck even to one's bare fingers. Lembogi came up beaming, with a couple of prize burrs on a plate, and assured me that in cases of sore throat a burr should be attached to the finger and rubbed briskly over the inside of the throat until bleeding ensued and the patient was cured.

After dinner that evening, I took up an empty petrol tin (used for heating the bath water) and practised roaring into it. I heard Abdi call out: "Lions!" in a hoarse stage whisper, and the boys chaff him and explain that it was only the Memsahib. It was a pretty compliment, and I was trying for an even deeper note when, to my amazement, two lions actually grunted in answer. I grunted back and again they answered, coming nearer and nearer till just beyond the embers they suddenly broke out into a tremendous roar. Next to my puny effort it was magnificent and deafening, and I roared again with all my lungs to encourage them. Then they roared in concert till the air thrilled and shook with vibrations, and the glorious waves of sound rippled out into the night and were held to the last echo in the amphitheatre of the rocks.

They were now so near that I could hear the dry grass crackle beneath their feet ; I could even hear them catch back their breath before opening out their lungs to roar again. Abdi ran up with the rifle, saying that they were too dangerously near. I forbade him to shoot, for I might wait a lifetime to hear lions roaring so close again (the Zoo held no comparison to the beauty of this sound under the open sky), so he put the rifle into my hands begging me to fire soon, and left me to enjoy it.

Lions in the wild state roar only after they have fed, never when they are hunting, and I could detect no anger in them. I believed that they roared in perfectly friendly contest one against the other, glorying in the sound for its own sake. Their attitude towards me was one of good-humoured amusement, and with that kindly superiority of the pro. they were showing me how it should really be done.

But by and by they drew in even nearer, and I reluctantly fired a shot into the air. Perhaps it was as well that I did so, for though it seemed like ingratitude and put an end to the entertainment, I found, next morning, that while the lions had been roaring near my tent a lioness had prowled within a few paces of the kitchen. I could not bear to admit such a motive, but it was just possible that the lions had roared so as to direct attention away from her. And although my roaring may in part have drawn them, the smell of a freshly killed sheep in the fork of the tree over the kitchen tent was, I fear, the stronger lure. My shot had no doubt scared the lioness before she had traced the smell to its origin ; but on the following night she came back, climbed up the tree to a height of twenty feet, and stole the sheep without any one being the wiser.

I followed her spoor for a little way, and then went to look for the spoor of the lions to see how near they had really been. The story of their visit was plainly written in the dust exactly thirty-seven paces from my tent. I could see how they had lain down, one with his nose towards me, the other at right angles ; for their bodies had hollowed troughs in the dust, their claws had furrowed it, and there were long, shallow grooves where their tails had beaten from side to side. Near by, I found the fresh spoor of the two rhino who habitually grazed round my tent at night ; and I had just come in to breakfast when three elephants advanced slowly through the camp and bore up under the hill to join their usual path.

This path, which followed under the mountain fifty yards above camp, led to the river and was used daily by rhino and elephant. In fact it was their main road, and I had unwittingly pitched my tent in the middle of one of their favourite grazing grounds.

I hunted for the elephants next day, and came upon them at noon in the thickest part of the forest, resting from the heat. In the silvery patterns of sunlight and the deep shadow they were at first almost invisible ; but I presently recognised them for the same four whom I had chased with the dummy, and I still felt guilty towards them. But they were in a big peaceful frame of mind that was very like forgiveness. They stood swaying gently on their feet, dozing and hugely rumbling, and sometimes fanning themselves with their ears ;

and when at length they noticed me, half hidden behind a tree a few yards from them, they eyed me tolerantly and without suspicion.

It was intensely hot, and the air was redolent of the smell of peeling bark and bruised, sappy undergrowth, of the sweetness of the thorn tree flowers, and above all of the warm and friendly smell of the elephants themselves. The stillness was so breathless that the droning of flies came murmuring through the aisles of the trees like a choir of voices. One of the elephants rested his tusks against a branch and fell asleep ; and while he slept, motionless as a rock and very blue in the shadow, a big yellow butterfly hovered round his head. This somehow gave the last touch to the intimate peacefulness of the scene, and I felt that I had only to lay down my camera, tiptoe up to the elephants and sit quietly beside them.

Never would I be so wholly free to do so as I was then, and yet it was just at times when I had a real opportunity of putting my cherished theories to the test that forgotten conversations jumped unbidden to my mind to hold me back : " And of course you promise you won't take risks " ; " if anything happens *we* shall get the blame." It was a pity to have promised, but there had been no other way of coming. These were not merely convenient memories in case (when it came to the point) I jibbed at the experiment, for, curiously enough, as I stood near those enormous friendly beasts towering above me I felt a sense of complete security and confidence in them untinged by fear. I was well enough acquainted with fear, and long practice at spooring and hunting, keeping one's eyes wide open and ears strained to catch the faintest sound, keyed one up to a sensitive pitch of intuition that in civilisation might have seemed like a sixth sense. It was no longer a matter of deduction or of reading danger signals ; if there was danger in the air, you could smell it, just as you could read the minds and moods of animals.

This kind of telepathy, unblunted by the power of speech, is probably highly developed in animals, which is why they can always tell if people are afraid of them. But if I could smell danger I was equally conscious of its absence ; and although to have walked up to the elephants would have seemed outwardly a crazy risk, I believe that at that chosen moment there was no risk at all.

As I watched them, one began rubbing his back against a tree. How often had I seen trees that bore the muddy, shiny marks where an elephant had rubbed himself, yet never before had I watched one doing so ; and by and by I saw something much rarer than this, for another elephant moved round in the undergrowth and lay down.

The cover was too thick for any good pictures, and for once I watched them in peace, and crept away at the end of half an hour without their knowing. I was convinced, then, that what they minded was not my being there (for they plainly saw me) but the metallic noise of the cinema. It always disturbed and puzzled them, filled them with a vague uneasiness and ended by exasperating them past endurance. It meant that one of them was constrained to drive me away, and that invariably ended in trouble and bad feeling.

The other insurmountable difficulty was that they could never become used to my smell. The smell of mankind would always fill them with unreasoning terror or anger ; and if, while I had watched them, the wind had sprung up in the wrong quarter, it would have instantly changed these four gentle elephants into savage and dangerous beasts. My safety hung always on these trifling eddies of air.

It is difficult to imagine the degree of fear and antipathy that mere smell can evoke in wild animals, because we can never experience it. There are to me few better smells (in its own way) than the smell of the elephant house at the Zoo. But to the elephants themselves, even after years of contact with the human race, a Bank Holiday crush may still have a smell that is subtly disquieting. The lions, whose sad, far-away look haunts you for days afterward, are not always, perhaps, dreaming of liberty and the great open spaces. They may be quite prepared to admit that the food is excellent and not hard to work for, that the crowd of human beings for ever watching them is a thing to which they can become fairly reconciled; but knowing how strongly wild animals feel on the subject, I cannot help thinking that they must sometimes say to one another :

" All this I could bear, but I just can't get used to the *smell* ! "

Abdi looked unwontedly gloomy as I rejoined him and we walked beyond earshot of the elephants. This time it seemed that I had gone too close to them even for his liking, and he shook his head reproachfully. I was up in arms.

" The wind was true," I said; " the elephants in a perfect mood. Aren't you enjoying it ? "

" You go up close," he answered, " and this time all goes well and the next and the next; but it will happen once too often."

And of course I could not explain to Abdi that this time, although I had never gone so near to them before, I had never felt so safe. But I guessed that he was secretly elated by our success, for he beguiled the long way home with some of his very best elephant stories.

" Once upon a time," he began, " there was an elephant who caught hold of a native of Somaliland, and lifted him up in his trunk so as to have a good look at him. Each time he waved him in the air the Somali cried for mercy, and at length the elephant set him down very gently upon his feet, and bolted."

Another story was about an elephant who lived at Marsebit (a grassy crater on the Northern District Frontier). This elephant met a safari, and systematically unloaded the sacks of flour from the backs of fifty donkeys, scattered all the flour to the winds, and went his way. Then there was the rather gruesome story of the horse whose rider had been plucked from the saddle by an elephant. The poor horse evidently sustained some kind of mortal wound himself, for he bolted back to camp and was quite intact till they *undid the girths*, whereupon his inwards fell out, and he died.

Abdi declared that he had seen with his own eyes an elephant fall into such a rage with a rhino who had arrived before him at his favourite water-hole, that he seized a branch in his trunk and beat the rhino until he " yelped like a dog."

The recounting of this delightful jungle book brought us to a bend in the road where the forest fell away before a magnificent view of Kilimanjaro. Its snows were already crimson in the sunset, and as I beheld the glory of it my stride lengthened and I forgot the hot and dusty road. Temporarily I even forgot the elephants, as I swung along wholly absorbed in the great and splendid theme of reaching the summit of this equatorial mountain more than nineteen thousand feet high. Only the day before, I had had the good fortune to meet, on his way to Nairobi, one of the few people who had climbed Kilimanjaro. He told me that I could pick up a guide and porters at Moshi, and he drew me a rough map of the climb. This fired me more than ever to make the attempt. I had, of course, no climbing outfit with me ; but the difficulties, he said, were not in the actual climbing. It was a long grind, and success depended not on skill but on one's ability to withstand the high altitude. His parting words were that I must make the attempt soon, before there was any risk of the rains setting in.

By the time I reached camp I had, in imagination, fought my way through insuperable barriers of jungle, scaled the snowy dome itself and looked down into the crater ; at which point these pleasant castles in the air toppled and fell in ruins at a single blow. Karua was waiting for me, and even at a distance I perceived that all was not well. His usual cheerfulness and the alacrity of his greetings were clouded by some misgiving. I at once jumped to conclusions : " Was it the lorry ? " Alas, I had divined the truth; he waved his thin, deprecating hands, the lorry had indeed broken down once more and had been towed to Nairobi for repairs. A matter of a month or six weeks at most, he earnestly assured me. But what was the good of that to me ? In a month's time the short rains would have begun, which would mean fresh snow on Kilimanjaro, and climbing conditions would be hopeless. And there was no other available lorry.

I quickly dispatched a runner to recall the syce who had taken Marouf ahead to El Kinunet. He arrived back about a week later, like Cassius " looking lean," and told me that the heat in the plains was like an inferno and that the mosquitoes at El Kinunet were more terrible than anything he had known. I saw that I was very well off at Namanga. One look under Marouf's girths confirmed my suspicions that the syce had again indulged in some reckless riding.

Apart from this ambition to climb Kilimanjaro, which I relinquished with sorrow and heart-burning (for since the morning in the Game Warden's office I had set my hopes on that climb) the sacrifice of the rest of the programme held immense compensations ; for I had never really wanted to leave Namanga. Had I then known that the future held two months on Mount Kenya, I should have welcomed the fallibility of the lorry as a blessing in disguise, for given the choice of the two mountains, I should always have chosen Kenya first. The glimpse, years before, of its snows and crags, had stirred a longing I could not forget.

Namanga was a paradise of wild animals, the like of which I might roam far and wide over the face of Africa before finding a second time. Besides that, I had now stayed there so long that my roots had gone deep. I was no longer a traveller journeying impersonally through an alien land, taking photographs of wild beasts as curiosities to bring home. Namanga *was* home, and the beasts were beginning to accept me for a neighbour. Their friendship, to me so priceless that I treasured the smallest sign, was, of course, only relative, perhaps partly imagined even; but at the end of these first five weeks I had spent among them, it seemed that they were indeed becoming used to me: the shy animals were no longer quite so shy, nor the dangerous ones so hostile.

It was a big step forward. It meant more to me than climbing Kilimanjaro; and I now determined to stay on at Namanga till the rains hounded me away.

Chapter VII

LONGIDO. MORE ABOUT RHINO. ANT-LION
AND ASTRONOMY

UNTIL I had climbed Ol Doinyo Orok I had looked across
to Longido with an easy heart. It was a fine mountain,
gracious to the eye, but it had remained impersonal. Now
it became a disturbing presence that filled me with restless-
ness. Look whichever way I would, my eye unconsciously
focused upon it and I snatched up the glasses for the twentieth
time to plan a line of approach, noting with a quickening of
the pulse that I should probably need a rope for the summit
which I saw rising like a bare finger of rock above the vegetation. It took away all peace of mind, it taunted me daily
like an insistent question-mark till it finally drove me into
discussing the possibilities with Lembogi.

He was keen enough, but for some mysterious reason
flatly refused to sleep over the border. As the mountain lay
some seventeen miles away and Lembogi held mulishly to
his resolve, I could do nothing till Karua visited his store
again. Although the lorry was out of commission he had a
box Ford, and as soon as he arrived the boys waylaid him
and brought him to camp to talk it over.

If only the Indian population could be composed entirely
of Karuas, life in East Africa would be very nearly Utopian.
He was not seemingly obliging, and taciturn or sly beneath
the surface ; but quick as a live wire, a born optimist, reliable
and honest as the day. He drove at break-neck pace over the
pot-holes day and night, and appeared never to spare a moment
for sleep. It was the busy season, he told me—he took away

hides and brought back calico and ghee and other commodities—and every time I saw him there seemed to be a little less of his emaciated frame. To look at him you would have thought that a puff of wind would blow him away ; but in the pallor of his face, framed by lank black locks, his brown eyes burned with an unquenchable fire. In all the vicissitudes of the road or the capricious behaviour of the lorry, I never once saw him lose heart or patience ; in fact he struck me as being of such outstanding character that I felt certain he must know the *Gitanjali* by heart.

He was now quite unsurprised and perfectly cheerful when I unfolded my plan that he should drive me to the foot of Longido at three o'clock in the morning, wait there all day and bring me back to Namanga in the evening. He agreed at once, saying it would give him an opportunity to transact business at Longido village ; and, although he knew that I had no other means of going there, his price was reasonable. What was so remarkable about him was his respect for time. I had said three o'clock, and he did not arrive somewhere about sunrise : he came precisely at three.

The boys packed themselves in with the rope, provisions and lanterns at the back, Siki and I sat in front, and in what seemed the dead of night we started off with a lively roaring of the engine and scraping of gears under a bright starry sky.

I know well that it was merely the folly of conservatism, but I still ranked motoring in Africa with climbing mountains by the help of a funicular. It was indubitably convenient to be able to cover two long marches with the climb thrown in during the space of nineteen hours, yet try as I would I could not enjoy it with a clear conscience. To arrive by any means other than good honest marching felt like cheating, and I was always surprised when vengeance in the shape of some frightful kind of breakdown forebore to overtake me.

By the time we arrived on the scene of action and Lembogi

had found the path, it lacked only an hour till daybreak. I lit the lanterns, and bidding farewell to Karua we picked our way among the bushes. Lembogi went first, blithely swinging his lantern so that it either shone in my eyes or, when he turned a corner, went suddenly out, leaving me to stumble in total darkness among the roots and stones. But apart from this, I cannot help thinking that half the charm of climbing lies in these early starts.

We went silently, and only the lanterns now and then squeaked rustily in the stillness, or an owl hooted ; and as the path meandered its leisurely way among thorn trees and ant-hills I watched the veld slowly waking around me. The partridges were the first to call, then a dove, and some heavy kind of bird blundered in a tree overhead. The stars paled, the sky reddened, and the world gradually began to take shape beyond the circle of lantern-light. Lembogi stopped to blow his light out, and presently a covey of guinea-fowl ran across the path.

Till then, my only contact with my surroundings had been through smell : the sharp, delicious smell of dew on the dust and dry grass, and sudden currents of air laden with the poignant sweetness of the thorn tree flowers. Sometimes the smell of Lembogi predominated, a definite though not un-pleasant smell, because I immediately associated it with every trek through desert or forest where I had ever followed a native guide. It was an integral part of the march, just as was the play of muscle over his back, and, with each step, the way the groove of the spine dimpled and jerked from side to side under the finely wrinkled and satiny dark skin. The rhythm of it had always fascinated my eyes subconsciously as I tramped behind him mile after mile with my mind far away.

Now as the light came, myriad little undefinable sights and sounds swelled the chorus of stirring life, and the earth rose and shook off sleep. Two jackals slipped like shadows over the rocks, and a herd of impala moved softly among the trees on their way to water. The air was full of the singing and calling of birds, and behind Longido the sun had risen.

Longido turned out as different from Ol Doinyo Orok as any two mountains in the same locality could be.

The approach was easier, the final climb more difficult. The forest, though full of the same trees, was in a more sombre mood, and the flowers were not so numerous or varied, though some, notably the giant begonias, were new. I found no traces of elephant, yet the mountain seemed otherwise to be full of game ; and besides rhino I saw several reedbuck (much lighter coloured than those above Kidongoi) and klipspringer and bushbuck.

Another interesting point of comparison was that while Ol Doinyo Orok during the Great War had been the natural fortress of the British, Longido, facing it across the frontier, had been the stronghold of the Germans. Many a place we came to where Lembogi halted and pointed out the remains of a camp, or an ambush on a pass between two valleys, or farther on, the scene of a battle. " Many men fell on this mountain," he said, and it seemed he must be speaking of some long-forgotten epoch, so unbroken was the silence to-day, so golden the peace.

It was a deceptive mountain, full of surprises. Ol Doinyo Orok, from the point at which I had set out to climb it, had actually looked nearly as far off as it proved to be ; but Longido, seen from camp nearly eighteen miles away, appeared to rise from the ground in one straightforward plane to the top, and it was only when I started to climb it that I found that it was in reality enclosed behind a defence of foothills. We threaded our way among them to a long valley of thorn trees which eventually led up to a grassy shoulder, and there I was amazed to see the summit suddenly appear above me. It was barely seven o'clock, and as is the way with summits in the early sunshine, it looked much nearer than it was. A couple of hours, thought I, and we are there ; but it took nearer six (that is to say, eight hours from the road, where I had left the car).

After the first glory of the sunrise, the mists came hurrying over the downland, hiding everything but the narrow game track edged with dewdrops which I followed ; till a shadow fell across the blank whiteness before me, and the track dived into the forest. Here our very footsteps were muffled, not a breath stirred the limp wet leaves, and there was no sound but of the sullen drip-drip from the branches as the mist sped past, coiling among the dark wet trunks like a thing alive. As I climbed higher, bamboos began to lighten the gloom with their pale feathery leaves, and I came to a clearing beside a stream. The summit, more than ever deceptively fore-shortened, looked down fleetingly between the mists that poured across, and reckoning that I should soon be at the top, I called a halt and waited for the sun to draw up the mists. Collecting the least sodden bits of bark, I was trying to induce a little fire to burn (for it was perishingly cold) when a breeze no stronger than a sigh shook down a quick patter of drops, the sun burst through, and the grey sky was suddenly deepest blue above the trees.

The boys at once broke out into cheerful talk, and as the sun dried and warmed us we eagerly started off again. An hour's stiff climb among the trees brought us out onto a headland of bare rock.

" This," said Lembogi, " is as far as we can go," and indeed it seemed that there was no gainsaying him. We stood directly below the narrow rocky summit, and as I faced it across a green trough of jungle I could see at a glance the difficulties confronting me. It towered above me in an impregnable wall of rock several hundred feet high. To the right (its north face) it fell down far below in a splendid precipice unstained by weather, so that where the sun struck it beyond the long cobalt shadows it shone red and yellow, as though the rock had been newly split, and the edges gleamed sharp cut, as yet unrounded by the mellowing hand of Time. To the left, the impenetrable jungle surged up to the rock like the Atlantic against a cliff.

Through this jungle lay my chance of success, and memorising the line of approach I climbed down from my crow's-nest and dived once more beneath the canopy of leaves.

It was then like hunting in the dark; but if I could steer by guesswork to the point where jungle and rock met, I could gamble on being able to climb upward and round to the back by hugging the foot of the rock. Mountains that seem formidable head-on often relent by allowing you a way up at the side or back.

Abdi received this hopeful theory with marked lack of enthusiasm, and it was clear that he was not enjoying himself. He was ready for any kind of hunting, but he could see no point at all in climbing to the top of this mountain; and since he was greatly looked up to by the camp (not laughed at like poor Mohamed) his opinion carried the more weight. Even Asani was won over against me this time; and Muthungu forgot his rôle of humble scullion, to whom the outing was supposed to be a treat (though he had, of course, to carry the provisions), and had the temerity to raise the unpopular topic of getting lost. Kabechi, leaning on his spear, chewing and spitting out bits of leaf, showed complete indifference either way. Lembogi alone was keen, and I turned and followed him as he climbed upward and lopped the branches out of our way.

It was at first so steep and slippery that we had to cling to the roots with our nails to save ourselves from slithering down. We worked slowly up through the matted undergrowth, now on hands and knees, now scrambling over or under branches which were swathed in hanging moss that trailed out like seaweed ; then ploughing waist-deep through plantations of giant begonia, where Lembogi, with a neat flick of the wrist, carved out a passage through the juicy pink knotted stems. The place reminded me of Muhavura, the volcano where, years ago, we had hunted the gorilla.

Now we passed into dark jungle where the ground vanished altogether beneath the tangle of creepers, and we hauled ourselves up like monkeys among the branches. The twilight was deep and green, and the wall of rock I sought was itself so green with moss that I almost ran my head against it before I saw it. The relief of finding it, at last, made me pause to wipe the sweat and crumbs of bark out of my eyes ; and looking down I realised that I was not only dishevelled and dripping, but scratched and torn, covered with mud and blood and smeared with green slime from the mildewing trunks. The boys were in no better plight, and by the look of us we had so far had the worst of the struggle. There was something about that steaming jungle that was not merely oppressive but positively suffocating, and I longed intensely to climb out above it for one good clean breath of air. The place stank with the acrid and fetid smell of the vegetation which had grown there and died and rotted in successive layers, generation upon generation.

We must escape from it, and the sooner the better. So saying, I felt my way along the dripping wall of rock, and between it and the wall of vegetation I could just squeeze my way. This was plain sailing, and I was beginning to think that I was past the worst, when my narrow corridor stopped short before a precipice. I wormed my way back again and, looking for a way up the rock itself, I found a ledge of heather running above my head. I scrambled up and walked freely at last. But my triumph was short-lived, for after a little way this welcome ledge also ended abruptly before the same precipice as the corridor below it.

I was now getting into serious difficulty, for where I had confidently climbed up I could in no wise climb down again ; I could not go forward, and above me the blank face of rock if not vertical, sloped uncompromisingly and showed no handhold. I cast about this way and that for a way out of the dilemma.

I was now above the blind clutches of the jungle and could see my position. I found that I was farther round to the back (south side) than I had dared to hope, and it was only a short last lap that threatened defeat. The peak rose in a succession of terraces like the one I stood upon, and each terrace was divided from the one above it by a rib of rock just too steep to climb. It was a perfect staircase for a giant, and in imagination I stepped lightly up from terrace to terrace with a careless scorn of merely human stature.

I called to Lembogi, waiting below, to come up and have a look at it. For the first time he was dubious. I thought that if only I could succeed in scaling this first twenty-foot slab, Lembogi would follow me ; and telling him to stand below and break my fall if necessary, I tried to draw myself up on the flat of my palms (by suction like a salamander) and my bare knees. Three times I came to within arm's length of the fringe of heather waving tantalisingly above me, and each time I reached up to grab it I inevitably began to slip down again. This put Lembogi on his mettle, and at my third unwilling descent backward he whipped off his sandals and ran up the face of the rock like a cat on a roof.

The second terrace ran upward and across in the right direction, but like the first it soon petered out, and the slab above it was even higher. Lembogi again took a run at it and, lying flat in the heather at the top, he reached down his spear to help me. I found that my rubber soles gripped well enough, but the spear was none the less a comfort, for one false step and I should have been hurled over the cliff below. A last terrace and a short slab (which even I ran up) and our troubles, it seemed, were really over.

All this had taken time, and the boys were now anxiously calling from below. The sound came up to us like the mournful bleating of sheep. Grinning broadly, Lembogi ran down the slabs like a tight-rope walker to show them the way up. It was a pleasant sop to my vanity to see the fuss they made over it. They tried first with their boots on and then with them off. Then they sat down and said that the thing was impossible. Lembogi ran up and down the slab like a performing dog, showing them how easy it was, but though they watched him with grudging admiration, it was the rope that finally saved us. The moment they had the rope like a life-line to hold on to, they came up hand over hand without a word ; and each one as he came over the top wore his own particular expression of studied indifference.

We breasted through half an acre of white woolly leaves which Lembogi called the blanket plant, and he shouted back that we were there.

We had climbed up by a spiral course which started below the front of the peak and came out on a bare shoulder at the back. But we were not on the summit, and sixty feet or so still rose up like a monolith. " If only I had brought a ladder," I sighed, and reluctantly climbed some rocks on the shoulder a little way off from where I could at least see onto the top.

The boys arrived in their own time and flung themselves down full length in the heather. It was well past midday and we were all a good deal exhausted. But to be beaten at the last by a measly sixty feet (it may have been even less) was hard to endure, and I could not take my eyes from the rock. I was now facing the back of it as three hours before I had faced the front, and as I scanned intently what at first appeared to be a seamless block of stone, my eye fell on a vertical fissure where the stunted little grey bushes turned over silver in the wind. It led up from an overhanging chimney filled with heather. I pointed it out excitedly to the boys, but they only shrugged their shoulders and laughed grimly, as much as to say that they had put up with enough already, and they were not going to break their necks on that.

So I slipped off to find the faithful Lembogi, who apparently felt none of the fatigue of the climb, and had gone off on an exploration of his own. He had been in his element all day, not only as guide, but also as medicine man, and I had observed him during the ascent continually picking, sniffing and tasting different plants. I came upon him close under the summit, which now looked like a huge boulder the size of a house, and found him burrowing on hands and knees feverishly pulling up roots, just as you may catch sight of your Swiss guide surreptitiously digging up gentian.[1]

I persuaded him to relinquish his treasure for the time being and to come and look at that fissure in the rock. He was my last hope, and he had done so much for me already that I did not expect him to do more than shake his head, spit regretfully, and say like all the rest that it was impossible. But I had misjudged him. He was only waiting for me to give the word, and he at once began to pull down the dead heather out of the chimney, and climb up. There was a tricky piece of overhang at the top, but he scarcely hesitated. He swarmed round it, and I saw with disappointment that the rope would not, after all, be needed. He gave me a hand up, and once we gained the fissure, the little bushes gave us stout purchase. We were rapidly hauling ourselves up when Lembogi, who was ahead, stopped and called back :

[1] A fine liqueur is made from gentian roots but, in the interest of Alpine flora, digging them up is strictly prohibited.

" Look ! We are not the first "—and he showed me a slender branch that at some time or other had been sliced clean through with a knife. Though we both sighed involuntarily over the discovery, I had never for a moment imagined that Longido had not been climbed before. And at all events there was not an aeroplane in sight.

We dragged ourselves up over the edge and stood upon the summit, on the very spot where, but a short while ago, I had watched two crows perch and had envied them. It was a flat top composed of broken slabs, and wider than I had expected, for there was room to walk a few steps. The boys cheered from below, but although I urged them to come up, and Lembogi provocatively taunted them, not one of them made a move.

The view swam under an amber haze through which the light played down in columns alternately smoky and iridescent. The clouds hung motionless above, mapping out the plains in imaginary lakes and forests with their ponderous shadows. Near by, Ol Doinyo Orok stood out curiously black in spite of the sunshine ; while far off, other mountains took shape vaguely—Lembogi pointed them out in turn— Gelai, Naseri, Ketumbaine, Mt. Meru (I should have liked to climb them all in turn) ; but Kilimanjaro, which I had looked for in vain from the top of Ol Doinyo Orok, was again invisible in the clouds.

From Namanga I had debated which was Longido's highest point : the peak, or the shoulder which ran upwards to its farthest end. The map gave only one height, 8,581 feet. The boys had held unanimously for the peak, I for the shoulder, and now that I stood on the peak, the shoulder rose higher, but when, after half an hour's climb beyond a dip I reached the shoulder, the peak soared up, and I was never able to decide between them.

We climbed down and started for the shoulder, and on the

way I came upon a beast lying down in the open which the boys declared to be a waterbuck. Only when I put him up at close quarters did I see that he was an enormous bushbuck. He was so black that the white markings showed up on his flanks like snowflakes. The ewe who broke cover at the same time was also exceptionally large, but her coat was the ordinary fulvous red.

I was leading the way up a game path winding among rocks and bushes when the stillness was rent by a sudden crash, and before I knew what had happened I was enveloped by a noise as terrifying as escaping steam. I glanced round, saw the boys scatter, and while I hesitated which way to turn (for the noise seemed to come from every side at once) they yelled to me to run. As I doubled back downhill a rhino burst through the bushes, and swift and terrible as a steam engine came charging down on top of me. I had no time either to dodge or run ; as he thundered down upon me I flung myself sideways to the ground. I saw his horn like a bludgeon driving past me, then the grey mountain of creased belly rushing over my head. The stones rattled on me like bullets, and the smell of him and of dust and flint struck my nostrils hot and pungent.

Shielding my head with my arm, I lay half stunned waiting for him to come back. But his speed and the steepness of the mountain saved me ; for whether he would or no, he carried on in his mad rush and went crashing down into the forest and out of earshot.

The boys ran up to me with scared faces, unable to believe their eyes at seeing me alive and unharmed ; for, looking on, they had thought that the rhino had first rammed me with his horn and sent me flying, and then trampled over me. Poor old Abdi looked quite grey with apprehension and said that he had never seen a narrower escape. He had not dared to shoot for fear of hitting me instead, and could only look on powerless to help me.

Oddly enough, I had started off on this climb with so strong a sense of foreboding that before I left Namanga I had taken a last look round my tent, wondering half whimsically whether I should see it again. The forest and the mountain, however trackless, had been friendly, yet I had been unable to shake off the premonition. I had connected it with the climb. The two crows flapping about my head as I crawled upward to the summit seemed like an ominous warning, and when I reached the ground again in safety, I felt lighter-hearted. But when the rhino suddenly charged, the thought flashed through my mind : " So it is *this*," and with the feeling of fate strong upon me I had already embraced the thought of death, and felt a dazed surprise at finding myself alive.

Indeed, the presentiment had so deeply coloured my mind that I could not look upon the adventure as a chance escape from a rhino ; but rather that death had been intended for me, and that at the last moment, for a reason I could not understand, the decree had been altered and something had intervened to save me.

I now resumed the climb, and although my knees still shook beneath me I sniffed the smell of heather hot in the sun with a sharper joy than ever before, and exulted in the kindly solid earth under my feet. It was my birthday, and I was alive ; I tingled keenly with this consciousness of being alive, and thought that I had never before been grateful enough.

When I reached the top of the shoulder it was only two o'clock, and I called a halt for food and rest. Taking the rucksack with my luncheon from Muthungu, I wandered off till I found a dip in the heather out of the wind; and rolling a cigarette, I lay watching the big white clouds towering up to bridge the rents of unimaginably blue sky.

The beauty of that solitude so far out of the world, so free and protecting, shamed me for my fears. And yet, except that life itself was so glorious, out there you lost all fear of death. Living in nature you came to understand more and more how death is a perfectly natural transition, to be as naturally accepted as all things that come to you : sleep, food, the glory of sunsets, dew and daybreak. As I pondered, it came to me with new truth how one's gladness and strength lay in the whole-hearted acceptance that :

" Everything harmonises with me which is harmonious to thee, O Universe. Nothing for me is too late nor too early which is in due time for thee. Everything is fruit to me which thy seasons bring, O Nature. In thee are all things, from thee are all things, to thee all things return."

The notes of a forest bird echoed musically—half melancholy—among the trees far below ; the shadows were lengthening and it was time to start down. I plunged into the forest, and the moss-covered trees held the westering sun golden and green among their branches. There was no need to hew our way, for the rhino themselves had made a fine zigzagging mountain path—indeed I could have made the ascent at this point with half as much trouble. At every clearing I looked back to the peak now soaring up remotely in blue shadow.

Out once more upon the open downland, I was watching a pair of klipspringer when Kabechi stopped short and made a grab at Siki's collar. There in front of us were two rhino, a cow and calf, asleep in a dust pit. As I watched them the mother rolled over on her back, then settled down again voluptuously in the pleasant sunshine. They had rolled so much that they were exactly the same colour as the red earth around them, like a couple of chocolate truffles, and hardly visible.

I went up with the cinema as near as I dared, which was not particularly daring, for there was not a blade of cover and my nerve had been badly shaken. They were soon awake and suspicious, and stood up looking towards me. Suddenly, without warning, they made a rush in a bee-line for me. There was no possibility for retreat ; so Abdi fired over their backs and they turned and galloped away, raising a cloud of dust that hung in the air long after they had gone.

That was the last of our adventures, and another hour brought me to the valley and the foothills as dusk fell from the deep red sky. I had left the car before the stars had paled, and when I found it once more they had again been lit.

Karua brought us back to camp at ten o'clock that night, and I gave out cigarettes and small presents all round, explaining to Jim that it was in double celebration of our climb and my birthday. It took a great deal of explaining, for apparently birthdays are not a native custom ; there is much song and dance at the birth, after which the event is forgotten, and no native can tell you his age.

An even more intricate subject were the roots which Lembogi had collected. He had told me that the Masai put them into their soup and at once became " as strong as lions." He had given me four or five of these roots, which resembled salsify, and I was eager to try the experiment ; but Jim, very mysterious and enigmatic, told me that if I ate them I should become extremely fierce, and he promptly annexed the lot for his sons in Nairobi.

Next evening I climbed up above the camp to make a sketch of Longido in the sunset. It rose up from the dusky plains, its rocky tower catching the last rays of the sun till it shone like gold. How much more personal does a mountain become as soon as you have climbed it ! Some one has

1a. (*top left*) Vivienne de Watteville's mother, Florence Emily Beddoes (1879–1909). Vivienne inherited her mother's dreamy wistfulness and her subtle sense of humour. This photograph may have been taken soon after her marriage to Bernard de Watteville in October 1899.

1b. (*top right*) Vivienne's father, Bernard Percival de Watteville (1877–1924), photographed at Madeira in 1916. Bernard, known as 'Brovie', was Swiss, a gifted landscape-painter and a dedicated hunter-naturalist. He died in September 1924, after being mauled by a lion near Lake Edward in the Congo.

1c. (*left*) Alice Mary Blandford, Florence's unmarried elder cousin, whom Vivienne called 'Semi-lini' or 'Aunt Semi'. Alice Blandford helped to bring up Vivienne after Florence's death and Vivienne later inherited her house at Hopesay, in Shropshire.

2a. Florence and Vivienne about 1903. The de Wattevilles, after their marriage, lived close to Florence's family home, Hesterworth, near Hopesay, in Shropshire.

2b. Vivienne holding one of her beloved teddy bears. The bear, a civic emblem of the Swiss capital, Berne, inspired a favourite childhood game in which Vivienne and her father pretended to be the 'Bärlies', a Swiss family of bears.

2c. Vivienne, aged nine, in a pensive mood, photographed the year her mother died of cancer.

2d. Vivienne in her teens, in a typical pose. She and her father had the same tranquil, direct gaze which betrayed unwordliness and introspection.

3a. As a fashionable young woman in her twenties, Vivienne cut her hair short. 'Aunt Semi' Blandford firmly disapproved of Vivienne's bobbed hairstyle. To please her aunt, Vivienne grew her hair long again during the 1923–4 African safari with Bernard.

3b. Vivienne, aged 33, with her husband 'Bunt', Captain George Gerard Goschen, and their baby daughter, Tana. Vivienne named her daughter after the Tana River in Kenya. A friend described 'Bunt' as 'one of the real sunshine-makers of this world.'

4a. Vivienne and her father on safari in Kenya, 1924. In front of Vivienne are the skull and horns of a bongo which Bernard shot in the Aberdare mountains. The bongo trophy is interesting, the horns being long and set unusually close together. The dog near Bernard is probably Major, with whom Vivienne and Bernard hunted bongo and giant forest-hogs. The unidentified man playing the accordion may be Major's owner.

4b. The interior of Vivienne's tent during her 1928 safari along the Kenya-Tanganyika border. Vivienne's unused .318 Westley Richards rifle is propped in a corner. Nearby, her little dog, Siki, lies dozing. Vivienne tells how she took 'enormous pains to design a travelling bookcase and other contraptions' which gave the tent a homely atmosphere.

5a. Vivienne's picturesque camp at Namanga in Kenya, from which she climbed Longido, 'a fine mountain, gracious to the eye', here seen in the distance.

5b. A man-eating lioness shot by Mohamed (centre, with rifle) at Kidongoi. 'The death of the lioness lifted the sinister cloud that had hung over the camp, and the sun shone with a more friendly benevolence.'

6a. The hut at 10,000 feet on Mount Kenya where Vivienne lived alone for two months early in 1929. The hut, in Vivienne's words, 'set snugly in a little dip sheltered by giant heath', was built for the use of all-comers by Ernest Carr, a Nairobi businessman.

6b. Looking westward to Mount Kenya along the Nithi Valley. Mount Kenya, sighted by the missionary, Dr J. L. Krapf, in 1849, was first climbed fifty years later by Sir Halford Mackinder, accompanied by two Alpine guides, the brothers César and Joseph Brocherel. Vivienne first saw the mountain in 1923 from the Meru Forest.

7. The twin peaks of Mount Kenya — Batian (17,058 ft) and Nelion (17,022 ft) — were named after two celebrated Masai chiefs. The hanging Diamond Glacier between them was so called because of its covering of exceptionally hard ice. The lower peak, Nelion, was first climbed in January 1929 by a small party led by the late Eric Shipton. Shipton's successful ascent of Batian on the same expedition, during which he met Vivienne on the mountain, was the first since Mackinder reached the summit peak in 1899.

8. The Nithi Falls. In what she called 'this dewy paradise', Vivienne bathed and watched swallows skimming the surface of the pool below.

written that to paint a tree is temporarily to become a tree ; and so it is with climbing a mountain. You come to know and understand it, to feel its individuality and even to share in it. Afterward it is always a friend—holding out an intimate message. The world is full of such friends : mountains, individual trees, favourite reaches of rivers and well-remembered boulders.

And, of course, this second climb had still further whetted my keenness to climb the really big mountains of Africa.

As I sat watching the fading glory, my attention was caught by the sand spurting up in tiny jets at my feet where an ant-lion (*Myrmeleon*) was hard at work making his pit. As he flipped up the sand with his broad head (himself buried out of sight) the walls of his pit became more and more conical, and the sand ran down from the top, evening them round to a perfectly shaped funnel which was now ready to trap any unwary ant who should fall into it. Once the ant falls to the bottom he rarely manages to escape, for the sides crumble relentlessly under his feet as he tries to climb them, and the ant-lion (in clearing the pit of the falling sand) flicks fresh sand over him the while, till at last the ant, weaker and weaker through his hopeless struggle, becomes half buried ; and, as you watch this little drama, you see that the ant-lion has now caught him by a leg and drawn him down out of sight.

This time my sympathies were with the ant-lion, because I had watched him make his trap with such pains, and there was not an ant in sight. I went to look for one, and this led me to the discovery that ants *squeak*. I caught one (a big soldier) in my fingers by his mandibles so that he could not nip me and, fancying that I had heard him make a sound, I held him close to my ear and clearly heard his shrill little squeak for mercy. I thought what a brute I was, and put him back where I had found him.

And so the ant-lion went hungry and I walked home

thinking how difficult it was to be consistent. I could never refrain from taking sides, and one of the hardest lessons to learn was to let Nature work out her own laws, and not to interfere.

Night had fallen and the sky was wide with stars. Living under them month after month I came to learn much of their rising and setting, and how in the passing of a few hours the face of the whole sky is changed. It was then late in August, and Orion did not rise till midnight. I had been reading astronomy since early morning and I could think of nothing else. As I looked up to the Milky Way, stretching above me like a misty sheen, I tried to realise that our glorious sun is but one of the millions of its stars ; that if one could travel as fast as light—300,000 kilometres a second—it would take four hours to reach Neptune, the farthest planet, and *four years* to reach even the nearest star. And one could go on travelling— always at 300,000 kilometres a second—for a hundred years, or a thousand, or a million, yet never reach the end of other worlds and other suns.

Flammarion[1] wrote : " The centre is everywhere, the circumference nowhere . . . there is neither above nor below— neither zenith nor nadir—neither east nor west—neither left nor right. In whatever direction we picture the abyss there is Infinity in every sense. In this immensity, the groups of suns and worlds that constitute our visible universe form but an island in a great archipelago, and in the duration of eternity, human life—the life of our whole planet itself—is but . . . the dream of a moment."

To try to realise—but we cannot realise it, for this is thinking in forms outside our knowledge, beyond the limit of imagination. In trying to strain our eyes into the Infinite, in trying to grasp this tremendous, overwhelming conception of God, the mind strains and stretches itself to breaking point. It is like

[1] This was before the books of Professor Jeans had appeared.

trying to contain the ocean in a thimble. Yet I found consolation in the thought that one drop of the ocean is as truly the ocean as a million tons.

But when you return from this terrific, inconceivable journey, the earth seems very little and very much your own, and how should you feel lonely ? For everywhere you are in it, living where you belong. Not just one little hamlet or province or even continent, but the whole earth is your home. It is overwhelming to think of life—human beings—on this planet thousands of centuries ago, yet in the universal reckoning this is but the intake of the breath.

You can go wandering among the stars and lose yourself in immensity, or you can come back and study the ants or the science of the atom, and find as marvellous a cosmos in your own body.

The world is full of hundreds of beautiful things we can never possibly have time to discover, and there is no time to waste in regrets over tiny individual dilemmas. Life is too short and too wonderful. There is no time to be unkind or envious or ungenerous, and no sense in enslaving the mind to the trivialities of the moment. For you can be equal to the greatness of life only by marching with it ; not by seeking for love but by giving it, nor seeking to be understood but learning to understand.

And when it is all over, there will be an agony of remorse because one spared the effort and did not make more of that little span of opportunity ; and knowing reality at last, who knows but that one will look back with unassuageable regret upon one's pitiful little faith.

Chapter VIII

HOME AT NAMANGA. TROUBLE WITH THE MASAI. PROFESSIONAL PHOTOGRAPHERS

THE charm of camping in one place for a long time was that special charm which grows out of familiar surroundings. The same trees greeted me on waking, and the birds now hopped down with a look of expectancy, waiting for me to put out their food and water. A lizard had adopted the tent as his home and came out to sun himself on the rifle-case, while the mud-building wasps (*Eumenes maxillosa*) looked upon the tent as such a permanency that they built their nests against its walls.

Jim said that if these wasps build in your house it is a happy omen ; and though it meant dodging in and out with immense care and circuitous manœuvring (for they hung poised in the air endlessly before they could make up their minds to land) I did nothing to discourage them.

No one worked harder than they. From early dawn through the long, hot hours when all else slept, they made their patient journeys, bringing each time a microscopic pellet of beautifully prepared clay. Very slowly the nests began to take shape, till after weeks of toil they resembled tiny gourds (half an inch in diameter) strung together one above the other in three or four, and sometimes five stories. There were no slap-dash modern methods about the mud-building wasps ; each gourd was a labour of love, rounded and finished off with a delicate precision that gave it the look of fine terra cotta.

These wasps were not only lucky, but, according to the boys, they had a very poisonous sting, so that I felt both flattered and a little frightened by their patronage. They were about an inch and a half long and had a striking and rather sinister beauty. They had personality which you could not ignore (or it may have been the knowledge that they could sting very hard if they took a dislike to you) and it became an integral part of camp life to watch them as they poised humming in mid-air, their purplish wings blurred with swift vibration and their bulbous, steely blue-black bodies curved sharply inward to waists so long and incredibly thin that you marvelled how they managed to hold together.

I noticed that as they advanced in their building operations the ichneumon flies (*osprynchotus*) began to follow them in and out of the tent. These, at a casual glance, were the same size as the wasps ; but in reality they were different craft altogether, and so gracefully slender, with long, narrow wings, that they made the wasps look old-fashioned and clumsily rigged beside them. This stream-line impression was further carried out by the two lance-like ovipositors projecting from the tail. The ichneumons also hung poised, and their orange legs (in daring contrast to their shining black bodies) hung down limply in a bunch like those of the hawthorn fly. But it was the relationship between these insects that puzzled me. What was the motive that linked their destinies ? You would see an ichneumon cruising about in a disinterested kind of way, but as soon as the wasps were safely out of sight making their bricks, the ichneumon would pry furtively into the nest.

One day the nest was finished, four stories high with a round opening, wide-lipped like the edge of a decanter, left at the side of the topmost story. Presently the wasp flew in with a large green caterpillar (in which she had doubtless laid her eggs) and after pushing it down carefully inside the nest she flew off to fetch more clay. Next time I chanced to look up

I was astonished to see the ichneumon emerging from the hole. The wasp returning with the clay soon completed her work by hermetically sealing up the hole with it.

It was not till years afterward that the mystery was explained to me, and I learned that the ichneumon fly is the parasite. As soon as the mud-building wasp's back is turned, the ichneumon seizes her opportunity to lay her own eggs in the caterpillar. Her eggs hatch out first, the larvæ destroy those of the mud-building wasp, and feed on the caterpillar intended for them. The ichneumon fly in her turn also has a parasite. So that what starts by being the incubator of the mud-building wasp is appropriated by the ichneumon, who may herself be deposed by a third insect which finally triumphs and eats its way through the walls of the nest to the threshold of life.

I need not, after all, have held the mud-building wasps in such servile veneration, for I was told that their sting is very bearable.

Lastly, there was a pair of tiny green and gold bee-eaters. They had a favourite thorn bush close to the tent, they were nearly always there, and they always hunted in the same manner : one perching on a branch while the other darted upward after a fly, swooping with pointed, kite-shaped wings outspread, and the moment she alighted the other would fly off for his turn. If they were not there, I knew where to find them in a similar bush higher up the hillside ; and they not only did all their hunting from these two special bushes but always chose the same twig for their observation post.

It was a happy place. Day after day the world about me woke to silver as delicate as filigree against the blue sky, the spurs of rock quivered in the heat ; and the sweet silence was broken only by the drowsy murmur of doves, the faint tinkle of cowbells or the chopping of wood. Even the autumn held no feeling of sadness or finality, though every breath of wind brought down a few more dead leaves, and the mountain-side was bleaching to russet and gold, stabbed here and there with scarlet.

They were halcyon days blessed with the care-free happiness of childhood, full of the bubbling irrepressible joy of Haydn's little trio in G major which I loved to play there, and holding all that the heart could desire : forests to roam, elephants to photograph, books with the leisure to read them, mountains to climb, a river to dream by, and the freedom and friendship of the sky and wilderness.

It was not due entirely to Africa, it certainly was not because I was achieving anything, for outwardly I was merely leading perpetual summer holidays : this overflowing happiness and well-being, I now understood, was due simply to the fact that there one lived in Nature the whole time, without being for a moment separated from her. In civilisation you feel restless and unhappy because you are spending quite three-quarters of this short and precious life indoors. Out there you lived under the open sky, and at worst there was only a strip of canvas between you and it. From your bed it was but a step, and the earth and rocks and trees were all there waiting for you. You were never for a second banished from them. Nothing was a waste of time any more, not even eating or sewing, and at last you lost that thwarted feeling of always *missing something*, and the reason was because you were always in it.

Living in civilisation is like looking at Nature through the window, or going for a walk in gloves. You never really mingle with it. The first green grass I see after London fills me with an irresistible longing to have a good roll, like a horse when his saddle is taken off ; and there must be heaps of people who feel like that who yet sacrifice their natural impulse to the tyranny of custom.

When I looked back to civilisation I wondered how I could ever, of my own free will, give up this freedom for that little circumscribed and artificial life. Yet none can escape it for long, and so many not at all. And even if circumstance compelled one to live in a city, there is one immensely consoling thought : the breeze, the sun, the width of the blue sky above—these things will be with one always, wherever one is till the day one dies ; in these things are security and one's innermost delight, and they shall never fail.

It was all very fine to take this lofty view about eating being a waste of time, but events came suddenly to a point where it looked as though there might soon be nothing left to eat.

The Masai, for some reason which they would not divulge, refused to let me have another ounce of meat or another drop of milk. The deadlock lasted for five days. They refused to come and talk, and I refused to continue as public dispensary. I hated this futile retaliation, and the position was frankly absurd, for there was no real ill-feeling upon either side. I knew that I had only to make a sign, and the District Commissioner would settle the affair in two minutes ; but I was loath to call for help and to admit that I was no match for them myself. The situation was a delicate one to handle, for I could not persuade them to sell me meat at any price, and had I used force and raided their cattle, one could never tell but it might have provoked a Masai rising on a grand scale.

It was all very unpleasant : the Masai greeted me with sour looks and the boys began to grow discontented with the poor fare, so that on the sixth day of this unaccountable siege I issued an ultimatum. Either they would come to terms by sunset, or I would send a message to the District Commissioner. And dismissing the matter from my mind I took Lembogi, the one faithful Masai left, and went off to look for elephants.

I found the same four (whom I now knew well) in one of their favourite haunts at the edge of the forest. It was a piping hot day, and they stood motionless under the trees, fanning themselves with their ears. The wind blew too uncertainly for a close approach, so I sat down in a glade for an hour or so waiting for them to move into the open, and at last they wandered along the edge of the swamp to feed.

There is nothing in the world so whole-hearted as an elephant feeding. The air was filled with the swish of grass like the murmur of waves, as they fed and moved among it. While three of them went deeper into the swamp, the fourth fed at the edge ; and I watched him twisting his trunk round and round each sheaf of grass—as one might twist macaroni on a fork—and then wrench it away. You had only to try to break one of the stalks of that coarse elephant grass to discover how much strength was needed to pull away a whole armful at once ; and it was protected by sharp stiff hairs which I found as difficult to extract from my hands as caterpillar hairs, and very painful.

The wind for once blew so true that Abdi did not even bother to test it with his bottle of ashes, and I crept up confidently to within fifteen yards. The elephant saw me perfectly well and even paused in his feeding to look at me. There was an amused little twinkle in his eye and, there is no doubt about it, he was literally *smiling*, as much as to say : " I know quite well you're there," as he turned back with friendly tolerance to his meal.

I felt positive that if I could have seen those elephants every day for a year, they would have ended by feeding from my hand. One of my dreams (if ever I become an eccentric millionaire) was to have lorry-loads of bananas and sugar-cane sent down to Namanga daily, so that I could give the experiment a proper trial. Abdi's imagination did not carry him quite as far as that, but he did say that the elephants had already told us quite plainly that they did not consider us any more as intruders, for only the other day one of them (a cow) had picked up a little stick within a few yards of us, and played with it, tossing it up and catching it in her trunk ; but as soon as she caught sight of the party of professional photographers she very nearly charged them.

Abdi was worth his weight in gold, not only for his impossibly wild stories, but because he had the gift of investing animals with personalities. We enlivened many a weary mile homeward with imaginary conversations between the elephants, and the joy of fairy-tales was ours because we really *believed* them. Asani occasionally contributed ideas of his own, but I am not sure how much he really loved the elephants, for he was usually out of sight by the time I wanted the second camera.

I had four cameras : a Bell and Howell half-gauge cinema camera, a Victor half-gauge cinema camera which could take slow-motion pictures, but I put little faith in this one for it had an exasperating habit of jamming at the most critical moments, and I used it only as a reserve if I wanted more film in a hurry. I had also a good Reflex quarter-plate for still photography, but found by experience that my little Zeiss vest-pocket camera (which I carried on my belt with the field-glasses) was far handier, and the enlargements were so clear that I could never afterward distinguish between them. I did not develop the films on the spot, for fear of being unable to keep the water sufficiently cool, but sent them to Nairobi whenever chance offered. I paid dearly for this error, for I could not see the results and profit by my mistakes soon enough, and only found out after I had left Selengai that all the telephoto work on birds with the Reflex was a failure because there was something wrong with the focusing of the telephoto lens. But the Bell and Howell made up for it, and the photographer's letter acknowledging the last three hundred feet of elephant film described them as distinctly good, which at once fired me to try for something even better.

Next day, the village elders arrived in ceremony, and we

held a great pow-wow lasting for an hour or more with most satisfactory results. A cow and a goat were sacrificed, and the past was amply washed out with at least a gallon of foaming milk. The old men were quite carried away by their own eloquence and their promises of goodwill—anything, in fact, so long as I would recall my letter to the District Commissioner.

But they were too late with their truce, for Karua had taken my letter overnight.

I had merely written for a line of advice, and great was my consternation on the following evening when Hugo arrived in person, post-haste, to learn what the trouble was about. It was greater still when I found that he took so serious a view of the matter that he was determined that I should leave Namanga at once and return with him to Kajiado.

We argued it out over dinner, and I was fighting a losing battle when in the middle of it all one of my tame rhino came round to change the conversation. Hugo was obviously taken aback by the grazing rights of my camp, and I quickly followed up my advantage by telling him how two and sometimes three rhino made a habit of feeding round my tent almost every night, which gave me ample protection from an army of ill-intentioned Masai. The rhino who had broken in upon our conversation continued to uphold me by drawing near enough to preclude further argument.

Having won my point, I was immensely grateful to Hugo for coming ; for he arranged with the Masai to *sell* me their cattle, which is what I had wanted from the first. It was unfair to them that they should have been obliged to keep me in meat over so long a stay, however much doctoring I did for them.

It turned out that there was more in this embargo of theirs than met the eye, and that they had been using me in some involved way as a stalking-horse for making trouble among themselves. Hugo's intervention not only saved me from any future experiment of this kind, but invested me with an imaginary importance in their eyes, and they thereafter appealed to me as a sort of intermediary between themselves and the Government. The old men would come and request me to write letters for them pleading all kinds of new concessions. One of these was naturally connected with the border rights. "Why," they asked, "if Kenya Colony and Tanganyika Territory both belong to Kinki Georgey, why should there be all these regulations about the frontier between them?" It was in truth very tantalizing, for their cattle were dying off daily from starvation in full view of an untouched grassy expanse, golden as ripe corn. This was the quarantine zone between the two countries, and no animal was allowed to graze there from either side.

A week later another contretemps (which I also failed signally to put right) was the unforeseen cancelling at the last minute of the Namanga cattle auction. The vast piebald flocks which had been assembled for it, and were slow to disperse again, not only ate up every bit of the scanty remaining grass, but attracted all the lions of the district; and the night was made lively by lions grunting, Indians shooting at them from the store, natives yelling, cows lowing, dogs barking and a pack of howling and snickering hyenas.

The lions took toll of the cattle to the tune of three bulls, and I went out next morning to spoor the drag along the road, hoping that Abdi might handle the rifle to more purpose than I the pen in my pseudo-official capacity.

Coming round a bend of the road, I caught sight of a white man standing beside his car. He had his back turned to me, and quick as thought I retreated noiselessly and slipped into the forest. It was fun to sniff danger and dive under cover like an antelope, to feel oneself on the side of the beasts and able to look at man through their eyes—an intruder to be feared and avoided. Extraordinary creature, Man ! Cunning in his own way, admittedly, but contemptibly lacking in jungle-lore ; he couldn't even smell his enemy, however the wind blew, and was so dull of hearing that you could walk into him at ten paces and he seemed totally unaware of danger.

But the day was ordained for sociability, and on my way home from the elephants that evening I ran plumb into another car round the corner. I jerked the rein, wheeled Marouf under the trees and clapped my heels to his sides. But I was too late. The car pulled up and out jumped a man whose face seemed vaguely familiar. He promptly hailed me and introduced his friend. We had been shipmates in the *Mantola*, he genially informed me. They had had a wretched trip from Moshi with breakdowns most of the way, and as it was then about sundown I offered them the hospitality of the road.

I was still puzzling over that face. It was as tantalizingly elusive as the odd piece in a jig-saw puzzle. Only towards the end of dinner did the fantastic truth dawn on me that he was no other than the ship's very blackest sheep, almost permanently (though quite harmlessly) inebriated, and unanimously barred from polite society. But I began to think that the ship had been unjustly harsh with him, for he never broke out into anything more serious than :

" I say, you know, this *is* rummy," varied with :

" I say, you know, you had such pretty frocks on the boat, and then we meet you out here all alone on a mule ! "—which striking proof of the incongruous continued to occupy him till they left. Only one other thing worried him, and he frequently recurred to it. Although he talked a good deal about the Wide Open Spaces, he would suddenly look around him (the hyenas were already making the night dreary with their howls) and with a shiver ask me if I didn't get the " Wullies." I had no very precise idea what the " Wullies " were, but soothingly reassured him.

His friend was one of the old school, a rough diamond in the best sense of the word, who had pioneered the wilds of East Africa for the past thirty years. He had lived alone on the veld and had not been lonely, and he had that understanding —depth of experience, or what you will—which lifts men above race, class or prejudice to the plane where they are human. We talked of Tanaland (in itself an unfailing bond) where he had worked for years on the lovely Bellazoni estate, which had left in my mind a vague, happy impression of flame-trees, swallows crowding along the tops of the doors, and pine-apples whose flavour I have never found again.

Karioki excelled himself, and Jim, deft and silent, anticipated our every want ; though he was heart-broken when I rather impulsively put the three remaining eggs into the mayonnaise.

It was after ten o'clock when the travellers started off again, and they hoped to reach Nairobi, at the end of nearly a hundred miles of dreadfully bad road, before the night was out.

I came back, stirred the logs to a blaze, and longed, for once, for some one to talk it over with. Musing on these chance encounters I thought that if one were a tree spreading a shade for travellers, this is what it might feel like. A little disturbance, the sound of voices, and they are gone. And you ? You rustle your leaves in the breeze, and wonder, and settle back into the peace of the forest with a sigh of content. In reality, this rather too complacent reflection only came into my head some days later when two strange women, motoring to Tanganyika, caught me in camp unawares, and ingenuously explained that they had heard of me from some natives at the ford, and wanted " to see what I looked like."

I cannot think why it seemed to me an inescapable duty to ask them to tea. I quickly regretted it, for their duty appeared to them even more urgent, and they took me to task and scolded me so roundly for the dangers I ran and my misguided choice of occupation that I felt as if I were sitting between the Red and White Queens. I should not have minded that, but when they were rude about my tame rhino, my ears went right back. The incident, trivial enough in itself, made me feel that I was alone, and that what I had such a longing to express was after all incommunicable.

The night was gloriously lit with stars, and the slender sickle of the moon hung low in the west. I listened to Mozart, and Schubert's Trio in B flat minor, and they reassured me again with a sense of profound companionship that all I felt had been felt before, and superbly expressed.

I rose from the fire and went up and sat among the rocks. Camp slept already, the moon had gone, and the silence was so absolute that the earth withdrew into the shadows and you were aware only of the stars scintillating and fluttering in the velvet depths of space. You felt suddenly nearer to them than to the earth, and losing the friendly touchstones of east and west, above and below, was, after all, not so very terrifying. Travelling slowly down the sky through sapphire depths and fiery constellations, my eye came back again to the tent. It looked very snug with the firelight playing over it and the tree sheltering it, and beyond it the fond curve of the mountain black against the stars.

Aching with a strange happiness, confident that this time I should be able to pin down a truer shade of meaning, I ran back, lit the lantern and opened my diary. But the words eluded me and slid away. I wanted the purple splendour of language but could only write haltingly of happiness that it is something that brings you into a realm beyond words ; words express it only as a blob of cadmium yellow can express the sun. It is this wonderful melting into all things and belonging to them. Lying on the earth and feeling " we are the same substance," and all things spring from it and return to it in an endless cycle of joy. And being all the time transported out of yourself in the sheer love of things. The breeze from the stars kisses your eyes, and the blue sky wraps you round with light. The clear, sweet colour of things sings to you and bears away your heart on silver wings into infinity.

This morning (I continued) I ran up among the rocks to hail the red rising sun ; and after breakfast I lay under a favourite tree and watched the vultures sailing in circles far above me, and the pair of little green and gold bee-eaters chasing butterflies. I say " watched," but for the time being there is no I and they : I *am* they.

Although cars occasionally passed by, the place was immune from any organised hunting or filming parties, for they were not allowed into the Game Reserve. There was, however, one exception, namely the party of photographers above mentioned. The leader of the expedition was a world-famous hunter and photographer, and he had permission to go where he liked.

They camped at the river for three days on their way to Tanganyika, and were eager to see what I had now come to look upon as *my* elephants ; so I offered to guide them, and they gave me a lift in one of their cars. I then learnt for the first time how game photography ought to be done, and I was secretly glad that I had not found it out before, because it was such a business in itself that the element of hunting was of necessity eliminated altogether. There was no thought of coming into touch with the animals themselves, nor would you have had a spare moment in which to lift your eyes to the blue sky above, or to sniff all the forest smells about you.

The leader and his young studio expert were both possessed of cameras weighing about 200 lb. apiece, complete with tripods fit to bear machine-guns. A young settler friend was also of the party, and we set out from the cars a long Indian file with porters staggering under the equipment. Fortunately the elephants were in a perfect mood for co-operation, and we found them without difficulty, 'twixt swamp and forest, just where I had hoped they might be. Lembogi pointed them out, and I whispered :

" There they are ! "—anticipating that the photographers would now creep stealthily forward. Which only showed how little I knew about it ; for instead of that, a halt was called, the cameras were unpacked, fitted, and adjusted, and the tripods were also unpacked, fitted, and adjusted.

My elephants were monuments of patience, and I felt proud of them. For usually you had just one and a half priceless minutes while they crossed the open, and then, either the forest had taken them among its shadows or the swamp had drawn its green curtain after them.

However, once all the parts were assembled, I imagined that the word of advance would be given, and that the thrilling moment was about to begin. But these cameras being fitted with magnificent eight-inch and twelve-inch lenses, the difficulty seemed not so much to draw close enough as to get far enough away to include the whole elephant on the screen. Anything under seventy yards was useless, and these powerful lenses at a range of thirty yards or so would probably have recorded nothing but three rings of his trunk or six hairs on his tail.

My own cameras had dwindled to the size of peas, and I felt far too bashful to admit that they were effective only at a miserable twenty yards. But I could not keep it dark for long, for the photographers assured me that they had exposed as much film as they wanted, and pressed me to take my turn.

I then had an exciting time on my own. Crossing a little stream to the elephants' side of it I lost Abdi, discovered that an elephant was walking down upon me and that I could not get away. The swamp cut me off in front, the stream trapped me on my right, and on my left was the elephant. The one ford back through the impenetrable wall of rushes I had already left a hundred yards behind me. At that moment, Abdi was re-crossing the stream in search of me, and ploughing such a desperate passage that I thought he was another elephant close by ; while he thought the same of me, so that instead of meeting we were running in opposite directions, and playing a ridiculous game of hide-and-seek.

Meanwhile, the elephant loomed up over the top of the grass, his trunk lifted above his head as with delicate, swan-like motions he felt for the wind ; and he had nearly reached the hedge of rushes along which I had come.

My only chance of escape lay in slipping back to the ford, but my only way there lay between the elephant and the rushes, and this the elephant had now narrowed to a mere alley. It was now or never, and I made a wild dash for it, scuttling back under the elephant's very eyes and feeling exactly like a field-mouse doubling back as the last blades of corn fall under the reaper. I overshot the opening to the ford, rushed back again and scrambled through to safety ; while the photographers had a fine picture of the elephant as he broke through the rushes in search of me, with his ears spread and my wind in his nostrils, before he gave up and turned back for the swamp.

After that, a couple of wart-hog ran towards us, and a baby waterbuck ; and finally, after the leader of the expedition had gone home, snorting something about blood pressure— and it *was* hot—we had a splendid view of the elephants. The two young men, in the absence of the restraining hand, now squared their shoulders, discarded the telephoto lenses, and prepared to enjoy themselves with some close-up work.

The elephants soon picked up our wind, however, and came towards us very deliberately ; and I admired the way in which the young studio expert, who had never seen a wild elephant before in his life, stood his ground before these three horribly daunting elephants bearing steadily down upon him. Perhaps it was partly the bravery of ignorance, and I did not like the look of things at all, for to make a stand before oncoming elephants when you know that they have got your wind is to court trouble, and no one can expect to make a nimble retreat with a 200 lb. camera. The first golden rule of the game is to make sure that the wind is your friend.

Another thing the elephants had taught me was that they are, of all animals, the most temperamental, and you must respect their moods. There are days when you can go right up to them and they bear with you with a big-hearted benevolence ; and there are other days when you know instinctively that they are not in the mood to brook liberties, and fifty yards is too close. This was their mood now, and Abdi and I read the signs of their impatience with extreme apprehension as they turned and circled and advanced again with their ears outspread. The photographer and his friend naturally enough resented my warnings and told me that I had been much nearer to the elephant myself. But they seemed not to be aware that the elephants were frowning their displeasure as plain as could be, and were now really angry.

I was thankful when we got safely away, for nothing made me more uneasy than these tactics of going up to elephants in a crowd. We were, including their porters, an army of about fifteen people. It felt a great deal safer (even though I did go nearer) to take one trained gun-bearer and carry my little Bell and Howell in my hand. The amusing part of it was that on the way home Abdi and Asani both said the same thing of their own accord, which kind words were balm to me ; for on the way out they had gasped with wonder and admiration at the professional cameras, and I had resigned myself sorrowfully to the thought that they would ever afterward despise my own methods.

Now, out of the corner of my eye, I saw Abdi spit on the ground and declare with audible disgust that it had been

" no good at all to-day, but what can you expect if you don't watch out for the wind ? " and so on, treating the photographers' boys to a highly fanciful version of our prowess in the past.

I had expected that when they met another party, my boys might get out of hand ; and it warmed my heart the way they rallied round me before strangers, taking orders at the salute (which was all their own idea) and generally proving to the outside world that we were a co-ordinate and happy unit with no weak spot in our defence.

I sundowned with the photographers, and their leader entertained me with stories that would have made even Abdi's eyes round with astonishment.

Next day I gave them Lembogi, who had already located the elephants, and settled down deliberately to write up my mail.

Scarcely an hour had elapsed before the cowherd arrived, full of excitement, to tell me that there were elephants just below camp ; so I set off at once, happily reflecting that after all we each had our elephants. But when I found them I I had grave misgivings that they were my own four friends. Abdi chuckled, for although he did not hold with the combining of forces of the previous day, he did not fall in with my idea of sacrificing our own opportunities, either. Lembogi had found the elephants at the far end of the swamp, and the fact that they had now come back to us was enough for Abdi, who immediately inferred that they had talked it over among themselves overnight, and said :

" Who are these strangers invading our swamp ? To-morrow we will return to the camp of our own people ! "

But I am afraid that the more obvious explanation for their leaving the swamp was that a grass fire was raging there.

I watched them for a long time pulling down branches and feeding with whole-hearted concentration ; and I was filming the cow elephant who was playing with the little stick afore-mentioned, when the two young photographers arrived on the scene and began operations. I quitted at once, having had more than my share already, and they joined me later on for tea.

The elephant had turned crusty, and they were describing how she had nearly charged the camera, when their gun-bearer interrupted the story by signing to one of them to hand over the matches. With a bravado that incensed me he then proceeded to light a cigarette inside my tent. I took him up coldly, for I was very angry—the kind of anger when you pick your words and lower your voice—and he was so much surprised that his apology was at once disarming.

It was not for me to admonish some one else's servant, but all this had happened in front of Jim, and as it passed unchallenged I could not forbear. If a white servant had behaved like that, some one would doubtless have kicked him ; and a black one, who has as little malice as a child, will cheek you for the fun of the thing. It is the easiest thing in the world to spoil natives in the wrong way.

The studio expert was American and very young, and he was a tremendous idealist about all men being brothers. We argued it to and fro with the heat that such questions unfailingly provoke. Africa was not yet ripe for that point of view, I told him ; it was still a country where each white man was outnumbered by many hundred black. But even—for the sake of argument—admitting the idea of brotherhood, liberty and licence would always remain the poles apart. The ideal was to come in touch with your men so that you won their confidence and affection, and at the same time to maintain as near as possible military discipline which, at heart, they were the happier for, because if they ceased to respect you they ceased to think you worth while.

What retort the studio expert made to this counsel of

perfection I cannot remember ; and his friend, who was a settler and had far more experience in the management of natives than either of us, wisely held aloof from the discussion. It was then near sundown, and we strolled back to their camp and satisfactorily buried the hatchet in a mixed vermouth.

They wanted the elephant pictures to incorporate into a film they were producing in the form of a connected story, and, having obtained all the pictures they needed, they left Namanga a couple of days later.

This gave me the idea of making an introduction to my own film ; and I set to work to paint the title with iodine on sheets of foolscap, which ran :

The 4 Patient of Namanga. The pieces were then glued together in one strip which, held by Abdi, Asani and myself, was brought close up to the camera till it (I hoped) became legible.

Once started on the idea of composing the film, I thought of making the boys take part in it. This caught their fancy, for they loved acting above all things, and laughed uproariously throughout the rehearsals.

The film was to open with Siki asleep, and me reading in front of the tent (camp idyll) when Kabechi and Lembogi run up to tell me (in pantomime) that they have marked down the elephants. I then seize the cameras, by which time Abdi and Asani arrive with Marouf. I leap into the saddle (in true Hollywood style), and we start off.

No one had explained the meaning of all this noise and bustle to poor Marouf, who was thoroughly bewildered and drove his forefeet into the ground, refusing point-blank to come into the picture. He was dragged forward by force and ignominiously pushed from behind, so that his contribution had to be filmed again.

After going along a stretch of road under spreading acacia

trees, I leave Marouf and we begin spooring and hunting, then sight the elephants from the top of an ant-hill. Here, some genuine close-up film of the elephants is introduced ; after which follow serious Polytechnic pictures showing the country, the water-holes, the spoor, the trees they have rubbed themselves against, or stripped of bark, or pulled down ; and close-up pictures of the different green-stuff, earth-nuts, etc., which they feed upon.

On the way home, I actually came upon the elephants themselves. They were in thick forest, and after waiting my opportunity for an hour or so, I managed to film the big bull in a lovely setting, framed among the trees and reflected in a forest pool.

Chapter IX

ALL ABOUT ELEPHANTS

A few days later, a tremendously lucky thing happened. The boys declared that it was the best of all good omens, for each of us individually, and for the whole enterprise, and that Fortune smiled upon us.

But I am anticipating; for to begin with, Lembogi merely came in with the news that there were five elephants close by.

As so often happens when one thinks one has only to walk a stone's throw, and sets off blithely in the noonday heat without bothering to take a bottle of cold tea, I walked for miles and saw nothing. The elephants had disappeared into the thickest part of the swamp, and a long round eventually brought me to the water-hole where I had once successfully ambushed a herd of zebra. I arranged a better hiding-place, and waited; but as there was no sign of any living creature I started for home.

On the way, I filmed two diminutive little goatherds shepherding their flocks. They were perhaps four or five years old, and whistled and drove the unruly goats with delicious gravity. They finished my last few feet of film, and I sat in the shade to put a new hundred feet into the camera. This, as it turned out, was the most inspired thing that I could have done; for I was no sooner ready than I heard the elephants coming out of the long grass.

I waited at the edge of the swamp, between them and a herd of cattle and donkeys that began to stream past into the grass where the elephants were yet partly concealed. I edged closer with the camera ready, wondering what would happen when they encountered, and managed to film the elephant and the cattle browsing peaceably side by side. It was an incredible sight, and you might have rubbed your eyes and wondered whether the millennium had dawned, when the lion and the lamb shall lie down together.

By and by the elephants began to consider that the cattle were presuming too far upon their privileges. The largest elephant came out into the open, walked down upon them shaking his head with a big admonishing grunt, threw out his trunk as you might crack a whip, while he literally herded together the straying cows and donkeys and sent them stampeding back. This done, he swung round, and with gentle deliberation rejoined his companions; and the cattle fell once more to grazing.

If this had been one of Abdi's stories I should have thought it a very good one. But seeing it with my own eyes I felt that I was at last seeing elephants as they really were, not as they appear to be when they suspect that human beings are watching them. There was such big forbearance in that act or, I would rather say, such perfect adequacy. With just a flick of his trunk he could have dealt death around him, or by moving just a trifle faster he could have trampled a dozen beasts in his stride. But the mutual understanding was perfect : the cattle were not seriously alarmed, but they thereafter kept at a respectful distance.

Elephants are probably aware, to a fine fraction, of their own strength. Only watch one in the Zoo, how he will crack a hazel-nut under his foot without crushing it ; but it is in trying to do it yourself that you can appreciate the nice judgement that is required.

Still I waited, hoping that the elephants might show themselves again, when suddenly, with the sound of waves running upon a beach, the tall grass parted before an elephant emerging back foremost dragging a second elephant after him by his trunk.

It was then that Abdi almost jumped for joy, exclaiming in English :

" Oh ! *Good luck !* "—and Lembogi flung restraint to the winds and capered madly, throwing his spear into the air. Abdi then explained to me that, although the white man does not know it, every native in Africa believes that to see elephants playing is the luckiest omen that can befall him.

Unique as I knew the film must be, it needed more strength of mind than I possessed to keep my eye to the finder, which was as remote as looking upon this alive and palpitating scene down the wrong end of a telescope, and I could not resist looking up now and then to enjoy the close reality.

By this time, four elephants had come into the open, leaving a cow elephant with a calf in the shelter of the swamp, and they circled and divided and circled again, executing a kind of strange rhythmic dance.

Then two of them interlocked their trunks and began a stupendous tug-of-war. Their trunks became living bands of steel as they tugged and swayed, and their gigantic grey haunches were braced back to the strain. First one would yield a step and then the other, as they strove in mighty deadlock ; then with a sudden wrench one of them rushed backward, dragging the other after him at a run for twenty yards. They then loosed their grip of one another and sparred till the ivory rang. The terrific brute force driving behind the clashing tusks made me understand why so many elephants have the point of a tusk broken ; and even in this friendly game I marvelled that the ivory did not splinter under the impact.

I am not sure how much it was play, and how much the serious business of ousting the young bull. The old bull certainly won, and stalked back, leaving the younger one standing pensively under a tree, almost thinking aloud.

Then the old bull returned, edged up alongside and rested his head very gently against the younger one's. It was as if he said that he had not really been in earnest, and that it was only a game ; and by and by the young one was soothed of his wounded feelings and they began to amuse themselves by pulling down the tree. The big bull took a branch over his tusks and under his trunk and levered.

But they were in no mood for work, and they soon gave up and wandered back to the swamp, shoulder to shoulder, through the long blue shadows of the sunset, till the grass closed behind them.

On the way back to camp I heard the thunder of approaching hooves and, leaving the boys behind, I quickly ran up and ducked behind an ant-hill as a herd of zebra, a couple of hundred strong, came galloping down on me like a division of cavalry. It was a great moment. My ant-hill, like a rock in the flood, momentarily diverted them ; they went streaming past on either side stretched at a tearing gallop, with a roar of hoof-beats that shook the ground, and joined up again behind me.

Whatever had alarmed them in the first place must have seemed trifling compared to the fright which they now received when nearly stumbling over me they got my wind too late to swerve. To me, crouching behind the ant-hill, smothered in red dust and looking up at the forest of legs flashing past, it was very much like the chariot race in *Ben Hur*. Every now and then against the confused background of sound, flying hooves and whirling dust, a clear-cut picture would emerge : striped knees drawn up for the forward plunge, round, pony-like buttocks, hocks striking back like pistons, a tail streaming out, or a neck bent low with its short, stiff mane curving downward and the ears laid back.

I was still crouching there while the thunder died and the dust slowly cleared, when an impala ram, alarmed by the stampede, ran silently back and took cover so near me that I could almost have touched his heaving flank. He was beautiful to watch, as all unconscious of me he stood looking back over his shoulder and listening with every nerve strained to the alert. Assured that danger was past, he whisked his tail with an air of nonchalance, and walked away with neat, clipped steps among the bushes.

Dusk had fallen, and taking a short cut back to camp by a new way, I came upon four little mounds covered with stones and laid one next to the other in the earth. I thought that they might be soldiers' graves, and prayed a prayer over them in passing. They looked so little and forlorn, and I, by comparison, so insolently full of this brief life. . . . " And yet," as it seemed to me Epictetus might have pointed out, " why grieve ? A little while and thou wilt be there also, and God grant it may be in half so good a place." But despite the philosophers, I promised that when the rains came I would come back and plant flowers among the stones.

When I awoke next day, and watched the smoke curling lazily upward into the golden light, while the air was full of fluttering wings and the freshness of very early morning, I realised with sudden poignancy how many lovely things I took for granted, and how seldom I stopped to consider the gladness of them.

Yet I could never look at the pale-eyed starlings without a catch of the breath in wonder at their beauty as they flashed through the sunshine, bright as gems, sapphire and amethyst, like the wings of Brazilian butterflies, contrasted with fiery cinnamon. Every day I saw some strange and lovely bird ; yet sweetest of all were the pearl-coloured doves, and I never saw them but I was filled with longing to stroke my eyes and lips against their little breasts. Even the crows ceased to bring me uneasy warning, for I had at last made friends with them. A pair used to walk under the verandah of my tent exploring among the chop-boxes, and when I saw them close to, with their white capes and intelligent bright eyes, I thought shame to myself for having looked upon them as harbingers of any kind of evil.

Nor can I forbear to mention a sugar-ant which I found " frozen " into the butter. I thought that he was dead, and scooped him out onto the edge of my plate, when he presently began to move. I held him in the palm of my hand so that the butter should melt faster and free his legs and antennæ. He had probably been imprisoned all night in the butter, under water, and was much more dead than alive ; yet as soon as he could move, the first thing he did was to clean himself meticulously all over and start away briskly to his labours.

Of course, you may say, he was merely doing what was perfectly natural to him ; nevertheless you could not but have been touched had you spent half an hour watching him—trying to get inside his mind—touched by the incredible bravery of Nature. And it is the same always, from the smallest moving thing to the largest, and you may observe this same great-heartedness even in trees and plants. In Nature, such a thing as giving in is simply not recognised. No hurt, nor check, nor disappointment can deter or clog that tremendous will to live and act ; only death itself can wrap the body in inanimation.

If I fell into the error of thinking of myself, because I happened to be a human being, as something higher, I learnt again and again that, relatively speaking, the smallest of living things outshone me in fidelity. They who never seemed to teach and who never intruded their wisdom, were my real teachers, and the nearer I came to them the deeper and truer became my reverence for all life. This reverence has been dwelt upon a million times and throughout the ages, but the day came when I discovered it for myself, and only then did it become my own living truth. Life, which one destroys so light-heartedly, Man with all his creative genius : yet all the nations of the earth might sit and weep over a single dead ant nor bring back to it one flicker of life.

The swamp was daily changing for the better. Although the farther end of it was still rank and green, and parts of it several feet deep under water, the middle was drying up. You followed a narrow path that dived into the wall of elephant grass and wound its way to the heart of the swamp. Instead of advancing into an ever-darkening jungle, you stepped out into the blinding sunshine on open ground as firm and bleached as a stubble field. It was several acres across, and shut in by a high barrier of golden grass standing like corn still uncut. Every day the herds of cattle (and probably the elephants themselves) trampled a little more of the corn and added another strip to the stubble. Here and there a rivulet neat as a furrow bisected it, and here and there a pool still remained, though visibly shrinking in its basin of caked and cracking mud. Pot-holes made by the elephants' feet surrounded these pools ; those on the outside already hard as cement, and the recent ones, close to the water, deep and soggy in the chocolate sludge.

The elephants (when the cattle did not forestall them) were very fond of this stubble field, and I now began every hunt by drawing it on the chance of finding them there. The only disadvantage was that I had to approach them across the open, but the fact of its being open made it an ideal place for photography.

Creeping through the barrier of grass one afternoon, I chanced on them when they were bathing. The sun was behind me and shone full on them, and they were boldly outlined, dark and immense against the pale stalks, and towering above the light, bare ground. The pool they had chosen was to them about the size of a hip-bath, and they took turns to plunge into it, each one sitting down, rolling his head back, stretching out his trunk, and happily wallowing with all four feet in the air. The water was no deeper than what was adequate for a hip-bath, either, and they came out with huge wet buttocks comically black in contrast to the rest of their grey hides.

Suddenly one of them saw me and sailed towards me with ears spread out and trunk curled up, looking angrier than I had ever seen an elephant look.

It is hard to say wherein an elephant's expression lies, for his great head, rough as granite, is scarcely to be played upon by the shifting light of expression. Yet there is no doubt that when you have studied him daily for many weeks on end you can read his every shade of humour like an open book. When he is undisturbed, his natural expression is one of smiling benevolence ; but when angered he seems to draw himself up to twice his natural height, the clumsy mass of him narrows and becomes clear cut, long of leg, intensely alert, alive and wiry, and in his lifted head and calm brow there is a look of cold displeasure beyond mere frowning.

I retreated before him across the stubble with as much dignity as can be combined with post post-haste, for a mob of natives had collected to watch the sport and they were firmly convinced—so I was told—that Abdi and I drank some enchanted brew that banished all fear of elephants.

I turned away heavy-hearted, for the elephants had not been disturbed by getting my wind. The trouble was that they were often disturbed by the natives driving their cattle to and fro round the swamp. Noise and shouting they could bear with, but the smell of humans upset them past endurance ; and on particularly bad days when the wind jumped round in circles, they were ready to charge at sight. But the presence of the cattle (from my point of view) had its compensations, for the elephants were accustomed to them and their owners, and there are probably few (if any) other places in Africa where elephants would tolerate day after day the presence of human beings.

I left the elephants in peace, and took a beat beyond the end of the swamp on the chance of coming upon other game. All at once I heard dogs barking and growling in the bushes, and creeping up saw three wild dogs devouring a dik-dik. Two of them were having a fierce tug-of-war over a haunch little larger than a hare's.

After this, I continued up-wind among the bushes when I picked up the unmistakable smell of waterbuck. Abdi laughed and shook his head, but round a bend we came upon three waterbuck feeding.

It is odd that natives, living as they do such a completely natural life, should yet have a very undeveloped sense of smell. They never use their noses, and so I suppose this fine and pleasurable sense has atrophied. Many a time I picked up the scent and stopped to ask the boys whether they could smell giraffe (or waterbuck, or whatever it happened to be) when to me the air was warm with these particularly individual smells ; and they would pause and sniff blankly like disappointed spaniels, and grin from ear to ear as though suspecting a leg-pull.

But to return to the waterbuck. I was in the midst of a careful and fairly successful stalk with the camera, when Siki slipped her collar and tore after them, full cry. The lighting was perfect, and Siki had again spoilt a very pretty picture. I finally caught her and gave her a perfunctory beating, perfunctory because I had by now come to accept the fact that nothing could ever break her of chasing.

Personality, even in a dog, is a curiously inviolable thing never to be conquered by force. To the last, Siki remained charming to everybody, exasperatingly obstinate and entirely independent, and I could only compromise and take what she offered in the way of devotion. Jock of the Bushveld comparisons were no longer mentioned.

Jim had personality, too. In fact he was one of the strongest personalities I have ever met. Not that he was overbearing. On the contrary, he was an excellent servant, combining the duties of butler, house-serving-cum-laundry-maid, and head boy. To have accused him of slackness would really have grieved him, for he had that obsolete quality, the pride of work. Without being in the least pompous he had an innate reserve and dignity that a Cabinet Minister might have envied. It inspired tremendous respect. In his own way he was devoted and most particular about the treatment I received from others ; but like all old servants his devotion lay so deeply buried under an unremitting austerity that I felt I should have to achieve something as improbable as sweeping Ol Doinyo Orok away with one arm to win a smile of approval.

He was often amusing, and had a quaint way of saying things. When he missed killing a mosquito in the tent he merely remarked with patient fatalism :

" His day is not yet ; when his day comes, then he will die ! "

There was also the incident of the strange native who arrived from Moshi on his way on foot to Nairobi. Asani said that he was his brother and would I write a letter to help him to get work. Incredulous of such coincidence, I insisted several times was he really his *brother* ? till Jim came forward with the enlightening explanation that they were " not really out of the same womb."

Asani doggedly maintained that they were brothers, for all that, and that they had been playmates as children in Tanganyika during the Great War ; and he drew altogether such a beautiful and affecting picture of past joys and present necessities that I wrote eloquently on behalf of this " brother " to the Game Warden, and gave him a few shillings to speed him on his way. I was swayed less by his kinship than by his astounding pluck : a single native without money or any means of sustenance, without possessions, except for the rags he stood up in, without even a spear for protection, setting off on foot on a three-hundred-mile journey, most of it through lion-infested country.

What with the elephants feeling on edge, and Siki chasing the waterbuck, it had been rather a bad day ; and I sent Siki home with the boys, and branched off on my own to the river.

I found a huge baobab tree whose trunk was already gilded by the westering sun, and sitting at its foot I composed myself to what Izaak Walton calls studying to be quiet. The monkeys played in the branches over my head, and a hyrax (looking like a small beaver) came and sat in his doorway at the foot of the next tree, basking and sometimes twitching his whiskers, or sociably blinking at me. A beautiful little golden bird with coal-black head flitted among the leaves, and as I watched him I caught sight of a bird even smaller, with red wings and peacock crest.

The monkeys were firm allies of all the beasts, for they were invariably the first to give the alarm, and since they trusted me, the impala, too, thought that all must be well, and they browsed happily along the opposite bank. They were perhaps fifteen or twenty yards away, and every now and then the sun would pick out their curving horns, or light up a rufus flank among the shadows, and the monkeys played almost between their feet.

It is wonderful how animals can distinguish notes of danger. Had I but snapped a twig they would have been off on the instant ; but the monkeys tossing the branches, throwing down pieces of stick or fruit, and making so much noise that had you not seen them you had held your breath waiting for some big animal to break through the undergrowth—for this the impala did not even lift their heads.

Such moments as these broke down all barriers. It was no

longer they and I, we were all equally a part of the unity in the divine scheme. That word *unity* had repeated itself in my dreams, and like some insistent message stamped itself on my waking consciousness. These sudden glimpses revealed its meaning, and indeed the whole answer to life in a shining vision of the nearness of God.

The vision remained unforgettably as the sun set and darkness crept down over the hill, when like an after-thought the sky again became bright, and a suffusion of lovely, splendid colour spread upward so dazzling and liquid that you could scarce keep your eyes upon it, but turned them to the solid mountain to ask could this be real? In the darkling east the clouds caught fire once again, but gently, soft as a thousand roses you could have crumpled to your heart; and as I turned to look at them they rolled back before the full moon. It was this that was so wonderful, for the moon at sunset is not fully wakened, it does not even glow; yet now it shone forth upon the pink clouds, sending down the bright beams of night. I stood dumbly before the glory of it, overwhelmed with the joy " that throws all it has on the dust, and knows not a word."

Next morning I went early to a favourite pool in the forest which I had named the Glade of Butterflies. I never went there but I found a cloud of butterflies hovering above the water by a moss-covered stump. I loved to sit quietly on this stump, when they would brush past my face like petals as they drifted to and fro in the sunshine, the big white ones turning the rays in burning opal from their wings. There were cinnamon golden ones intense as flame, and many different kinds of blue, brown, green and gold, and pale yellow. There was also a particularly beautiful and rarer kind that flashed past me with the flight of a swallow (and I could feel the wind of his passing) whose long wings were black like velvet and set with lapis lazuli.

The elephants were near by; among the tall trees and

chequer of light and shade they looked immense, and the forest was here open enough to reveal them.

There were few things so fascinating as wandering through this open forest watching the elephants when they were wholly unconscious of my presence. Such moments were like being admitted to the sweet intimacy of Nature no longer on guard against me.

When I watched them stripping the bark with their tusks, and how deftly they used their trunks, taking hold of a little bit of frayed edge which I could scarcely have taken hold of with my fingers, I came to believe that they might easily have been capable of threading a needle. There is nothing so brutally strong and yet so tender and mobile as an elephant's trunk. With it he can bend the barrel of a modern rifle into an arc (I was told this by the hunter to whom it had happened), and yet you can watch a couple of elephants—as I did then—standing side by side, and one would put up his trunk as sensitively as a finger and thumb and give the other an affectionate pinch on the lip ; and they stood thus for five minutes at a time intertwining trunks in the most gentle and loving caress.

I was absorbed in watching them, and stood motionless among the crackling leaves, half hidden by an ant-hill, when a third elephant saw some tempting green fronds beyond his reach. With incredible agility, for the sides were almost sheer, he climbed onto the top of my ant-hill, and his outstretched trunk rose up twenty feet above my head. He seemed positively gigantic, and though the feat might have put you in mind of a circus elephant climbing onto a ten times ordinary-sized tub, standing up there with his forefeet on top of the pedestal of red earth, and his neck and trunk outstretched against the sky, he towered like a stone archway between the trees.

Even then, some of the choicest branches eluded him ; so

he climbed down and deliberately pushed the tree over. It was a big tree, sturdy as an oak, and he pressed his forehead against it, moving slowly forward till the roots cracked and it leaned out and fell, and he straddled it with all four legs. He walked round to the top, delicately plucked the tenderest shoots, and strolled off into the forest.

The wonder was that there were any trees left standing, for there were trees great as cedars felled by the elephants, and almost every day another well-remembered landmark had gone.

By this time it was midday, and the heat beating up off the ground sent the wind eddying about treacherously ; so I left the elephants before it should betray me to them. It was about three miles from camp, and I had not realised till then how torrid the heat had become. The cracked and baking earth scorched through the soles of my boots, and the glare swept up in hot waves against my face.

Chances never came singly. I had waited and watched a hundred times hoping I might see an elephant pull down a tree, and I saw it happen for the second time that very afternoon.

I found the elephants beyond the swamp and in the open. For once conditions were perfect : the sun right, the wind right, the approach right, and the elephants themselves—the usual four with the big bull who sometimes joined them—stood together throwing up the dust in their trunks, scraping the earth with their feet and turning up roots with a kind of nut growing on them which, I afterwards discovered, had a good taste and aroma like pine resin. Abdi knew all about them and said that they made very good cough mixture for small babies.

When the ground is bare, elephants appear to be much nearer. I put the distance at twenty yards, but pacing it afterward I found it made a full thirty-five.

The wind turned fickle and compelled me to retreat several times. And just then the camera jammed, and I thought that the chance of a lifetime was lost. I unscrewed the lens and worked the shutter, and all was well ; but I know of no more exquisite torture than trying to screw in a finicky little lens before five advancing elephants.

They vanished into the swamp and I sat down to change the film, and was no sooner ready than I heard one returning. Without waiting for Abdi, I dashed to the spot where I expected the elephant to appear. He climbed out of a hidden pool and towered above me ; even in the finder he was immense, and when I looked up I felt suddenly overwhelmed by his nearness. He saw me and sailed about with his ears spread, and tail up, and the water glistening on his hide.

They all came out beyond the zebras' drinking-place, and then it was that I saw the big bull, silhouetted darkly against the emerald swamp, beginning to pull down a thorn tree. I dashed forward, eyes only for him, when I found myself sinking up to the waist in liquid mud. I plunged and struggled, squelching my way back to firm ground where Abdi scolded me severely, saying that I might just as well have gone in over my head.

We crept round the edge and wormed our way to a clear view between a high hedge of green-stuff on our right and the quaking bog on our left. The elephant was stripping the bark ; then, half straddling the tree with his forelegs and gripping it with his trunk, he swayed it back and forth as though it were a young sapling.

It was a great subject, and beautifully lighted. Yet I dared not go nearer, for on my left, hidden in the swamp, was another elephant. Abdi tugged my sleeve, and looking over my shoulder I saw in horrified amazement the third elephant on our right quietly looking at us through the leaves at our side. We had already *passed* him, so that between the bog and the elephants we were completely ringed in. With beating hearts we turned and slipped back out of that narrow circle of death.

While I was at dinner that evening, Jim rushed up in tense excitement and whispered :

" Catch hold of Siki, there's an elephant standing behind your chair ! " I grabbed her collar and looking round saw in the shadowy moonlight, not an elephant but the dim outline of a rhino. He began to walk deliberately towards me, though he probably had not an idea that he was near camp, for he was walking down-wind. We waited in silence, and when he had drawn to within a dozen yards he swerved uphill to his favourite bushes and I soon heard him contentedly cropping.

This was the perfect adventure, and I fell asleep that night to his friendly munching. Later, Siki woke me with a bark, and the sound of munching again stole into my consciousness. It was now much louder, and on both sides of the tent at once, and listening to the sound I detected not one rhino but three, all apparently browsing among the tent pegs. In reality, they were twenty paces away, and two of them were on the far side of a deep trench (made during the rains by a watercourse) running down on my starboard side. This trench had proved a great protection, for the rhino who grazed up to its farther edge never crossed it.

I went out to make up the fire as a signal to them to refrain from walking over my patch of ground ; and they acknowledged it with many an outraged snort of indignation. I sympathised with them, for I shared their feelings every time strangers invaded our solitudes. I do not think that they felt any lasting rancour ; as for me, I had only warned them as the elephant had warned the cattle and, so long as they left my tent intact, I loved having them round me.

But it was destined to be a night full of incident, and Jim woke me in the first grey light with the words :

" Simba ! " (lion) " in the trench close by ! " I was broad awake on the instant, thrilling with excitement, and my first impulse was to leap out of bed and seize my rifle. But then I remembered, and turning over said as sleepily as I was able :

" I can't shoot him, he's all right, let him go."

The boys told me later, that at daybreak a giraffe had come galloping straight for the camp, and swerved left-handed among the trees ; and that a big black-maned lion in pursuit had almost reached their tents before he was aware of the camp, then swung up past my tent and leapt across the trench. A second lion slipped into the trench, and they caught sight of a lioness. I made no doubt that they were the same three who had roared so splendidly some weeks before.

It was an extraordinary thing how much more deeply impressed the boys were by an idea or a superstition than by a commonplace reason. They were bitterly disappointed over my indifference to the lion. To their minds, I had let slip a golden opportunity, and the old argument came up again : Why wouldn't I shoot a lion in camp ?—and that I had permission from the Game Department to do that much. So at last I told Jim my secret, explaining to him that if I killed anything it would cross my luck ; that I was absolutely protected and could go among all the beasts in safety so long as I kept the pact. If the lion ever came inside my tent then I would shoot, but that morning he had not taken arms against me, it just happened that my tent had lain in his path.

Jim was beginning to grasp the idea, and there was enough mystery about it to catch his fancy. A gleam of understanding spread over his face as he put the next question :

" Can Abdi shoot ? "

I said that of course he could, and that his shooting had nothing to do with me.

This solved the whole vexed question, and after that the

boys did not merely bear with my belief, they came to believe it themselves.   Jim even went so far as to transport a scorpion out of my tent in a tablespoon rather than kill it ; and at night, when the rhino snorted alarmingly near the camp, I would hear the boys stoutly asserting to one another with a conviction that would have done credit to a Christian Scientist :

" Rhino are *not* bad animals ! "

Chapter X

A BIG TUSKER. THE RAINS. DIGRESSION
ON AURAS

THE drought had now reached its climax, and paradoxically enough all the trees, released by the magic of a single thunderstorm, burst into leaf; so that the softest spring green veiled the silvery branches, and hung in luxuriant shadow above the baked earth and brittle grass. This produced an effect at once unreal and very lovely; and the transparent colours in the early morning—autumnal for clearness, springlike for tenderness—were so beautiful that when I awoke I could only exclaim in wonder, and know how good it was to be alive.

Even the praying mantis responded to this sudden change. They had darkened to drab brown with the fall of the leaf, and now when they flew onto my table at night, attracted by the lantern, they were palest green like the tendrils of young peas.

The " stick " insects remained like the grass, bleached as straw; and catching sight of one moving over the ground—his joints exactly resembling the knots in grass-stalks, and his head hidden between his long, projecting front legs—you might at first think that a piece of dry grass was being blown along by the wind. He has a ridiculous way of walking, for each step is accompanied by a lilting, swaying motion backward and forward. This (I supposed) was to make you think that he was an aimless bit of stubble not bent upon any destination in particular; but there was an infectious hilarity about him that persuaded me that he practised this legerdemain partly as a huge joke.

The elephants had temporarily left the swamp to look for fresh feeding grounds round the other side of Ol Doinyo Orok. They appeared to have a set programme and to make a continual round tour of the mountain, so that if they disappeared in the north you could count upon their reappearing from the south a few days later.

They had now been gone for some time, so that when at last one was reported, I had a well-organised hunt for him all through the forest.

But it was to no purpose. You would think that anything so large as an elephant must be easy to find, yet in fact no beast can be more elusive. I have watched an elephant, who meant to slip away without my knowing, move over crackling twigs and dry leaves like a shadow. He had the same marvellous astuteness as a woodcock, who will sometimes get up with such an ado that you are too much surprised to throw up your gun, and at other times will fly off as silently as an owl before you have even seen him.

When the elephants did return, I had such a day with them that I dreamt about them all night long. Whatever else I dreamed of, the bushes would divide before the huge head and slowly waving ears of an elephant.

I found three of them directly after breakfast, and followed them all the morning as they ambled through the forest. Eventually they stopped at a water-hole to drink, and I crept up very close to them. They filled their trunks with water, then slowly and solemnly tipping their heads back they poured the water down their throats, and I heard it go gurgling down like water poured into a tank. They then made their way into thick forest and I waited for a couple of hours for the chance of a photograph. I could see an eye—elephants have surprisingly green eyes—or an ear above the branches ; and below, as one sees feet moving to and fro on the stage when the curtain is down, I could see their legs, the loose skin creased like a hillside scarred with dry watercourses ; or a tail with the tuft of black bristles at the end, swinging slowly from side to side among the dusty sunbeams.

The wind was horribly uncertain, blowing right round at regular intervals and keeping me retreating and advancing and retreating again.

Once, when I was very close, in the shadow of a bush, two of the elephants unexpectedly came towards me looking for fresh grazing. Suddenly they suspected my presence—though providentially at that moment the wind held true—and they stood motionless with their ears outspread attentively listening, and their trunks poised questioningly just clear of the ground. One movement of mine would have confirmed their suspicions ; and, with the close-set bushes at my back blocking retreat, I stood petrified in the shadow, holding my breath. I now seemed to be looking up into their green eyes and counting the hairs all the way up their trunks ; and their scrutiny at last became so unbearable that I edged sideways, and the leaves drew a kindly screen between us. Picking my way on tiptoe I rejoined Abdi and breathed freely again.

In all our adventures his coolness inspired me with complete confidence. He had at last learnt the invaluable secret of standing motionless as a statue under an elephant's sometimes very penetrating gaze. I could never make him understand the idea of stereoscopic vision and that all animals lack it ; but I did convince him that, when the slightest movement might be fatal, immobility transformed him into an unheeded tree trunk.

When in the afternoon the elephants began to make their way back to the river, I ran ahead and filmed them as they came towards me ; but the best chance they ever gave me was when they fed along the top of the bank. I climbed down into the stream and scrambled up the far side, which here made a steep drop of twenty feet. With this moat between us, I crept opposite the elephants ; and the fact that they were slightly above me made them seem all the nearer, so that they towered up like pillars between the trees and the sky. Had there been a bridge between us, I suppose it would have spanned seven or eight yards, and I could certainly never have stood my ground had there not been this protecting fosse—about three times the width of the fosse between the bears and the public at the Mappin Terraces—dividing us. The elephants also appeared to consider it a safeguard, for they continued their feeding quite imperturbably, though eyeing me the while.

The tangle of hanging creeper sometimes hid them entirely, and I could see only a trunk coming through, feeling about like a hand in the dark, then tearing down an armful of succulent herbage.

One of them presently put into her mouth a length of white wood like a small gate-post. She turned it over reflectively in her jaws till Abdi whispered that she meant to throw it at me. It was a terrifying thought, and although I still kept one eye in the camera I kept the other anxiously on that nasty-looking missile, for the wicked twinkle in the elephant's little eye, showing a corner of white, made me put the more belief into Abdi's assertion. And then she broke the post in two, as you would break a stick of barley sugar, and ate it.

After a time they began to lose patience with me (and small wonder, for I had infringed upon their peace and privacy all day) and the big bull walked clear of the trees to a part of the bank that was quite bare. I could see him only by climbing down halfway on my own side and tilting the camera up at him, for the branches above me hung in my way. Abdi was by then wrought into a state of frenzy, and entreated me to climb back; while the elephant raged to and fro putting now one foot over the edge, now the other, shaking his head and trumpeting angrily. Then, seeing that he could neither reach me nor frighten me away, he spun round and they all three made a bolt.

I foresaw that they intended to cross lower down, so I dashed ahead to cut them off, and arrived in time to see the last elephant fording the stream below me.

I found them again beyond the forest; and the big bull made a splendid picture framed between two trees, the light and shadow crisply drawn by the red rays of the sunset. He stood quite still, watching me patiently, and my heart melted at the sight of his patience; for though I had meant them no harm I had plagued them more than enough. They probably did not mind very seriously, but felt the rising irritation one feels towards a persistent fly; indeed, they were wonderfully merciful.

Abdi—keener than mustard now that we had more than a mere gap between us—urged me to take photographs, for the wind held true and the opportunity was good. But I felt that this, if ever, was the moment for a little gratitude; they had forgiven me for the Mappin Terrace incident, which was obviously an unfair advantage to me, and I walked resolutely away determined not to give them fresh cause to regret it.

Elated by our success, Abdi thought of some more elephant stories. He told me that he had seen elephants *carrying* their new-born calves that were too young to walk. They laid them across their tusks and held them round the middle with their trunks. He also said that an elephant that is shot down in a herd will sometimes be carried away by his companions to a remote spot where the hunter will never trace him.

Abdi was ill next day with dysentery, and I made him an infusion of edelweiss which had been given to me in the Alps as a certain cure. This was the only opportunity I had of giving it a trial, and its effects were immediate and miraculous.

The elephants now had three days' complete holiday, not, I am afraid, of my own free will but through force of circumstance, for I was laid up with another attack of malaria. As always, fever destroyed all sense of proportion, and I felt lonely and troubled in spirit. But Nature can never see you out of tune but she has compassion, and suddenly, wonder of all wonders, the shy little roller bird who at Namanga was not to be seen once in a month, and then only far away through the field-glasses, flew down at my very door. (Moseli-katse's Roller *Coracias caudatus caudatus*.) Such colour as his was a message of gladness ; for he was plum-coloured and rusty green-gold, and his wings unfolded every shade of blue, opal, green and turquoise like the deeps and shallows of a lagoon when the sun plays over them.

Even lying in bed seemed no longer a waste of precious time, for the trees were there all round me, bending their heads in the exquisite grey light, and the mountain was modelled grey and green against the soft sky.

Nevertheless, the feeling of coming separation hung over me. The tender colours of evening caressing the earth, lingering a little moment before fading imperceptibly into the warm dusk, filled me with a love for it all so overwhelming that I felt suddenly as big as the world, able to clasp all the earth to my heart and to mingle with every stream, to crush the little trees in my arms for love of them, and to kiss the mountain-tops. I prayed that all this lovely wilderness would not forget me, and the answer was always : " It is not *I* who will forget, it is for you to find your way back." That is the everlasting message of the Divine through Nature. And because she never intrudes her love upon mankind it is so often passed by unheeded, yet it is there always for any one who will seek it.

" Man, stretching out his hands to the stars, forgets the flowers at his feet." In this all-engrossing quest for the new, the unknown, the untasted, our vision is out of focus. Often it is the best that is in our possession, but it is so near us that we cannot see it. Even God Himself we relegate to the unfathom-able blue heaven where we can never reach Him ; as though we were blind and deaf to the eternal assurance expressed through every flower and hill and dewdrop that He is here all round us, much closer to us than anything else can ever be.

When I was up again, a Masai brought me a young baboon, and I paid three shillings for his ransom. He sat, tied by a rope, on the lamp-hook halfway up the tent-pole, and ate dried apricots and drank some milk which I held up to him in a saucer. But although he was so tame and gentle, I could not endure the wistful look in his eyes, nor refuse him his liberty. He was so much surprised when I let him loose, that instead of making one dash for his beloved forest he kept stopping to look back.

The rainy season was drawing inevitably nearer. Dark days succeeded one another with leaden skies, and all Nature waited in breathless suspense. Lightning flashed round the horizons, thunder rolled like the distant sound of drums, and on the languid air was now borne the smell of rain. But no rain fell and, although I knew that it must make life in the tent depressingly damp, I longed for it to come and break this oppressive stillness, this tense waiting for something to happen. My head ached from the thunder, and through the unnatural hush came the incessant shrilling of cicadas, maddening as the sound of knives being eternally sharpened on a grindstone, and the calling of doves and hoopoe in endless insistent repetition. And, as in some spell you cannot break, the flat-topped thorn trees loomed fantastically green between the black clouds and the pale dust beneath.

The elephants were not far from camp, and I found them at their favourite occupation of digging up "pine-nuts"; and later, a single bull, with the point of his right tusk broken, chest deep in the water-hole.

Standing thus among the reeds, half submerged and well

below the level of the edge of the pool, he seemed farther off than he really was, and I walked to the very brink to photograph him. Suddenly he came plunging towards me, the water breaking back in a wave from his shoulder. He was still somewhat below me and I was holding up the camera when, without warning or apparent effort, he climbed out of the pool beside me, towering like a mountain of glistening wet granite. At the same moment Abdi, tired of urgently whispering " Andoka! Andoka!" into my ear, dragged me backward by the arm ; so that however remarkable the picture I could not continue to hold up the camera, and we scuttled away like rabbits till the elephant lost us and wandered off into the forest.

Next day, I came upon a glorious old bull with a pair of long, curving tusks. We recognised him at once for the lone bull I had pursued in the early morning above camp some weeks before, who was so daunting and who, when I found him later in the swamp, charged me at sight. He was a seventy-pounder and unmistakable, not only on account of his superb tusks but because he was a giant among elephants. His companion, grey and insignificant beside him, reached barely to his shoulder. He was altogether of a mightier structure, and impressed me at once with the colossal weight of bone and skull, sharp-etched in light and shadow, moulded like rock, as he towered up like a mammoth, rugged and dark.

He was intolerant from the first moment because—Abdi explained—he was fully conscious of the worth of his lovely ivories, and the instant he saw me he made a lightning charge down upon me. I held up the camera for a second, but Abdi dragged me back by the shoulder and I ran for my very life with the pounding and crashing of the charging elephant filling the whole forest behind me. We both ran helter-skelter (very much like the frightened cattle when the elephant drove them off) and when we turned round he had stopped, and stood angrily shaking his head.

Although I could have wept over my failure to take more photographs of this magnificent charge, I had been gorgeously frightened ; and I know of nothing more completely terrifying than running away from a charging elephant when he is really in earnest. His speed is unbelievable ; he is on you before you have time to think, and as you fly before him, dodging this way and that among the trees with that deafening crash behind, you feel that nothing on earth can save you. Had he got my wind it is probable that nothing would have.

Whether he meant to catch me and lost sight of me, or whether he meant merely to drive me away, I cannot tell ; but I realised then more than ever before that photographing elephants at close quarters is a perilous game. It was only by amazingly good fortune that I had come in contact with four or five gentle and patient elephants all those months. Now was the time to be more than usually careful, for the lack of water over the country might bring many new and possibly uncertain-tempered elephants to Namanga.

The more I studied elephants, or indeed any animal, the more chary I became of generalising about them. One can lay down no definite rule as to how they will act in any given circumstance. They have each their own individual character as have human beings, and no theory of race, environment and past experience can allow a margin quite wide enough for individual impulse.

On the way home I again came upon elephants fighting. Or maybe they were only playing ; it was hard to tell. They were two cows on the edge of the swamp, and engaged in a tremendous tug-of-war.

Abdi was beside himself, and told me again that in all his experience of elephants he had never before seen this happen, and he was convinced that something incredibly lucky was in store for us. I have never personally met any one who has seen elephants fighting, and Abdi confirmed my belief that it was a rare experience.

With this in mind, it was an abiding regret to be robbed of an interesting and indeed valuable piece of film. The sun was already near to setting, and threw a lurid red light over the scene with unreal purple shadows. The two elephants tugging in perfect profile, rushing back now this way, now that, shone in this theatrical lighting like bronze, and their slim curving tusks gleamed out from the sea-green swamp in unnaturally sharp relief. The effect was so strange that they looked huge as primeval monsters. But the light was only deceptively bright, and the film came out (as I knew it must) hopelessly under-exposed.

A day or two later, while looking for my four old friends, I unexpectedly ran into the seventy-pounder and his companion. He was feeding in the forest close to the road, and, though he did not get my wind or hear a sound, he must have had an inkling that I was there, for he came out onto the road and twice patrolled it systematically up and down.

I fell to wondering what would happen if some luckless motorist came along, and had no sooner thought of this possibility than I heard the horn of a car. Followed by Abdi, I ran out onto the road as the car—driven by a wild-looking Somali—tore round the bend, and then there were suddenly elephants charging from every side at once. The car had arrived at the psychological moment when the elephants had elected to cross the road, and the big tusker, whom I had imagined to be a rogue, and probably pining to try conclusions with a passing car, took to the most ignominious flight at the first toot ; while the second elephant lost his head completely and rushed first across the road and then back again in front of me.

But if the rogue had found his match in Henry Ford he was

not to be outdone by myself, and he no sooner saw me drawing near than he swung round for a fresh charge. By then the sun had set, so I left him ; and he stood with his enormous ears spread, puzzling over the sound of my policeman's whistle, which I blew for the syce to bring Marouf.

I hunted in vain throughout the next day, and had I found the elephants, the sky had been too dark for photography.

The whole world was dark and silent, silent but for the frogs croaking in frenzied welcome to the rain. The oppression lay upon me with the weight of steel as I walked on and on in a dream, and the very beasts seemed all as black as the sky above—three wart-hog and the slate-coloured guinea-fowl, the clumsy flapping vultures, zebra, and even the impala moved like dark shadows before some impending fate.

Out of the stillness a roar of wind smote my ears, and across the open came a whirling column of dust and leaves high as a tower. It passed us closely, at fearful speed, and Abdi told me that if one of these wind-devils caught the tent it would wrench it from the ground and carry it bodily upward.

Siki chased some giraffes, and I was trying to catch her when I almost stumbled over a poor little native calf all crumpled up and dying. We managed to make him stand on his feet, and I thought that if I could bring him back to camp and feed him he might recover. At that moment fell the first big drops of rain, so leaving the boys to drive him in, I took the cameras and galloped Marouf back to camp.

The rain soon fell in sheets, drenching me to the skin and, what was far worse, wetting the cameras. The lightning stabbed in front of me with blinding flashes and the earth was so slippery that Marouf, in water to the hocks, could hardly keep his feet. By the time I reached camp it was nearly dark, and putting the cameras safely inside the tent I turned back to meet the men. Fearing I might miss them in the thick bush, I whistled all the way, but received no answer, and when at last I found them they were not much farther advanced than when I had left them, and they were trying to carry the calf. He was wellnigh dead, and I was compelled to abandon him to his fate—which, poor little beast, was certainly hyenas—for we were all wet through and shivering with cold, night was upon us and camp two miles away.

The rain cleared off on the following afternoon, and I was hunting up-wind through the forest where Lembogi had marked down the elephants, when Abdi snapped his fingers, and looking round I saw through the foliage the ear and slim, curving tusks of a cow elephant directly *behind* me. I retreated as best I could, biting my lips with vexation, sure that I had given her my wind fair and square. When we approached her again, however, she was unconcernedly feeding ; and watching her long for an opportunity, I presently noticed that her eyes were tight shut, and that swaying gently from one leg to the other she was fast asleep. She awoke by and by and strolled unconsciously towards me, but, as always, the clicking of the cinema gave me away, and she turned and walked off through the forest.

As I followed in the wake of those immense, creased hind-quarters through the dividing and closing bushes (the steaming heat drenching me like a bath), the sun, biting down between thunderclouds, drew out of the damp earth and the new-blossomed thorn tree flowers a fragrance so passionately sweet that I had to stop every now and again to breathe it in more deeply. It might have been an April day at home, and this forest some tender, springlike woodland ; then the exotic butterflies flashed across my path, those great posts of legs came into view again, and I was back in the heart of Africa.

A little rain had transformed the world of dust and drought to a pleasant land where flowers bloomed on every side and sparkled in a glint of sun with burning dew-drops. The birds found their voices again and filled the air with song, and the

Masai (whose cattle had been dying like flies) rejoiced over the end of the famine. A thousand rivulets broke from the mountain-side in happy tumult, and all the earth sang of deliverance : " The wilderness and the solitary place shall be glad . . . and the desert shall rejoice and blossom as the rose."

But these showers were only the forerunners of what was to come, and now the rains broke in good earnest.

Ear-splitting thunderstorms smote upon every side, wrenching the tent from its moorings, filling it with spindrift from the torrents lashing the ground. In the space of two minutes the waters came swirling round, and every tent-peg had drawn, driving me out at all hours of the night into the blinding downpour to hammer them in again.

It put me in mind of our trek round the Lorian swamp, years ago, and although there was no longer the constant anxiety of looking after the skins, I soon found that a caseful of books, a gramophone and records and cameras and films were unpractical things to have in a tent during the rains. But they were never more welcome than now ; and, during the long dark days when I was weatherbound, I forgot the damp and discomfort while plunged in the adventures of Doughty and Kinglake, and in re-reading *Othello* and Isaiah. I shut out the monotonous drumming of the rain on the canvas with some of the Beethoven quartets (especially op. 135 " Es Muss Sein ") though the andantes were scarcely audible above the clangour outside.

It was not until the first terrific downpour that I discovered that the tent was pitched head-on to the storm, instead of presenting a low-roofed flank ; and we spent the following morning re-pitching it. The men re-pitched their own tents in a better position and cut deep channels around them to drain off the water.

An ox was sacrificed to put a little cheer into the camp, but even with so much feasting I saw clearly that we could not hold out much longer against the rains. The men were miserable, and small blame to them, huddled in their little tents with no change of clothing. They were stoical, and in spite of a night which (even in my big tent) had sickened me of tents for a while, they greeted me cheerfully next day.

Having spent most of the day in trying to keep everything sheltered from the fiercest storm I had ever known, my dream was to reach a land where tent-pegs would not draw and where I could get really dry again. Going to bed or getting up was only an exchange of dampness, and I could no longer imagine there was a dry stitch in the world. Books and leather began to show patches of green mould, metal was stained with verdigris, even the bread tasted of mildew ; and under the ground-sheet the wet earth threw up curling and sickly white shoots furred with damp, and full of spiders, scorpions, white ants and centipedes that had sought refuge there.

I snatched the one fine interval during the day to escape from this dank misery and go and look for elephant, and had no sooner found one than he charged me across the swamp at sight.

It is extraordinary to watch an elephant preparing to charge. He gathers himself together, sinks himself down like a lion about to spring, then suddenly shoots forward with a shrill and terrifying trumpet.

He was soaked with rain and looked as black as bitumen. The rain and the thunder had no doubt upset him as it had the rest of us, and put his nerves on edge. The swamp was a dismal place for him, the reeds beaten down by the rain, and the half-burnt elephant grass all sodden and charred black on greyish white like porcupine quills ; so that it was little wonder if my arrival was the last straw to his patience.

I left him and squelched my way home as the deluge broke over my head.

The Namanga river came roaring down like an Alpine

torrent, and the swamp was nearly impassable, which put very definite bounds to the scope of my activities. As I came in, a troop of sopping wet and bedraggled baboons went scurrying through the storm for the hillside, hoping, perhaps, for better shelter among the rocks. I wondered where the birds hid themselves and how the beasts found a dry corner. This was the one preoccupation of man and bird and beast—to keep dry.

Mists swept down the hill or lifted to reveal a wet steely flank of granite. Water rushed past the tent door and the skies bent low, heavy with the rain to come. In all it did, Nature was so gloriously whole-hearted.

At last there was a fine morning, and I set out through the radiance of the early sunshine to say good-bye to the elephants.

I found them at the far end of the swamp, and three of them were playing together—a farewell good luck to us, Abdi whispered. The old bull, standing apart, was scraping in the earth with his forefoot for " pine-nuts," and rolling them up and down on the inside of his trunk to free them of earth, an amazing feat, for he never dropped a single bunch.

What I had hoped for, but never dreamed of obtaining, was a chance like this when Abdi and I could go close up, and Asani could film us and the elephant all together. It was the best opportunity I had ever had, and when I had taken enough photographs, Abdi and I walked up a little nearer yet and, standing at attention, we gave a smart salute in farewell. At the same moment the elephant must have received a puff of our wind, for he spun round with ears outspread to acknowledge it, and gave me a dramatic ending to the film.

I wanted no more photographs, but I could not tear myself away from the elephants. This was my last day, for Karua with the lorry (fit for the road once more) was coming on the morrow to take me back to rail-head at Kajiado. There was no reprieve, and so, with a heavy heart, I sat down to watch the elephants for the last time.

Having been with them daily for the best part of three months, I had come to know all five of them individually : the old bull who had driven away the cattle (it was he who had acknowledged our salute), the cow who had played so gracefully with the little twig, and the bull with the broken tusk who had climbed out of the pool ; the younger bull who had been worsted in the fight, and the cow whom I had found sleeping in the forest. They had interwoven themselves in the scheme of everyday life and I could not bear to think that I should never see them again.

The wrench would have been less hard if I could have gone up to them and said good-bye. But it was only in dreams that I could do that. Then I went among them and explained about the detestable clicking machine, and they talked to me and led me through wonderful forests. They carried me on their backs and allowed me to watch their mysterious dances and to play with the little calves.

Even had I been able to remain among them for years, how, I asked myself, could I ever bridge this gap between dreams and reality ? Short of drinking a magic potion that would enable me to understand animal language, it was hopeless. I might as reasonably look for the rainbow bridge to Valhalla.

And while I sat and watched the elephants now peacefully feeding in the glad sunshine, and pondered the folly of my quest, something that I had read years ago came into my head. It was the theory (it came, I think, in a book on theosophy) that animals can see auras. I had thought little about it at the time, but now it threw a light on my darkness bright as a revelation. Achievement depended on no external miracle or magic. It was much simpler than that, so simple, in fact, that I had overlooked it. The means had been put into my own hands, for—taking the theory of auras as a working hypothesis—it was I myself who must become something different. My aura was probably red and rather turgid, and however much I loved them, until they saw that it burned with a pure blue flame the animals would never put their trust in me.

I saw now, that I had approached my goal from the wrong angle and that I was altogether unworthy of it. New vistas opened before me, and I suddenly understood that my desire for friendship with the animals committed me to something far greater and deeper than itself. Yet the two things were so inseparable that it was only by pursuing the greater that I could encompass the less.

I could never change the colour of my aura by sitting down in the wilderness with a carefully selected supply of stores, and servants to look after me. It would need not only a stoic simplicity, but an intense effort and concentration of the spirit beyond my present understanding. It was no use my practising a simplicity that was comfortable, solitude with a perfectly working domestic machinery, and an impulsive recourse to prayer merely in moments of spiritual grace. If I sometimes experienced the uplifting nearness of the spirit it was only that the spirit, knowing itself everywhere, could understand and pity. But my reflection of it was so weak and wavering that the animals could in no wise perceive it. What they saw was a very ordinary predatory human being whom they had no reason to suppose otherwise than hostile. Only through the power of the spirit made manifest could they be disarmed and reassured.

And this power of the spirit was not something one could have, but something one might become. There were no half measures. To come into close spiritual harmony with all Nature (and mankind) demanded the supreme sacrifice contained in the five words : Leave all and follow Me. The saints alone have found the way ; or perhaps many have fleetingly beheld it, but only a handful of rare and chosen natures have had the hardihood and courage, the faith, and, above all, the reckless and immeasurable love to follow it.

To these, the perfect communion with Nature came naturally. There is that lovely picture of Buddha in the wilderness :

> Oft times while he mused—as motionless
> As the fixed rock his seat—the squirrel leaped
> Upon his knee, the timid quail led forth
> Her brood between his feet, the blue doves pecked
> The rice-grains from the bowl beside his hand.

Or again, there is the picture—and this was the one I loved best—of St. Francis of Assisi surrounded by his birds and beasts. In such lives, friendship with the animals was but an incidental achievement which they took in their stride towards a greater goal.

Nevertheless, it was through his choice of the most difficult of all paths—that of giving up himself and his will to the spirit —that St. Francis came so near the spirit that the birds and beasts understood and responded to his love when he called to his Little Brothers.

" It will rain, Memsahib," said Abdi, who had come up and stood patiently waiting.

From the far-off unattainable silver visions I reluctantly withdrew my gaze and glancing upward saw that Abdi was right : the clouds were gathering and the sky, except for one stabbing shaft of sunlight, was black as ink.

The immortal and purifying fire was not for such as I, and I rose regretfully to my feet. It was, after all, as happy a leave-taking as I could have hoped for : the elephants saw me plainly, yet did not mind my being there, and when at last I tore myself away they were still feeding undisturbed. I turned my back on them and walked home before the coming storm.

Even Abdi was subdued, and there were no more elephant stories.

Left to my own thoughts I could not help dwelling sorrowfully on all the friends I was about to leave : the three rhino who browsed nightly round my tent, the lions who had taught me how to roar, and the herds of zebra and impala I saw every day, so that they now scarcely bothered to show alarm. There was also a pair of dik-dik close to the camp, and a hyrax, and a great number of birds, including two fishing eagles, a pair of crows and a green woodpecker, the pair of little bee-eaters, a tame covey of guinea-fowl, two partridges and flocks of starlings and doves which I fed daily.

Going over this long and varied list, I laughed to think how many people had asked : " But aren't you lonely ? " Even my tent I shared with a family of chirruping crickets, and spiders, lizards, mud-building wasps and—since the rains had come— almost too many scorpions and centipedes. Every night two little bats flew up and down over my bed gently fanning the air above my face as they chased mosquitoes. I loved to lie in the dark and listen as they brought up the end of each turn with a quick velvet flutter of wings.

All the rest of that day the tent rocked under the sudden frenzies of the wind, and the taut canvas resounded like a drum under the roar of descending rain. I shivered miserably, helpless to defy the cold, and turned with a heart of lead to my packing.

As I went through the stores, setting aside a well-earned heap for Karua, the thought of Karua reminded me that I was not only leaving the animals, but in two days I should be paying off the boys and saying good-bye to them also. And when (next morning) we packed into the lorry, not the brightest red blanket nor the shiniest of knives nor the puttees he so deeply coveted could enliven my farewells with Lembogi.

Towards evening the clouds lifted, and Siki whined and

urged me to leave my uncongenial occupation and go for a scramble.

Climbing up the wet slabs of rock and the rain-washed earth from which new life was already quickening, I felt the weight of sadness lifted from me. Up there, high on the mountain-side, the wind blew round me savage and triumphant, the mists whirled above my head ; while below, the rain-sodden land lay sombre with stretches of standing water, and brow drawn against brow in faint pencilling of new-born green. Longido stood up swathed in grey cloud and its foothills dark as indigo. Indeed, the whole world was dark and wet, yet curiously wide-eyed and calm, as after the shedding of tears. The wind dropped, and the voices of birds and of rivulets rose up clear and bell-like through the hush of evening.

The sky rent asunder forming a lake of palest transparent green, and in the midst of it, caught by the sun's hidden glory —the one point of light in all that vast and terrible gloom— Kilimanjaro shone forth, bright as a vision above the dazzling belt of clouds, the very symbol of promise.

Still, I thought, as I gazed upon it in wonder, chance might decree that I should some day scale those heights. Little did I then dream how that promise was to be fulfilled.

To the jungle photographer, who must toil and sweat in the heat of the plains, where water is tepid and butter oil ; where he is plagued day and night by flies and mosquitoes and a splendid variety of ticks, and no sooner over one bout of fever but he must succumb to the next, this vision of the eternal snows cannot but shine out in blessed contrast as the reward of his labours. And my earthly paradise was, after all, not Kilimanjaro, but the even more rugged and beautiful Mount Kenya.

Part II

THE MOUNTAIN (Mount Kenya)

Chapter XI

*IN WHICH I MAKE MY HOME IN AN
ALPINE HUT*

EVER since we had camped in Meru forest on the slopes of
Mount Kenya (hunting for elephant in 1923) and stepping
clear of the trees I had seen the snow lying like two petals
beneath the summit rosy in the dawn, I had longed to return
and climb the mountain.

It had been just one of those plans that lie at the back of
one's mind ; but now, while I was staying in Nairobi during
the rains, my friend the Private Secretary, who knew the
mountain well, fired me anew with its possibilities.

It was not merely a single mountain, he told me ; it was a
whole country of its own and parts of it were still unexplored.
His descriptions of its wild grandeur, its glaciers and precipices,
its valleys full of flowers and its surprisingly blue tarns set down
here and there in the wastes of rock, filled me with a longing
to be off. However strong the appeal of desert and jungle,
the urge of the mountains is strongest of all.

The only drawback, to my mind, was the scarcity of game,
but I came to appreciate that this in itself held one tremendous
advantage. For since there were no lions to guard against,
I should not need the rifle, and, better still, once installed in the
alpine hut I could send all the porters away. There would
then be no human being within about twenty miles, and I
could at last try the experiment of real and absolute solitude.

The best time to go was now, as soon as the short rains were
over, for December to March are the three best months in
the year on the mountain. It was December already, and I

looked despairingly at the low, leaden skies which showed no promise of a break. It was nearly Christmas, and every one said why not spend Christmas with a jolly party up-country instead of going off by myself again? But Christmas is a very special time to be with one's own family, and failing this, I loved the thought of spending it on the mountain.

The difficulty of inducing natives to face the cold was, like many another incidental difficulty, smoothed out by the Private Secretary, who said he would get in touch with Mtu Massara, the Mwimbi headman whom he himself employed on his climbs, and who could be relied upon to pick men who had already been up to the snow-line.

While others spoke of Christmas festivities, we withdrew with a pleasant feeling of conspiracy to pore over maps and write up lists of stores and equipment. I believe that it gave him very nearly as much anticipatory pleasure to draw up these plans as it would if he had been setting off for the mountain himself. I was still only toying with the thought, and humouring this whim of his—for the idea of going off to the mountain absolutely on my own, and allowed to climb and explore to my heart's content seemed too good to be really possible— but before I knew what had happened it was a *fait accompli* all cut and dried, with no margin for demur. I was to spend two months at the alpine hut which stands just above the tree-line on the eastern slopes of Mount Kenya, at a height of ten thousand feet.

It was a grand adventure. Till the last I did my best to keep it secret, for those who knew asked almost accusingly why on earth I wanted to spend two months alone on that gloomy mountain. There weren't even any elephants up there!

The excuse of photography had gone, but botany sounded very well. Plausible as it was, many friends shook their heads sadly. They thought it a great pity. And I could not convince them any more than I could convince the Red and

White Queens of Namanga. Now, I know that they were wrong, as those who advise against adventure must always be.

There still remained the question of my outfit. As I went ruefully over my threadbare tropical clothing, it looked chilly and inadequate for the high altitudes; and Nairobi did not seem to me the place to produce mountaineering boots with the right kind of ace-of-club shaped nails, or (except, of course, for that undying favourite the Balaclava helmet) warm clothes of any kind. As for a Whymper tent and an ice-axe, one might as reasonably look for sugar-cane in Spitzbergen.

"I can fit you up with most of the things you'll want," said the Private Secretary, who, from practical experience, was much more alive to their necessity than I was. "You can take my tent and fur-lined sleeping-bag and trench coat, and I've got a particularly good aneroid I can lend you. For the rest we'll go round and see what Melhuish can do."

Mr. Melhuish was another mountain enthusiast. After hearing what was toward, he smiled approvingly and leaving us to look at his beautiful (and now well-known) mountain photographs—by the help of which I hastily memorised some important landmarks—he reappeared with a pair of well-greased boots studded all round with the orthodox nails. With ski-ing socks inside they fitted me to a T.

Until his next leave they were more precious than gold, and as though that were not enough, he went to the limits of friendship by adding to an already growing heap of accessories his rope and ice-axe. Of all the many kindnesses which were showered upon me (and there were an incredible number) that ice-axe will always stand alone. It is a thing that I could never, by any stretch of imagination, have done myself. To lend any kind of tool or weapon demands a sacrifice of a high order; and an ice-axe is a very special thing. I often greased it. Although I had little chance of using it, it was an ornament to the hut, and lent to the enterprise an aspect both businesslike and picturesque. But then, anything to do with mountaineering holds for me perhaps a little more than its intrinsic glamour.

Now I was all ready to start.

At the last moment, another friend lent me a fur kaross (rug) which was to prove a boon at Hall Tarn, and a fourth his car to take me over the hundred and forty-eight miles from Nairobi to Chogoria, at the foot of the mountain. This kindness was all the greater in that they themselves could snatch no more than a fortnight's hard-earned leave to spend on the mountain, and they would have given worlds for my opportunity.

At last the rains cleared, and soon after five o'clock one morning the native driver began loading up the car with my kit, chop-boxes, spare petrol, and Siki.

To go by car over the Thika—Fort Hall—Meru road, the same road we had tramped along in the heat and dust over five years before, was a curious and poignant experience.

Owing to seven punctures and a collision with the road grader—who was very sorry to have stripped me of a wing but ingenuously admitted that he had neither pulled up nor given me room to pass because he had " hoped we were Indians "—owing to these long and frequent delays, I did not reach the Mission at Chogoria (my destination) until after ten o'clock that night.

Even so, what before had been a whole day's trek now took me no more than a bare hour in the car. I could not reconcile myself to that. There was something almost callous about it, a lack of respect. The advantages of a car are not lightly to be ignored, yet I think they are dearly bought. You may be superior to the road which before held you at the mercy of its every whim and caprice, but this superiority sends you through the country a complete stranger. For, when all is said, however long the road may have seemed afoot, it was a companion whom you came to understand and love. From a car, landmarks are too fleeting to hold a meaning for you ; trees are no longer friendly goals cheering you onward to the distant bend to linger a moment in passing beneath their leafy shade ; now, they flash by impersonally as telegraph poles, and are as swiftly forgotten. And the music of running water (rare enough on an African road) no longer charms your ear, for like as not, with the noise of the engine, you will pass by without hearing it.

But much as I disapproved of my present mode of progress, and guilty as I felt for coming back in this worthless fashion, it was nevertheless a peculiar joy to reunite myself once again with that road. Landmarks kept reminding me of other landmarks that lay ahead ; little bits of the road came back to me as vividly as yesterday ; so that I was for ever eagerly anticipating what was in store. It was a game between memory and reality. Here was our first march from Thika (how endless it had seemed !) and the swamp where we had bought sugar-cane off some natives ; there the long hill where Kongoni (my father's gun-bearer) had beguiled the way by teaching us the Swahili names for elephant, buffalo and lion. The single tree on a hillside where we had camped stood there unchanged, and below it the stream where Kasaja, one of the porters, going down to fetch water, had first played his fiddle, whose haunting little phrases were to become so familiar. Next came Fort Hall ; and the butterflies that had lured us from the road in pursuit still hovered above the green bushes along the river.

A puncture (I believe it was the fourth) delaying me by the big swamp near Embu, I struck off through the long grass to an ant-hill from where I could pick out the place where we had had many a buffalo hunt. I saw no buffalo, but the white egrets who accompany them rose up in a flock, graceful as terns, and wheeled above the vivid green swamp. As for Embu, that little oasis set down in a wild place, I would not look at it as I passed through, so fearful was I of losing the living first impression.

For some way after that, the road was new to me, for going on foot we had followed the switchback short cuts. As I skirted below our old camp, where three baby owls had sat in a branch over the tent, I picked up the thread again : here the river where we had found the bridge down and had waded across, there the corner that still smelt of pigs, and again I looked vainly for the tree that gave out this pungent smell.

Now I was in the real forest, and I waited for a certain bend that in memory epitomised the whole of that long trek, where the banana leaves caught the late sunshine with their luminous green, and opposite, the tall silver Mukui trees reached up to interlace their branches against the gloomy depths. At length I came to it, and found it unchanged and just as beautiful. It was too beautiful. It stabbed me with sudden misery, a culmination of this long day of reviving past scenes, so that I found it in my heart to wish that I had not returned.

Dusk came to blur the images, and then darkness. Turning off the engine and moving slowly and silently down the long hills (for the road was bad), the hush of night fell upon me. I could hear the call of night birds, and leaning back could see the half-moon through the roof of branches.

Climbing out above the forest again, I saw Jupiter rising red in the night haze, a dull orb, ungleaming. It was not like looking up at a remote planet, but rather as though one looked out across the tree-tops and across space to another sphere— a huge impression, almost frightening, yet strangely beautiful ; and the next moment the car went plunging down under the trees again, following the hairpin bends up and down the narrow valleys. The forest breathed out the scent of close-packed vegetation, pungent, acrid and sweet in the darkness ;

and the smell of earth and of dew and wood-smoke, the sound of water rushing beneath the bridges, and the liquid, bell-like notes of the frogs, brought the forest close around me though now become invisible.

Soon the head-lamps changed the road to a tunnel of light into which the overhanging branches came and went, and moths fluttered, and two rubies shining on the ground marked a nightjar sitting motionless, until the wheel was nearly upon him, when with wide, hurried wings he would fly up and vanish out of the charmed circle into the darkness.

Beyond Chuka I lost the way, and sent the driver to inquire at a village. A native dance was in full swing there, a monotonous sing-song and the beat of tom-toms throbbing endlessly with a kind of suppressed excitement through the pitch blackness, till it became woven into the silence.

At length the lights of the Chogoria Mission twinkled in friendly welcome through the trees, and although it was past ten o'clock, dinner had been kept for me.

I was given a delightful little guest-house to myself where the sun flooded in next morning as soon as he was up, and you looked him in the face across a bank of flowers to the bracken slopes drawn in silver lines of dew against the distant blue hills. Going round to the back of the house (for such a morning urged me quickly without doors to see all that there was to see) I suddenly beheld, above the primeval forest, the peak, deep violet in the liquid light. It called me to be off, and I fretted over the delay. But first of all the remainder of my stores did not arrive, and then it was Sunday ; so that it was not till the third morning that I started, by which time the days had passed so pleasantly that I was sorry to go.

Although the porters were assembled by seven o'clock, as always on the first day of a safari, much time was lost in making up the loads. Having satisfactorily disposed of them among twenty-five porters, and secured two more to carry native flour and ghee, I had still to take down their names and provide them with a couple of blankets apiece. They were then sent ahead unloaded for about four miles and, after we had breakfasted, Dr. Irvine drove me up in the lorry with all the loads. This was a fine saving of time and labour, and brought me to the forest fresh for the long climb. The loads were claimed once more, I said good-bye to Dr. Irvine and started off.

He had arranged everything for me, and had been most kind and helpful ; and before I had gone far, a runner overtook me with a parcel of five tiny roast chicken (prepared for Christmas, I knew, and to be ill spared), a parting gift from his wife to speed me on my way.

The path led under trees for a mile or two, till it came out into the sunlight where a bridge had been thrown over a stream, and the broad banana leaves sent quivering green flames across the shadows.

And then the climb again. It was beautiful forest, sometimes subduing the sun to a rich twilight, so deep was the roof spread overhead ; sometimes luminously green where a huge tree trunk broke through and stood darkly out against a background of leaves. Above all, it impressed you with its silence, a silence that broke in upon your thoughts so that you must pause to listen. The men's voices came echoing back as down the aisles of a cathedral.

We crossed another brook, purling down among the tree-ferns which threw out their fountains of green fronds twenty and thirty feet high.

Beneath the forest's welcome canopy, climbing was never hot, but the loads were heavy and the porters called frequent halts. Time pressed, and I spurred them on. Bringing up the rear, I often came upon a straggler sitting discouraged beside his load ; and helping him to re-tie it and hoist it onto his head I urged him unrelentingly onward.

I was to have reached the hut, nineteen miles away, in one march ; but by the time we reached the halfway camp it was already past three o'clock, and the men declared that the hut was still another four hours' climb. The danger of buffalo or elephant in the path decided me to give in, though with an ill grace, for it meant needless unpacking. By then we had left the forest behind and traversed a belt of smaller timber, and climbing a plateau of heather and tussocks bright with patches of pink and scarlet and golden immortelles (*helichrysum*), we reached the beginning of the bamboo.

I pitched the Whymper tent in a tiny clearing a few feet square in the first bamboo copse. It was so small that there was scarcely room for the tent and a fire, and the feathery tops met over my head.

I was glad enough to halt for the night, and was resting before getting to work to unpack and cook my supper, when the continued murmur of voices close by roused me to find out why the porters had not set about making their own camp. Looking round the flap of the tent I saw half a dozen of them sitting with their heads together intoning the Bible. This effectively disarmed remonstrance, and the best that I could do in the circumstances was mildly to suggest that there was a time for all things. They looked up in pained surprise, closed the Book and started about their duties with Christian resignation.

The second chicken and a cup of hot cocoa made me a splendid supper. Before the stars came out I crawled into my sleeping-bag, and, except to realise from time to time that Siki was snuggling closer and closer into the small of my back for warmth, I did not awake until six next morning, when Hezekiah came to call me.

Hezekiah was my new personal boy, trained to the mountain climate (which Jim could never have stood) though to nothing else whatever. I had told him to call me at five, so that I might be up quickly to pack—Hezekiah naturally knew nothing about packing—and start at daybreak.

But hurry as I would, I was numbed with cold, the porters were still stupid with sleep, everything was drenched with dew so that the tent was difficult to fold, and it was seven o'clock by the time we started.

It was a cloudless morning with a crisp tang in the air, and the path wandered and climbed beneath tunnels of bamboo and across flowery open spaces until it gained the real bamboo forest, ranked stem by stem, dark and green like the depths of the sea, and overwhelmingly still. Now and then the sun pierced through with golden shafts, and looking up to the leaves against the brightness you would see them caught in a warm aura like fluttering spears of light.

I fell purposely out of earshot and stood still, listening to the silence. The sun was behind me, and looking back I saw a hundred single cobwebs spanned across, flashing line on line in changeful hues against the shadows, as water does when the sun glints over it. How easily, I thought, could one be lost in such a place. As the porters advance, the forest echoes to the ring of laughter, the voices go warmly through the dank air, stirring it to life. Fall a hundred yards behind, and the silence flows back upon you, closing over their wake like deep waves of water. You strain your ears : not a sound comes back. Not a bird calls. A breeze may shiver through the leaves overhead, and one stem knock against another with a sound inexpressibly sad.

Except for some fresh elephant droppings I saw no sign of game, and I rejoiced that I had left the rifle behind. Elephant, rhino and buffalo were said to be a danger, but in that blind going I fancied that a rifle would have been of very little use.

The forest began to thin out, the little pink flowers captured the sunlight, shining like coral in the dew, and violets laid a purple mantle on the path-sides. I came to the last ragged out-posts—trees from whose bare branches waved streamers of pale moss—and over a rise of heather, without hint or warning, the peak, visible at no time during the climb, suddenly revealed itself.

One last glimpse backward to the descending hills of forest to the far plain, and next moment the first rampart of heather rose up to screen it off behind me, and I was in a new country, in the presence of the mountain.

In fine swelling lines of tawny and purple it rose up from gigantic moors, gentle curves soaring upward dark and light as the little clouds sailed across them. And above that, rock sheer and jagged reaching up to a patch of snow under the peak, which in turn went soaring up still more remotely into the deep sky.

Brave and inspiring was this sudden vision, and although the climb had left me with knees trembling, I could have yodelled for the joy and beauty of it.

And now the way slackened out benevolently, leading across the open and down through a grove of beautiful lime-like trees which grew to a height of seventy or eighty feet, the *Dombeya mastersii*. I stepped out joyously, pausing many a time for a picture of the trees framing the mountain, a group of cedars, or a graceful outcrop of bamboo beside a true moorland stream. Subjects to photograph formed and re-formed themselves with a beauty of line and balance that was irresistible ; yet even then, I knew that it was less form than colour : vivid colours, greens and blues and yellows set aflame by the glory of the morning, golden flowers against azure, colour so insistent that it almost burst into song.

Half an hour later, toiling up round the last bend, I came unexpectedly upon the hut, set snugly in a little dip sheltered by giant heath and a single green tree. It looked wonderfully welcoming in the midst of that vast solitude as, with a beating heart, I put the key in the lock, and opened the door for the first time on my home.

The porters had no wish to spend another night in the cold, and they started back as soon as they had put down their loads.

I kept Hezekiah and Magadi to do the rough work, and as I could not wait another moment for the excitement of moving in, we set about at once opening the windows, taking out the table, chairs and bunk-frames, and submitting everything to a good scrub with soap and water. I unpacked the stores, scrubbed the cupboard shelves, lined them with clean paper, and arranged the hut stores in one cupboard and my own in the one adjoining it.

It was dark before I had finished, and I was by then almost too tired to think about dinner. But it was Christmas Day and I had been given a plum pudding on purpose ; so I completed the feast by warming up a tin of the old favourite, Heinz's Spaghetti in Tomato Sauce ; and battening down the hatches against the cold, I rounded off the house-warming with Beethoven's Seventh Symphony.

There remained much to be done. To begin with, the boys came round next morning looking utterly wretched, and said that they had not slept a wink because of the cold. So the first thing was to send them off to cut bundles of grass with which to make themselves beds. They had a small room partitioned off at the back of the hut (generally used as a store) and they had tried to find comfort in three miserable blankets each, on a floor lined with galvanized iron, at a temperature that froze the water in the buckets.

Bringing a carpentering outfit proved an inspiration, and we soon improvised a lean-to for the kitchen with iron sheeting and wooden props. This took me most of the day, but there is nothing in the world so satisfactory as *making* something.

It poured with rain, and little did it matter, for the roof was watertight and there were no tent-pegs to worry about. And, what was such a vast improvement on a tent, there was heaps of room. In fact, the hut was an ideal home, at least eighteen feet by twelve. Before nightfall I put the last touches to it by unpacking the books, hanging up a picture of the mountain, and arranging a bowl of ferns and flowers gathered from the banks of the Mara, which flowed at the foot of the gorge under a natural bridge past my door.

Chapter XII

IN WHICH I SEE THE MOUNTAIN.
LAKE ELLIS. CORYNDON PEAK

THE fern grotto below the natural bridge in the rocks was the first thing that attracted me.

It was difficult to reach, for the cliffs that walled it in on either hand fell down sixty feet or more. At the bottom the Mara gurgled unseen among the soft depths of greenery. There was one place on the other side where the earth sloped under a face of rock, and here the porters of former expeditions had worn a tortuous and narrow path in their journeys to and from the water. It took me some time to discover it, and when at last I climbed down through the green tangle, I found myself in a fairyland of flowers and ferns and moss beside a little waterfall.

Having risen early to make my bed, sweep and dust the hut and cook breakfast, I felt to the full that sweet content which simple work is said to bring, and I sat a while idly dreaming by the water. When all is said, it is those idle moments that are precious. When all else is forgotten I shall still see that spray of golden flowers hanging against the golden gloom, and the stream running by like crystals over amber ; or in imagination look up to the beard-moss waving and floating out overhead, grey-green against the ribbon of deep, penetrating blue.

I had taken a bucket with me, for I wanted to practise hauling water up the precipitous path against the time when I sent the boys away. The first ten yards were easy enough but the way was very slippery, and long before I panted to the top, with half the water spilt already, I had definitely decided that there would not be any question of baths.

As I climbed out of the gorge, I saw that the mood of the day had changed ; and in a few minutes the sky became heavily overcast and the mountain dark and brooding.

But it was not yet ten o'clock, so telling the boys to collect firewood, I took my camera and a slab of chocolate and set off up the road above the hut.

Beyond the long rolling slopes of heather hiding the hut among its folds, I knew nothing yet of my surroundings, and unable to resist finding out what lay beyond each succeeding brow, I walked up past the Gates of Kenya—two dome-shaped hills with a rocky cleft between them—and followed the zigzags till the road at length straightened out and skirted high up round a great amphitheatre.

The road led part of the way up to Hall Tarn (where climbers usually camp on their way to the peak) and although overgrown it was well laid and, for a mile or two, even feasible for a car. I began by hotly resenting its intrusion in so untouched a place ; but when I strayed from it to photograph a fine tree groundsel about twenty feet high and in full bloom, I floundered hopelessly among the tussocks, the heather surged over my head, and my feelings towards the road when I regained it were chastened to gratitude.

I was still hoping to come to one of the lakes ; but when I had climbed halfway round this amphitheatre, I set the compass (the road, looking back the way I had come, faced due east), tested the aneroid, and sat down.

It was the size of everything about the mountain that was so overwhelming. You might have compared it to Norway : same plants, same smell, same precipices rising out of the heather with strewn boulders at their feet. Yet try to climb any gentle slope, or reach any minor summit, and it would take you not forty minutes but two or three hours. The going (apart from the road) was very laborious and the atmosphere deceptive, so that distances were much greater than they seemed.

In that huge amphitheatre, which fell away hundreds of feet below, and rose up about me on all sides to dark sweeping shoulders, cliffs, crags and a flat-topped volcano the colour of indigo, I sat and listened. There was not a sound in the world except the twittering of the sun-birds in an isolated bush beside me. They hovered above the flowers (which looked not unlike St. John's Wort) after the manner of humming-birds, and they had long beaks and tails and iridescent black and green plumage. Mists hung over the peaks, and every now and then out of the silence the wind would bring the sound of a waterfall so suddenly that it was startling. Siki was restless, daunted perhaps ; and had it not brought back the familiar scenes of childhood, had I not been bred to solitude and happy in it, alone in that vastness and unearthly silence I realised, almost with a shiver, that I might have been suddenly terror-struck.

Standing like a pin-point in the midst of that sunless and gloomy desolation of rock, was like standing face to face with the beginning of creation. And then, as the awful majesty of it became more than I could bear, the strong arm of pro-tection swept aside loneliness once and for all in the illuminating consciousness of God, and of the tremendous friendship of the earth.

I swung home bareheaded, singing an impromptu magnificat for happiness ; and coming round a bend I put up a duiker, the first living creature I had seen. Siki chased and ate locusts, and I picked delphiniums which here and there lit up the dark heather with shining blue, and farther on I collected over a score of different kinds of flowers to paint.

The picture of that extraordinary flat-topped and completely round volcano lingered in my mind, and next day I went off to reconnoitre. It rose up on the northern horizon, and was so far off the beaten track that I wondered whether any one had troubled to climb it. The boys told me it was called Karingo. But I found exactly what I had feared : miles of hills and valleys lying between, and the going all among tussocks. The going was indeed so bad that I could not possibly have reached the volcano and returned in the day. I now noticed for the first time a conical grassy mountain near by, which looked even higher, and stood quite alone, and on the following morning I decided to climb that instead.

The dark and frowning days were over. I was up with the lark and flung open the doors as the sun rose red upon the mountain-side. The full moon hung transparent as a cloud above the peaks, the bushes sparkled in the cold dew, and below me the rolling sea of fog curdled in shining opal to the horizon.

It was a morning that exulted aloud, so that you had to run, sing and jump for joy. It made me feel sad, too, as I sipped my coffee before starting off on the climb, to look out over that floor of clouds solid in the sunshine as mother-of-pearl, and to think that down there people were waking up and saying what a nasty dull day it was going to be.

That magic cloud-belt severed the mountain from the earth. One stood upon Olympus, or on the roof of the world, and breathed a rarer air. The sun shone on the colours in their first rainbow purity, unfiltered through any atmosphere at all, and everything was intensely bright and clear-edged as though the very leaves were cut out of metal against the sky.

As I started off through the rime, the sharpness pricked in

my nostrils and I could scarcely hold myself in to a walk. And yet, that such a day as this should be poured out on one human being alone was unbearable. Whatever I did I could never make enough of it ; and, in any case, my exaltation among those vast and silent hills was as significant as the frisking of a gnat.

At the end of half an hour the boys caught up, and leaving the road I struck off to the right and took diagonally up a mountain of heather and tussocks. Always the top seemed just ahead and always, having reached it, I found that a break in the rock divided me from a higher one. I learnt, then, not to climb each height but to steer a course up the valleys. The boys had small faith in my guiding, and went on climbing and scrambling, so that although they moved at treble my speed, when they looked down from a top it was to find that I had outstripped them from below.

I followed up a succession of wild gorges where the rocks fell away grey and broken to the fine grass—typical lie up for a hare, I thought—and among the boulders the tree groundsels threw out their cones of blossom overhead, burning gold against the deep blue sky.

Although the round hill, Mugi, the boys called it, was my ultimate goal, I wanted to find Lake Ellis first ; and after a long search I came upon it, hidden in a dip in the hillside. It is the largest lake on the mountain, about half a mile long and a quarter of a mile wide.

I reached it where it flowed out in a little brook, and there I put up a couple of duck (black with white bars on the wing). The way the wind ruffled the water to darkest blue, tipping the wavelets with white, and the sound of them lapping against the shore, was so exactly like our lake in Norway that without thinking I looked for the sailing-boat. I climbed down and walked along the brink where the giant lobelias stood like sentinels, when all at once through an opening in the opposite cliff the whole group of shining snow-clad peaks burst upon my sight.

I drank two cupfuls of icy, crystal-clear water, took some photographs, and then struck back east again for Mugi, which in my hunt for the lake I had already passed.

We had been walking for ten minutes when I discovered that I had left my knife by the lake shore. The boys at once turned back to retrieve it. Their good humour in mishaps like this always amazed me. I stopped them to put the cameras and rucksack down and, at least, to go back unburdened ; and tying my handkerchief to Magadi's spear to mark the spot (for it was a wide, grassy plateau), I continued slowly ahead. The wonderful part about natives is that they can run up and down hill like dogs and will always catch up however much start you have. Climbing the hill I put up five partridges that flew up from under my feet with such a whirr and screeching that I jumped into the air.

Mugi looked higher than it was, or maybe I erred on the other side this time. It took me forty minutes from the lake to the summit. By aneroid (at 11.45 a.m.) it measured 11,600 feet.

The summit, only a few feet in diameter, stood alone, and whichever way I turned, the view was immense. On one side lay Karingo, the flat-topped volcano, and running up from it was a long ridge called Ndugi, bounding the north. To eastward and far below me, hills and forests and plains dreamed under the sunlit clouds, while at my back the peaks, ephemeral with snow, swept upward in flowing lines of light against a sky blue as gentians.

Sky and earth brimmed over with rollicking blue ; the very wind blowing off the snow sped down on wings of light ; the hills danced and the heavens laughed for joy.

I lay in the hot sun with a tuft of heather to prop my head at the right angle for the view, and studied the twin main peaks—Batian and Nelion—through the glasses. Of course, without Swiss guides any thought of climbing them was out of the question ; and, of course, no one living in their sight and presence could help making the attempt. Many attempts had been made already but, so far, Mackinder, with his two Swiss guides, was alone in his conquest of Mount Kenya, when, in 1899, after bitter hardship and a night of exposure below the Diamond Glacier and close under the arête, he reached the summit.

But in the meantime there was that buttress of crags to the left, culminating in the Coryndon and Delamere Peaks. I studied a line of approach. It would be a big climb to manage in a day and return to the hut, a rise of between five and six thousand feet, but it was well worth trying. They had never been climbed (so I had been told) and I should be able, at last, to try out the aneroid in the interests of science.

I called the boys to show them the knife-edged pinnacles I had set my heart upon, but they were both curled up in the heather, fast asleep. They were very like a couple of friendly young pointers. When they were on the go they travelled so fast that they seemed to quarter the ground ; and the moment it was time to stop they went to sleep. Though they often maddened me with their indolence and good nature, I looked on them with much affection. You could not help liking them, they were so completely trusting and unsophisticated, like dogs or children.

I liked Magadi best. He was a raw savage and always smiling. He carried a spear and wore a tartan blanket looped up over one shoulder. There was a jauntiness about him which I think he must have owed partly to the way he wore his hair. It was close-shaved except for the top, which was clipped to a neat round thatch and slightly tilted, like a béret. I guessed that he had a touch of hero-worship for the initiated, Christianised Hezekiah.

As became his superior enlightenment, Hezekiah wore khaki shirt and shorts, and a faded green Homburg hat which rarely left his head. Learning and letters had an immense pull over mere savagery, and Hezekiah never let it be forgotten. He droned through page after page of the Bible at every odd moment of the day, from seven a.m. onwards, till I, distractedly trying to read or write inside the hut, would rush out in a frenzy of exasperation and think of something else for him to do. On these occasions I invariably found Magadi lying on propped elbows, drinking in every word with rapt attention. I wondered if Dr. Irvine had any idea how near he was to winning another convert. Perhaps he had foreseen the rich opportunity the mountain would afford for study and meditation, and had chosen out these two with an ulterior purpose. I would ask him about that later.

Meanwhile, there was no doubt that the heathen Magadi, the perfect fag, outshone Hezekiah, the Sixth Form boy. On our climbs it was he (Magadi) who had the initiative and a cheerful belief in our undertaking. Hezekiah had a way of looking prim and rather pained. When I felt particularly irritated with him I thought that he came as near as was possible for a native to being a prig. And then he would do something entirely disarming, and I hastily retracted these harsh thoughts. Once he presented me with a wooden spoon, carved out of red cedar wood with immense care and hours of labour. Another time it was a pair of butter patters. He even scrubbed the floor without my telling him, or I would come in and find a bright blue delphinium tied to the back of my chair.

And a little of the savage did still persist in spite of everything. It popped up its unworthy head one evening when I sat watching a duiker nibbling the grass close to the hut. Hezekiah came round the corner, and I put my fingers to my lips to warn him to keep quiet.

"I see it," he whispered back, his face lighting up with frankly pagan glee. "I will fetch my spear!" And I took a thoroughly mean advantage of his absence to give the duiker the alarm.

The difficulty with the boys was to find occupation for them. I endeavoured to teach Hezekiah the rudiments of cooking; I invented every imaginable kind of task to keep them busy. The first of these was to dig a hole for the old tins that lay about. They dug a pit large enough to trap an elephant, and then collected all the tins and bits of paper—the accumulated rubbish of years—and buried them out of sight. There was satisfaction in that piece of work. I almost wanted to put up a notice to future climbers on the use of this pit.

But the fact remained that the supply of firewood far exceeded the demand, the floor had been scrubbed and re-scrubbed, the washing had all been washed, the saucepans burnished with earth and ashes, and everything was spick and span. There really was nothing more that they could do. It was like being becalmed in the doldrums without sails to mend, and I wished I had thought of bringing a few gallons of Stockholm tar so that they could have given the hut a fresh coat. With too much time on their hands they yawned with boredom, felt more and more depressed, hated the cold nights and longed for the plains and their companions. The place held no charm for them, nor were they afflicted, as I was, with an insatiable urge for climbing. I understood how they felt, and was inexpressibly touched that they never once thought of asking me to let them go. I promised them that after our climb up Coryndon Peak they should have a week's holiday.

Knowing that it would be a long climb, I had planned a very early start; but Hezekiah, getting no response to his knocking at four a.m., weakly desisted, and it was seven o'clock by the time I awoke, full of remorse and reproaches. I ought to have put it off till next day, but I could not waste such a morning as this ; and with a furious concentration of hurry I managed to start within twenty minutes.

It was an even longer climb than I had anticipated. I never caught up that early start, and was all day a couple of hours behindhand and racing against time. I should have left the hut at four-thirty with the lantern, and left the road by the first light of dawn.

There was about an hour of road, and then I cut down left-handed and crossed the floor of the Nithi Valley, which shone like silver with young groundsel. Close to, they looked like artichokes (or cabbages) with the under sides of their leaves soft as down. As I climbed higher, their leaves were no longer filled with dew but each one held a tiny crescent of ice ; and the path was so hard with frost that the boys complained presently of needles in their feet, and we halted while they thawed them in the sun.

Till then I had been luckier than I knew, for I had fallen in with a little path firmly trodden among the tussocks, made, presumably, by duiker and such small game, for no native ventured up to these heights of his own free will. Now it petered out, and we battled and slipped and tumbled among boulders and tussocks in a long steep traverse. Insensibly I fell away from the steepness to a gentler gradient, then fought my way straight upward again, lured always by a cliff high above me in whose shadow there waved a patch of vivid scarlet gladioli.

When at last I reached the top, I found myself on a wide grassy back with the Nithi Valley on my right hand and the Hobley Valley on my left.

I walked over to the left till I could look into the Hobley Valley, and saw far below me a little tarn which lay as green as an ocean pool among the rocks. At my back the view was opening out, and every step upward widened the horizon. Over two hundred miles away to southward (on my left) faintly pink as a cloud above a yet fainter ring of clouds, was Kilimanjaro. On my right beyond the Nithi Valley, a corner of Lake Ellis flashed like a sapphire from a fold of the mountain-side, and the conical mountain, Mugi, looked from this proud height little more than a mole-hill.

The sun was hotter than the Alps in August, and there was not a cloud in the sky.

When, from Mugi, I had chosen out my line, I had not guessed that this grassy ridge I was now following might be severed from the peaks by a deep valley cutting transversely across it. Beginning like a broad back nearly a mile wide, the ridge narrowed as I climbed until I could look into both valleys at once, then to the width of a path like an ice-bridge, falling down in a precipice on either hand, till I foresaw the moment when it would be eaten through altogether and project like a headland over a rift between me and the mountain proper. But the isthmus held true, and led me across to the region of the peaks.

By then it was midday. Coryndon Peak and the rest looked little nearer than when I had set out towards them five hours before, and we were badly in need of a breather. I reluctantly decided to sacrifice a precious half-hour for a rest and some food. The altitude may have had something to do with it, but eager though I was to push on I could not have gone another yard.

A fresh factor against me—and once more I railed at those wasted hours abed—the clouds that daily swept up from the south and hung about the summits between twelve and three o'clock were now inexorably forming. Luckily, they were coming up only half-heartedly, forming, breaking, melting and forming again ; and, anxiously conning the sky, I thought the signs had never been more favourable. It was no longer one of those blue days that conjure up the big white clouds out of nowhere; it had changed to one of high, streaky currents with a hint of mares' tails which, though not so inspiriting as an unflawed depth of blue, is often more to be trusted.

After that rest, the heights of tumbled grey stone confronted me less forbiddingly, and I decided to climb to the top of the lowest part of the skyline and, if need be, to give up Coryndon Peak for that day. This decision (as I knew very well in my own mind) was the thin end of the wedge. Once on that skyline I would urge the boys to the next. Anyway, I argued, when they pointed to the sun overhead with one foot already in the western sky, we had been climbing only five hours; three hours for the return was generous reckoning, so that we could safely climb till two o'clock.

Although they were in a sense bred to the mountain, there was always an undercurrent of uneasiness in the boys' attitude towards it, as though climbing too near it were a kind of tempting of Providence.

Now as we started off again, the sun went behind the clouds, drawing after him the living colours; the shadows raced over the harsh and arid rocks clammily like bats; mists wreathed stealthily past, bound for the same direction as ourselves; the wind changed to a higher key, and whined forlornly among the desolate grey stones. In a moment we were shivering with cold. It was easy to fancy that the mountain had turned less friendly, and the boys doubtless read in this swift and sinister change a direct warning from the gods that dwelt on it. We had come a long way; reaching the top held no glamour for them, it was not even a point of honour, and it was but natural that they should plead to go back.

If I could have only fired them with my own example and struck ahead! But this was what I was quite incapable of doing, and although it was I who obstinately held for going on, it was they who made the pace. Magadi tore up those unending steeps like a dog, and whenever I raised my eyes as I struggled painfully upward (each step costing me several hard-drawn breaths that sent my heart throbbing in my ears) there was Magadi, far above, silhouetted against the flying clouds, his blanket streaming out on the wind, and Siki at his heels.

Up and up we toiled, now and then passing a giant lobelia whose single cone, mistily blue and standing rather taller than oneself, was so soft to touch and feathery like hackles; up to the shale, long slopes of it that went tinkling down like glass under every step; then into volcanic dust, an even worse element, for you sank in deep and it slipped under your weight a good half step back with each step forward.

And each new skyline was but an outer court, and although it admitted you one degree nearer, there was always another threshold to be crossed, and beyond it another wall to climb.

But the jagged cliffs on my right, my goals before, were now below me, and Coryndon Peak itself looked down from close above. And then I came to the edge of a chasm. Between me and Coryndon Peak lay a small valley. To climb down, cross it and regain my present level on the other side might take half an hour or more. It was now past two o'clock, and, retracing my steps to an opening on the right where I found the first patch of snow, I halted for a quick consultation. We stood on the edge of a fine semi-circle of precipice, and far below lay Lake Michaelson.

I tried to reason with the boys, who now besought me more earnestly than ever to turn back. I agreed that Coryndon Peak was out of the question, but let us only gain the lowest part of the arête which rose up before us, then surely, at last, we should be able to look across to the snows of the main peak. After all this, we could not give up for the sake of one paltry half-hour.

And so I pushed on, the boys unwillingly following; now the clouds lifting to show me my objective, now drawing a darker shadow over the sun, putting us into twilight, and scudding damp and chill past our faces.

Now we began to haul ourselves up from ledge to ledge, to look for handholds and to step warily. It was not intrinsically difficult, and had it been clear I should have thought nothing of it; but as it was, the dense fog put a spice of danger into the climb. Rocks would loom up, then the baffling mist blot them out, leaving us with nothing tangible but the ledge upon which we stood and the piece of rock to which we clung. I had no idea what lay ahead, how near or how far I was from the arête, and looking back I saw that retreat was also cut off. I had brought no chalk with me, the wind was now blowing half a gale, so tearing the pages from my pocket-book I wedged them under the stones to guide me back.

The minutes were precious, yet as in a dream I could not hurry my lagging steps by a fraction. But I was past the horrid phase of trembling at the knees and fighting for breath. The moment you come to a bit of real climbing and are caught in the thrill of getting somewhere near the top, you feel suddenly strong again.

And then, reaching up my hands in the unsubstantial mist, I found nothing to take hold of, and groping my way cautiously forward I came to an abrupt halt. The next step would have been into space, for I was actually on the sharp crest of the arête.

I took out the aneroid and found that the needle pointed to 15,120 feet.

As I peered into the dark swirling clouds, they rolled up before my eyes, revealing a great abyss and a wall of burning red, sunlit rock towering up to incredibly sharp needles. Near the top it was gouged straight through, and held a lozenge of blue sky. Below it the rock fell down hundreds of feet among the shadows. Beyond, Nelion—one of the main twin peaks himself—strode gloriously upward into the heavens, throwing a blue shadow over the glacier. On my left, sprinkled with fresh snow and not so very high above me, was Delamere Peak with an arête like the Eiger, and monoliths balanced against the shifting mists : fantastic fingers of rock, all top-heavy, holding on by a miracle. On my right also, the rock rose up, and below, framed in this inverted arch of precipices, lay Hall Tarn, a deep and tranquil blue. Beyond it there soared more pinnacles of rock, and beyond these again, immeasurably far off, lay the whole world.

I stood dumbly before the overwhelming beauty, the glorious imagination behind that universe of rock flung at random into this masterly construction and harmony of line. Out of chaos was order created. In my diary I wrote : " I stumbled then for words, and none would come but the flaming revelation—' this *is* God '."

It was now past three o'clock, and to reach the road before darkness overtook us would be a stiff race. With one last look about me I turned for a flying retreat.

Yet, even then, I could not go away like that, as it were casually. It was a tremendous moment, calling for a response deeper than anything I could give. I ran back alone, and knelt among the rocks and prayed. . . .

As I climbed down over the arête I thought that I understood why the saints and prophets, and indeed our Lord Himself, when they wanted to pray, chose to go up into the mountains.

Fortune was kind, for the mists had entirely gone. In spite of that, it was difficult enough to retrace my steps.

There was but one way in that rocky labyrinth, and a short cut would invariably give out at the edge of a cliff, forcing me to climb back and search again for the guiding pieces of paper.

On the shale I got my own back on that undaunted spirit Magadi, for he had never learnt how to put both feet together, lean back on his spear, and glissade ; and for once I left him standing.

Both boys picked up lumps of snow and called it " chumbe " (salt), which explained their frequent allusions on the way up to salt brooks, salt that cut your feet—they were ever pointing out traces of this peculiar salt. For them it would always remain mysterious and a little uncanny. Even for me it held an element of unbelief. To reach the snow-line and to hold a lump of snow in my hand, here on the equator, was an adventure I had looked forward to with childish pleasure ever since my arrival on the mountain.

Running, sliding and scrambling, we were soon off the scree and back among the tussocks ; and as we lost our hard-won height I pulled up to look round again and again, for fear that I might be missing something. Never was there such a view ; and now, in the gentle blues and violets of afternoon, it led the eye ever farther afield to the realms of enchantment. Out there, far below me, lay the hills of Maua where my father and I had once tracked (in vain) the largest elephant in Africa ; to the left was Siolo and Archer's Post. Through the glasses I picked out the hill where we had hunted Chanler's reedbuck, and beyond was the mountain called Kom, for which the elephants make when the Lorian swamp dries up. Only the mists of distance hid the Indian Ocean. A soft bank of cloud hovered above the plains, shedding down a blueness that was rather a light than a shadow, so that earth and sky, forest, mountains and plains were melted together in a sea of quivering light.

The immortal joy of the world lifted us out of ourselves, till I found that we were all singing as we went, and each a different tune in a different key.

After a long battle with the tussocks I eventually stepped onto the road again as darkness fell, and the peaks rose up like Valhalla toward the stars.

Chapter XIII

SOLITUDE AND THE FAIRY DELL.   HALL TARN.
THE CURLING POND

THE boys were up before sunrise, eager to be off on their promised holiday, and nothing would do but I must have breakfast at seven o'clock, an hour earlier than usual.   Their work done, they left me like a marooned sailor with a plentiful supply of firewood and every bucket and empty petrol-tin full of fresh water, and started off in the irrepressibly high spirits of a couple of schoolboys.   The holiday spirit was in the air, and as soon as their voices were lost in the silence I put aside my broom and duster and lay down in the heather with a sigh of content.

Swifts darted to and fro in the blue sky overhead and, taking courage from the sudden quiet, all the little birds came hopping down to find a breakfast.   This, I thought, is what it must be like when human beings leave a place.   The noise and bustle are gone, the tree shakes out its leaves upon the breeze, and it is as though all Nature said : " Ah ! " with a happy sigh, " and now to resume life ! "   When man is near, Nature shrinks unobtrusively into the background to become merely a setting.   When he passes on, she comes to life again, the fairies creep out one by one, shyly at first, and soon you find yourself in the midst of a silence not empty or lonely but full of the poetry of the all-important business of life.

How beautiful is real solitude ; not only living in the wilds, but giving yourself up to the spirit that dwells in them.   The spirit within one is shy also, and this communion can be won only in the boundless silence.   Solitude such as this was complete escape from oneself because there was nothing to bring one back to the consciousness of self. Spirit, like mercury, can be divided and encased in different forms, but when it can it will run together again with the Spirit that is everywhere in the universe. By and by it must separate once more and return to its own little prison of flesh, bearing a certain name, moving in a destined set of circumstances for an infinitesimal moment in Time. But the name or the rôle is no longer important or perturbing, for the spirit, having once united with itself, knows itself everywhere and knows itself free and everlasting. It wants nothing, for it is everything, and can pour itself out endlessly from the universal source.

There was so much to do that the days were never long enough. Besides collecting and painting flowers, exploring the mountain, reading and sketching, I wanted to make improvements inside the hut by putting up some more shelves and making curtains for the windows. There was something pleasantly domesticated about sitting in the doorway of an afternoon and sewing away at cretonnes. The hut itself, companionably creaking in the hot sunshine, audibly spoke its approval of these homely attentions. It had never been treated as home before. People had come and always left in a hurry, cleaning up superficially to meet the Alpine Hut Rules but never having time for the extra touches. Now it began to take a pride in itself. It was being lived in, and it settled down with a new sense of well-being.

I wasted little time in cooking, for I was reading Thoreau's *Life on Walden Pond* in which he shows that life can be very happily maintained on beans and rice. This theory appealed to me enormously, for the inconsistency of longing to make friends with the animals and yet eating meat, had always troubled me.

I came home in the evening to rekindle the embers and cook

my supper. The pot was cheerfully boiling as the last rays of sunshine caught the smoke curling up blue and straight above the roof. The far-away blue hills showed themselves between the fold of my valley where the juniper stood out grey-blue against them, and though the sun still gilded the tree-tops, there was already the damp smell of mist rising out of the shadows. A bird skimmed through the golden air, and the hush was so perfect that you almost held your breath with it.

Suddenly there came the sound of a man blowing his nose. It could not be, I must have dreamt it ! But reality came roughly round the bend—a little fairy tinkle of alarm, the unheard patter of fairy feet, as each ran to his post and stood motionless as though turned to stone—and the spell was broken, broken by the noise and clatter of three mountaineers and their twenty-two porters.

The mountaineers insisted that I should not turn out for them—though it was an alpine hut and they had as much and rather more right to it than I—so they pitched their tents and we dined together (not on beans and rice this time, for we all had plenty of stores). One of them was Norwegian, and it was a bond in common that in climbing here we should both be so constantly reminded of Norway. The other two were experienced alpinists, and time went by unheeded as we talked of their hopes of conquering the peak and revived memories of past climbs. They certainly knew their job, and were fitted out with crampons, alpine ropes, Swiss nails to their boots and ice-axes all complete, the sight of which filled me with an intense longing to be going too. There are few things that can give you the feeling of having missed everything worth while like watching a party of climbers setting off for the high mountains whilst you are left behind in the valley.

However, I had planned a trip to the glaciers myself a week

later, when Hezekiah and Magadi were to bring back the necessary porters.

In the meantime, one of the party had brought me some watercress roots from the Mission, and when they left next morning I took the plants down to the gorge.

The stream ran swiftly over the golden gravel, leaving no backwaters with the ooze which watercress loves best; but after paddling up and down through the shallows I found a place where I could make a little breakwater. A quiet pool formed behind it, and I found plenty of mud for planting by reaching my arm in under the hollow banks.

Every time I visited the gorge I was enchanted afresh. When you climbed down through the sprays of golden flowers to the grotto of ferns and running water, from where you could look up to the sun through a tapestry of green, you left the everyday world behind and stepped straight back into childhood. My time both with the elephants and on the mountain was a Peter Pan existence; the very fact of wearing shorts took me back to the spade and bucket years; but it was here, paddling and digging and re-shaping the course of the stream (getting wetter and dirtier than I should have been allowed to) that I most completely slipped back into the Golden Age. It is this being intimately in touch that is the secret of youth. Children know it, though not consciously, perhaps, and it is only when they begin to grow up that the veil drops between them and it, and they are driven out of paradise.

Across the pool in front of the little waterfall was a half-submerged tree trunk, upon which I could lie with my face close to the water and watch the most entrancing effects. First, the water churning white under the fall, and then a string of bubbles sailing past, each like a crystal caught for a moment in the sun against the shadow of the rock, and all winking like lights in a harbour, and suddenly going out. With my eyes shaded where no ripple intervened, I looked down to the floor of the pool as clearly as through a glass, and all the pebbles had a purplish bloom on them like mussel shells, and the water-beetles that skated about in jerks, faintly dimpling the surface, sometimes dived down, each taking with him a remnant of the upper air so that he seemed no more a beetle but an oblong of quicksilver. I caught one and found that he was much like an ordinary beetle, but had a tail projecting beyond the sheath of his wings which he flicked with much vigour, reminding me of the ant-lion, and it was not his legs but this tiny propeller which gave him his speed.

I collected several different kinds of fern spores to send home, and explored farther down-stream, paddling in the water itself, for the banks were too steep and overgrown. At every bend the gladioli flamed in the sunshine and delphiniums lent their blue to the shadows, while among the maidenhair and asparagus ferns were red tiger-lilies and tall white anemones.

Thoreau says that waterlogged timber burns thrice as long, so shouldering a good piece I climbed up again through the successive veils of green to the top of the cliff and home.

One of the remarkable things about the mountain was its immense range and variety of green. The giant heath contrasted pure olive and yellow ochre with silvery terre verte, lit here and there with the fat chestnut green of the Brayeras, the silvery bushes of Muhato (*Stoebe kilimandscharica*) or deepening to blue-green with juniper. The predominating harmonies were silver grey-green. They were lovely and maddeningly elusive. They would taunt and fascinate me till I left what I was doing and took up my paint-box. I always started off with the same enthusiasm, confident that I had only to slap it on boldly with a full wet brush and put down exactly what I saw. Then, after I had spent hours in persevering endeavour, those flat grey tones would laugh at me like little elves : " Only Constable could have caught us ! " they mocked ; and I flung down my brush, and sawed logs in a fury of frustration.

My week alone soon sped by, and on the evening of the day appointed the two boys arrived with half a dozen porters in charge of Mtu Massara, a tall, fine-looking old Mwimbi.

I missed Jim more than ever when it came to packing the loads, and although I started on them at dawn, it was nine o'clock before I left the hut. I intended to camp at Hall Tarn that night, but although it is reckoned a four-hour climb, what with the slowness of the porters it took nearer seven.

We were well above the Nithi Valley—indeed I could look across to the grassy ridge on its far side up which I had climbed to Coryndon Peak—when I called the first halt. Till then the day had been sunny with a dazzling sea of fog stretching out at our feet like some arctic land. As I sat watching it, the clouds above threw down their shadows, changing it to wooded valleys and snow mountains, till it gathered itself together, rearing up like a gigantic forest of oaks. That was the beginning of its advance upon the mountain, and within a few minutes the clouds and mist drove up, overtaking us and keeping a jealous guard upon all that lay ahead. Now and then it would lift a corner, giving a glimpse of the crags above to cheer us upward, and Lake Michaelson, far below, framed in mists and precipices, lit up the gloom for an instant with one stabbing ray of light.

It was folly to have called that first halt. It put the idea into their heads, and the porters clamoured for another every half-hour. Mtu Massara and I stormed at them and chaffed them by turns, but what seemed to help most was changing round their loads—though it reminded me of the coach-in-four in the pantomime when, to rest the horses, they took them out of the shafts and put them back in different order—but each porter preferred carrying any load rather than his own.

I thought that if I were no longer there to argue with, they might quicken their pace, so I struck ahead and crossed a small cirque.

It was the kingdom of the giant groundsel, and it was like walking among beings from another planet. Suddenly, out of the mist, those huge and incongruous vegetable shapes loomed up, passed by and vanished again. The very rocks, outlined against the valley, had grown to the shape of trees rather than stones : top-heavy boulders perched on rocky stems. The heather had given way to a low-growing plant, hazel with silver leaves, palmated and crinkly, with little points silky as a mouse's claws.

If you felt bound in ordinary civility to smile as you passed the giant groundsels with their charred and barrel-shaped bodies and green topknots, a giant lobelia would never let you go by without stroking it. Usually it was about one's own height—a shaggy cone, silvery blue shot with green and purple, and, if you parted the feathers near the top, silky yellow. These hackles were deep and soft like a bird when he fluffs himself out against the cold. They were deliciously warm and aromatic on their lee side, so that I was compelled to stop and bury my face in their softness. The flowers hidden away under the hackles were dark blue (with two petals, and five stamens and sepals) and about the size of Viper's Bugloss. The hackles fell down over them from top to toe, and a stiff fringe of leaves grew up round their feet.

I examined them carefully during the last interminable halt, which was above a grassy chimney on a little plateau. This was another curious phase of country : the rock all worn into the shapes that ice takes when melted by water flowing round it. Rocks which stood up on the skyline, the size of monuments, and little pieces of rock beneath one's feet were all worn to these same shapes. The giant lobelias were here in their infancy, and only about six inches tall. They reminded me of sea-anemones as their leaves flowed out to and fro on the current of the wind.

I was feeling my way in thick mist when the sun broke through, and I reached Hall Tarn.

Coming upon this blue, untroubled little lake lying in the midst of that wilderness of rock was even more thrilling than finding the first snow. There was a hatch of some kind of spinner on the water, and instinctively I should have mounted a fly-rod and gone off to catch a trout for supper.

Of all camps this camp at Hall Tarn was the most romantic. The tarn lies about fifty feet from the edge of a thousand-foot precipice, and it was on this narrow margin of tussocks that the men pitched my tent. It was like being in an eagle's nest. From my doorway I could very nearly dip my hand into Hall Tarn on one side and look down over the precipice to Lake Michaelson on the other. This headland stood up alone from the valley already deep in shadow ; and as the mists were magically inhaled out of sight in one breath of the golden evening, the peaks rose up like spires into the clear sky.

As soon as the sun was gone the cold was bitter. I was glad enough of my small tent, and as soon as Hezekiah had pushed a tin of hot soup under the flap I battened everything down for the night. I had a jug of water at my elbow, and when I tried to pour out some to drink at two a.m. it was frozen solid.

Buried in my sleeping-bag, fur rugs and innumerable blankets, I felt as snug as an Eskimo dog under the snow ; but the tussocks, which I had at first thought were going to be as good as a spring mattress, became harder and harder as the night wore on. Old campaigners will tell you that so long as you have a hole for your hip, you can sleep no matter how hard the ground ; and considering that the tussocks seemed to be all bumps and no holes, I slept pretty soundly.

If you have to strike a match to look at the time, the chances are that you will dream you are doing so and in reality fall fast asleep again. My luminous watch saved me from such a temptation, and as it pointed to five o'clock I was filled with sudden curiosity to brave the cold, put my nose outside, and see what everything looked like.

One glimpse, and the lure of a warm bed—the only warm corner in the world—lost its persuasion. For, as I now discovered, that meagre strip of canvas shut me away from an inspiration so beautiful that everything else was forgotten, and I dashed out of the tent to behold it.

The stars were still bright in the paling sky ; the Great Bear on my left, the Southern Cross on my right. The mountains were but shadowy forms half guessed at, for the life of the universe lay not behind me in the tangible rock, but in front, in that one bright band of orange encircling the sleeping earth. An ocean of mist stretched out to it, blindfold, unmeaning, frozen ; and above, the waning moon vanished like a pale green sickle in the purpling dawn. The glow of dawn pulsed through the sky, drowning the stars in a more liquid light and melting the mists in a clear rosy breath.

In the giant groundsel at my side a bird twittered, and looking round I found Hall Tarn running red with reflected glory—venetian red like the sails of ships—and the reflections trembled in the ripple that went sighing past, all in a moment, like a forgotten memory that sweeps across the mind out of nowhere, and is gone. The air was filled with the winnowing of wings as the swallows skimmed above the water.

I remembered Lake Michaelson, and peeped over the edge of the precipice to see if it had awakened. But it lay there darkly, like a shield in the night, polished black and still unflawed by the dawn wind, with only its outer rim gleaming faintly where it spread beyond the shadow of the cliff.

For all I had waited, stamping my feet on the iron ground, making a fire (and how gladly the flames leapt up to the coming day !) and cooking my breakfast, the great moment for which I had been watching took me by surprise. Suddenly the frost sparkled red beside me, and then, on the wings of his own widespread rays, the sun rose and heaved the world up into the light.

Although I had finished breakfast when Hezekiah appeared out of his tent, shivering in his blanket to call me " before sunrise," it was a good hour till I had the caravan on the move. Certain loads were favourites, others fought shy of, and always, at the last moment, there was an altercation over who should carry, in addition to his load, the lanterns and kettle.

The morning was cloudless and as clear as rhinestones, and the sky recklessly blue to set your heart singing. I struck out across the frozen marshes—still peopled here and there by the friendly giant groundsels—where a stream wound its way among broken ice, silver as cobwebs against the sun.

The peak was now in full view. I was marching straight toward it ; and as the sun warmed the rock, and the snows shimmered before my eyes, it seemed very near, indeed almost attainable.

To-day my objective was the Curling Pond, a frozen pool in front of an overhanging lip of ice (part of the Lewis Glacier, and about halfway down it). It might be large enough to curl on, though I believe that it has been used only twice in history, when Mr. Melhuish skated on it. But it is an important feature, for beside it is erected the second hut. It is the highest camp on the mountain (unless, like Mackinder, you camp on the arête itself) and it stands at approximately 16,000 feet, just a thousand feet below the summit. I had heard much about the Curling Pond, and seen pictures of it with the Lewis Glacier and the peak, or with Point Lenana like a long snow slope in the background, and I was consequently all agog to see it for myself.

At the head of the Nithi Valley, close under the peak, I came upon the three mountaineers' porters who were encamped there. It is the recognised fuel camp, and porters (who hate the cold at the top camp) make it their headquarters when possible. This was an inevitable excuse for my own porters to loiter.

Burning with excitement and impatience I struck ahead by myself, while Hezekiah, now far in the rear, still made a pretence of following me with the cameras. His book-learning had raised him above the porter's estate and earned him a soft job ; while poor Magadi, who on an occasion like this was after all only a porter, toiled and sweated under a heavy load.

The path climbed steeply between two narrow walls of rock till it reached a saddle, under which lay a little blue tarn girt by snow and black crags. As I stood looking back over my path, the water lay shining pale as the sky against the shadow of the valley. Below, now far away, Hall Tarn sparkled like a jewel crowning the precipice, and beyond it rolled the ever-present sea of fog—the Roof of Kikuyu, Mackinder called it. A solitary eagle cried overhead ; otherwise, except for the crunch of snow under my foot, the silence of early morning in the high mountains was unbroken.

While toiling upward I had eagerly pictured in my mind what I should find on the other side of the saddle, and as my eyes came level with it I looked over into a wide valley winding down into the distance between sides of rock bleached as the desert in the hot sun, with here and there a deep purple shadow where a cloud rested above. I pulled out my rough map and identified it as the Mackinder Valley. Ominous tongues of mist were already creeping up, and it did not look nearly so set for a fine day as on my own side.

The peak now reappeared soaring above the Kolbe Glacier.

Below it was Point Lenana, and I bore left toward it above a cavern of ice whose roof of icicles was already slowly dripping in the sun.

As I came under the shadow of the rock I was startled by the sound of voices. I could not place them; they seemed to float by me out of nowhere, like the voice of Ariel, yet to be so intimately near that I felt like an eavesdropper, and expected to find the speakers behind the next boulder. I quickened my pace, looking curiously ahead, but the voices came no nearer. And then by chance I raised my eyes to the peak, and there, standing on the topmost summit, were three figures diminutive as ants. So crystal clear was the air that their voices, not raised above ordinary conversational tones, had come down to me nearly fifteen hundred feet below.

I yodelled and cheered with all my lungs, and they yodelled back. Seeing the conquest with my own eyes (only the second in history) was very nearly as good as sharing in it.

And then a hundred thoughts crowded into my mind: perhaps it was, after all, not impossible; perhaps they would even take me up, next day. My heart leapt at such a possibility.

Building these castles in the air, I climbed up through the snow and slipping shale, little dreaming that I was completely off the track to the Curling Pond. The Kolbe Glacier, with yawning blue crevasses, suddenly confronted me. Hezekiah was nowhere to be seen.

Precipices cut me off whichever side I tried to climb, and there was nothing for it but a nasty traverse back to the ice cavern. I was thoroughly lost, and had no idea where the path was or the Curling Pond. It was uncomfortably steep and I climbed down over boulders and floundered waist-deep in the snow between.

Still there was no sign or sound of the porters, and I began to fear that I had missed them. Perhaps they had gone on. I paused to listen. The silence closed round me with a relentless grip. I was alone, lost, a little frightened and completely furious. I had climbed at least three hours out of my way, and I was obliged to drop down some hundreds of feet. Eventually I sighted Hezekiah, and shouted down to ask what Mtu Massara was doing. He was supposed to be the guide. But the porters at the camp had doubtless kept him in prolonged and vitally interesting conversation.

At last he came, beaming and mildly apologetic; and having set me on the right path, under the Tooth at the head of the Hobley Valley, he returned for the porters.

There followed an endless steep traverse on scree. I walked forward for a few steps, slipped, floundered, picked myself up and started again, while the mountain-side went pouring down under me in a stream of shale and dust.

"Poor ant," I thought, with the sudden compassion born of fellow-feeling, "this is what it must feel like to fall into the ant-lion's pit: always struggling up and up while the sand slips relentlessly down and down beneath you." It was so realistic that I vowed then and there never again to take the part of the ant-lion. On the contrary, I would make a point of delivering all ants from such unimaginable despair.

My own struggle across this diabolical stuff was protracted for another couple of hours, by which time, what with fatigue and the high altitude, had it not been for Hezekiah following close upon my heels, I think I should have lain down and wept. A rest and some food would have made all the difference, but the thought of food was nauseating (again, I suppose, the effect of altitude) and I had eaten nothing since breakfast, eight hours before.

At two o'clock, with the mists pouring down chill and grey, Hezekiah and I reached the Curling Pond and found what shelter we could in the lee of what had once been the hut.

It had collapsed in a sheet of ice out of which a coil of rope half emerged, frozen stiff as a hawser. It was a pathetic wreck—like a ship in the Arctic—back broken and the ice strewn with splinters of doors and walls. On the floor (the only part left intact) was an incongruous pair of high-heeled brown shoes, bleached and sodden as orange peel. As I sat shivering in the drearily howling wind with an inadequate jumper pulled over my thin tunic (the sun had been burning hot only an hour before, and my sweat had dropped in the dust) I looked disgustedly at those shoes with their senseless high heels. Who could have brought them there, and why ? I tried to picture some one walking in volcanic dust or over the rough jagged rocks in anything so absurd. It could have been only for a wager. Lying there side by side with faded elegance in this freezing bitter place, they testified to human folly till I could bear them no longer. I picked them up and hurled them out of sight among the boulders.

The mist was now so thick that I could see nothing around me but the Curling Pond and a ghostly line of the glacier's snout curving above it ; and guessing at the direction of the peak I shouted to the climbers. The answer came back so close that I expected them to arrive at any moment, and thinking to get some hot tea ready for them I hunted for a kettle in their tent close by, while Hezekiah busied himself with a fire. It kept our minds from the dismal cold, as did pulling about the wreckage and trying to make a shelter from the icy wind. There was every possibility of the porters losing heart and turning back, for it had transpired overnight that not one of them save Mtu Massara had ever been up to the snow-line before. This was not his fault. The number of good mountain porters was of necessity limited, and the mountaineers had had first pick. This would mean spending the night in that miserable shelter, and the later it grew the more earnestly I applied myself to building it.

At last, between four and five o'clock, the first porters arrived.

The voices from the peak sounded no nearer, and I began to grow anxious. The climbers had already taken six hours over the descent (from the time I had seen them on the summit) and only another hour of daylight remained. There was no moon, and the glacier lay between them and camp. To be benighted in that cold (and they were doubtless climbing light) might be desperately serious. As always in such cases, there was nothing that one could do except mentally to enact a thousand dangers ; but it occurred to me that to cross the glacier with warm clothing, food, thermos and brandy flask and a couple of lanterns might be helpful, and I prevailed upon Mtu Massara and Magadi to forget their fatigue and come with me. I even offered them my spare boots, but they were too small. They hated boots, anyway, and seemed to think that they were surer footed if they could dig their toes into the snow.

I reconnoitred the glacier for tracks above and below, and finding none, I climbed halfway up Point Lenana, from where the glacier looked safest, and we then roped.

All at once the clouds parted, and the peak stood out unexpectedly close above us, its whole length in knife-edged silhouette. High up on this outline I made out two figures, and a third in shadow. I was appalled by this discovery, and to reckon how far the glacier still lay below them. The wall of the peak was in shadow, but through the glasses I could make out the climbers, the rope showing up very white and linking them together. To watch them climbing down, swinging from ledge to ledge of what seemed a perfectly sheer precipice of a thousand feet, held me in a miserable suspense ; and a sudden avalanche of rock glancing against the side with a hollow ring put my heart into my mouth.

As for my being able to reach the spot at which they would

end up, I despaired of it with the passing of every minute. By
the top, it looked like a three-hour climb round ; straight
across, a steep fall of ice and a chasm (a real bergschrund) cut
me off. Below seemed the likeliest, but only because I
could not see it. I did not want to delay the climbers still
more by shouting, but it was my only chance. I shouted
very slowly :

" Did you cross a-bove or be-low ? " The answer came
back amazingly distinct :

" Be-low ! "

" Are you all right ? "

" Yes ! "

That was a huge relief, and I dashed back to the camp,
where I hastily made some hot tea for the three of us ; and
Mtu Massara and I, both blind with altitude headaches, swallowed thirty grains of aspirin each, and we started off. This
time we found the footmarks, and crossed over.

The mists had trailed off, and the glacier was now green and
gold in the slanting rays. Everything was safe and friendly
again : it was that enshrouding mist, cold and baffling, that
oppressed one with a sense of foreboding and insecurity.
When it came down you felt that it would never lift ; and
when it lifted it vanished like an evil dream, and the peaks
stood up serene and strong as ever.

I was nearly across the glacier when Magadi pointed :
" There they are ! " and the climbers reached the glacier as
we reached the foot of the rocks, and the sun set.

All my fears now seemed incredibly foolish, and they had
never been shared by the climbers themselves. They had
twice climbed to the summit and knew exactly how long the
descent would take them, nor had they been troubled by the
mist as we had. The lanterns were not lighted, nor the
warm coats put on, though the cake and hot Bovril did not
come amiss ; and afterward we all set off across the glacier

again, glissading light-heartedly among the crevasses where before I had tiptoed in deepest respect, and the boys had tugged backward on the rope like a couple of frightened ponies.

When we reached the Curling Pond I saw with gratitude that my tent was pitched on the floor of the hut beside my attempt at a shelter. I seized the tins that bore the most inviting labels, and the saucepan of potatoes cooked by the faithful Hezekiah, and joined the climbers. Their tent was even smaller than mine ; and shutting up every crack and crevice we successfully defied the cold, ate to our hunger, and I heard the story of the climb.

Told there, on the very scene of action, it held the glamour of an epic.

First, they had reconnoitred the peak from the north, and followed a route which they had decided on from the lower hut. It was comparatively easy, and they felt already sure of success when only a couple of hundred feet below the summit they were turned back by a blind overhang. " We could have thrown a biscuit onto the top of Nelion," they told me ; and they had had to climb down, shift camp and try the southern arête. Altogether, they had spent a week finding out the route. It was finally not Mackinder's route, for near the summit they had kept to the rock instead of crossing the Diamond Glacier, a little pendent glacier almost vertical, and so hard that it was scarcely possible to cut steps in it.

What had impressed them most was Mackinder's courage. They said that they would have tackled any kind of rock rather than go the way he went, crossing that perilously canted stretch of ice hanging over the void.

I put a hundred questions ; but even in that uplifting moment of achievement they continually drew the talk away from themselves and back to Mackinder. If he had been their hero before he was more than ever their hero now. In those days (1899) travel itself was difficult, and he had had to march with a caravan all the way from the coast to the foot of the mountain. He had had difficulties with the natives, some of whom were hostile, and all suspicious towards the mountain and himself. Afterward, when he had been victorious, there were people who doubted whether he had reached the real summit, who said that his summit, Batian, was not so high as Nelion. The three climbers had once and for all dispelled that theory (and they were gloriously indignant about it) for the clinometer proved that Batian stands the higher by forty feet (17,040 feet above sea-level).

The remarkable thing to an amateur, looking at that formidable face of rock, was that any one could foresee a possible route to the top. Early in the day I had cherished the thought of climbing it ; later, I had nursed the hope that they might take me up. Now I realised that not only had they been twice to the summit, and that nothing would induce them to face it in cold blood a third time, but that it was quite beyond any ordinary climbing knowledge. They were experienced rock-climbers, used to the test pitches in the Lake District and the more difficult mountains of the Alps, and in their opinion —taking into consideration the altitude, where one is apt to become more easily exhausted and less precise—Mount Kenya is as difficult to climb as the Matterhorn. They compared it to the Meije in the Dauphiné.[1]

As I walked back to my tent under the deep starry sky, and looked up to the peak standing dark and knife-edged in the silence of night, I thought again of Mackinder with César and Joseph, his two Swiss guides, making their bivouac up there in the freezing cold under the arête.

His description of the climb (quoted from his journal) has the authentic ring and, like the books of all the old explorers

[1] The three climbers were Mr. P. Wyn Harris, Mr. E. E. Shipton, and Mr. G. A. Sommerfelt.

and pioneers, it fills one with good healthy rebellion against the limitations of everyday life, and inspires one with longing to set one's foot in the path of high endeavour. Here it is :

"It took three hours to cut our way across the hanging glacier to the farther side of the gap between the two summits, and I gave it the name of the Diamond Glacier. At first we traversed the ice obliquely upwards, each step requiring thirty blows with the axe. There was a thin covering of snow. Then we turned a little towards the base of the lesser summit, but seeing no foothold on the rock we resumed our oblique course upwards towards the greater. The glacier was steep, so that our shoulders were close to it. Had we fallen we should have gone over an ice-cliff onto the Darwin Glacier several hundred feet below.

"At last we reached the stone again, and almost exactly at noon set foot on the summit, which is like a low tower rising out of a heap of ruins, for the lichen-covered rock is vertically and horizontally jointed. On the top were three or four little turrets close together, and on these we sat. . . ."

And later in the same day he wrote :

"The light effects were wonderful that evening. On the hanging glacier we had frequently been enveloped in the cloud, which shielded us from the equatorial sun, but at sunset we came again into the clear air on the top of the southern arête. All the eastern horizon was glorious, with a deep purple belt rising like a wall from the end of the landscape. Three hours later, as we trudged home over the Lewis Glacier, the great features of the mountain stood out as though boldly sketched with black and white crayons. The upper end of the glacier rose in snowy billows to the point of Lenana on the one hand, and on the other skirted the foot of the cliff by which we had descended, now black in the shadow cast by the moon. Below was the white expanse of the cloud roof flowing dreamily beside the solid texture of the ice. Most striking of all were the sheens and jetty blacks on the pinnacle of the Lion's Tooth.

" The midnight scene as we supped by the camp fire I shall never forget. The sound of the Nairobi torrent, swelling suddenly from time to time as the breeze changed, and even the occasional hoot of an owl, made no break in the silence of the great peak standing brown and white in the glare of the setting moon. The Pleiades twinkled over the centre of the Lewis Glacier, but overhead the stars in the black vault were steady and without twinkle. Our camp was on the broad floor of a deep valley shut in by steep slopes to north and south. To the west was a moraine of great blocks and tree groundsel. To the east were the red cliffs, and to the north-east the Lewis Glacier and the peak. Those evenings, this the most wonderful of them all, were spent almost monosyllabically, warming our hands and feet at the fire amid the mysterious shadows of the groundsel. . . ."

Chapter XIV

THE PEAK AND THE GLACIERS

I HAD willed myself to wake next morning before sunrise, and wrapping up as warmly as possible, I undid the fastenings of the tent and was seized at once by the full force of the gale.

The sun was barely heralded as I climbed over snow and scree to the promontory. Below me ran the deep Hobley Valley, purple with night and faintly lit by two lakes. Its farther side stood up in black pinnacles of cliff like a barrier before the curling white waves of cloud. The wind rushed howling past, advancing with a roar, retreating with a sigh, and the waves, for all the world like Atlantic breakers, rose up as though to dash themselves in spray against the rocks. The expanse of cloud curved unbroken round the horizon. And then, infinitely far off, calm and sphinx-like, Kilimanjaro alone was bathed in the red sun. Even as I looked, the rays pierced through the pearly sea, and Kenya, with the shrill winds whistling about her head, rose up from the shadows, plunging into the crimson fire and throwing out a violet shadow against the sky.

Only once before, when standing at sunrise on the summit of Teneriffe, had I seen this beautiful shadow projection.

The three mountaineers had invited me for a day of rock scrambling. It was a heaven-sent opportunity, for roaming about the glaciers or climbing would have been dangerous to attempt alone, and the natives were more of a hindrance than a help.

All day there was never a cloud to intervene between

us and the sun or to shadow the hyaline purity of the peaks. One might assume from this that a strong wind means clear weather and keeps the fog at bay, whilst a still, sunny morning is what the clouds like best.

We crossed the Lewis Glacier without a rope, for they held it to be the safest in the world. It was unlike any glacier I had seen, for the ice melts under the vertical rays of the sun and fills many of the crevasses brimful of water, which freezes up again at night. We followed down the scree slopes round Point John, at the southern end of the big arête.

From Point John the arête dips down to a narrow col and rises up again in a beautiful little pic, symmetrical as Cleopatra's Needle.

We reached the top of this col (after an exciting climb up a couloir of shale and loose boulders, which I should never have dared try alone) and found ourselves under a natural archway (15,300 feet). It framed a view of the whole southern side of the peak with the Darwin and Tyndal Glaciers, and we looked straight up to the wicked little Diamond Glacier, which seemed literally to hang between the two summits. Knife-edged arêtes ran up on either side, forming an amphitheatre; on our own side from Point John, which rose so sheer that it seemed to lean out above us, on the opposite side ending abruptly with Point Piggot, and falling away to Two Tarn Col, where two little lakes lay like emeralds in a basin of red rock bounding the earth before the rainbow-coloured distance.

We sat looking into this world of arrested motion : tumbling glaciers shining in sunlight, towering peaks and precipices warm and living against the deep blue sky. Even the wind held back from that perfect silence. As one's eye travelled up and down those sweeping, soaring lines, they sprang to life in the glory of rhythm : the very silence was a song of triumph.

We wondered that there were no avalanches, not even stone ones where the Diamond Glacier must melt over the rocks, and the frost split them. And we were speaking of it when there was a roar that filled the mountain, as an avalanche broke loose high up on the Tyndal Glacier and came rushing down under a swift-curling cloud of snow.

We went down and halted for a drink from the ice-cold brook flowing from the Darwin Glacier ; then crossed below the snout of the Tyndal Glacier which overhung a pool of water translucently green as an inlet of the sea. We looked up into a blue cavern of ice where the bright fluttering reflections slipped over the glassy walls and back into the water.

Another climb brought us out above the lakes, and we spent an hour or more lying in the hot sunshine looking up with shaded eyes to the dazzling peak. Nothing moved except an eagle's shadow planing to and fro across the face of the rock.

With the peak there before me, soaring up in lines that gave it beauty of poise and balance which I found hard to attribute to mere accident, I remembered that Professor Gregory had diagnosed it as " the ruined stump of an ancient volcano which, when in eruption, must have been thousands of feet higher than at present, and even loftier than its great twin, the volcano of Kilima Njaro. . . . The central peak consists of rock which solidified in the throat of the volcano when the volcanic forces waned ; it consolidated as a plug of hard rock which sealed up the outlet like a cork in a bottle This plug has now been left as the summit of the mountain owing to the wearing away of the looser volcanic tuffs which formed the walls of the crater and of the pipe."

I had resented these cold scientific truths and that wonderful peak being compared to a mere plug. I felt that the past belittled the present. And then I suddenly saw that in these geological facts lay the greatest poetry of all, and as I looked I tried to picture those gigantic convulsions which had shaken the mountain to its very roots. Knowing a little of the mountain's history, one was, as it were, brought into its confidence. It may have been a dead volcano, it was still the living rock ; and its immutability declared with every uprising line the glory of action.

I liked to think about its " throat" ; not even Milton himself, with the whole range of imagery and poetic licence to his hand, could with a single word have evoked a more stupendous picture, that at the same time touched the chord of human emotion. The scientists are the real poets ; they bring more human sympathy to their subjects than the rest of us can even dimly appreciate.

It is, indeed, from the south side that one must see the mountain. From the east, at the Curling Pond, one is already too high, and the summit is but a rock, a succession of jagged teeth only a thousand feet above ; but from here it gathers itself out of a much greater depth, and the twin glaciers lift it up on wings shining into the very sky.

Although we avoided the steep climb back to the col, and skirted round the end of the southern arête under Cleopatra's Needle (marked Midget Peak in the map), the way back seemed interminable. It was a heart-breaking climb over scree, or from boulder to boulder, steps that were much too big, like those of the pyramids, so that you were forced to bring your knees up each time in a doubled-up position which, at that altitude, made you pant thrice with every breath.

I found it a very humbling performance, for I was always last. The climbers were charming, and sympathetically assured me that they had felt the altitude just as much to begin with (though in my own mind I knew that I should feel it as much after a week) and they never minded waiting for me. The whole day was a saddening revelation. Not only was I a drag on their speed, but where they moved with cat-like precision I managed to dislodge a piece of rock that went hurtling down under me, and on one difficult bit there had been the ignominy—only it was too funny for so big a word—of having a brace of ice-axes brought up as foot-rests below me.

But I enjoyed myself too much to care. One never minds being *thoroughly* beaten. It is the half and half that is galling. Had I seen the peak alone, I should not have understood that I was beaten beforehand, and the peak would have dared me until maybe I had broken my neck upon it. But there is more in mountaineering than simply daring oneself. To climb a difficult peak when one is not a trained climber is like a novice jumping at a ski-ing contest or riding in a race ; and determination without skill is a bird without wings.

At the edge of the Lewis Glacier, under Point John, we had cached a thermos full of tea. The thought of it spurred my flagging steps, and when at last we found it again we sat down for half an hour's rest.

The sun, now near to setting, threw the shadows across the ice in wavelets of pure lilac, cobalt and green, while the facets tilted towards it burned like gold till they softened to pink and then deepened to rose. We had now only to cross the glacier by one long uphill traverse ; and we did not hurry.

It was then that I discovered that I had lost my hat. It had been tucked into my belt most of the day and I had no clear recollection of when I had seen it last. It was the only sunproof hat I had, but even as the calamity fully dawned on me I went on doggedly saying that it did not matter. Had it contained all I had in the world, I was past forfeiting one step of that hard-won climb to retrieve it. But turning a deaf ear to my protests, one of the mountaineers quietly slipped off his coat and began scrambling down over the way we had toiled up. In that vista of grey broken scree and big boulders which all looked alike, nothing was more difficult than to retrace our route, and it was by great good fortune that after a time he actually found my wretched hat. I put it away safely in the rucksack, and we followed the others across the glacier.

I no longer took this glacier very seriously, but I found that it could conceal some quite formidable crevasses, after all. Following more or less conscientiously in the steps of the mountaineer, I suddenly slipped through the snow and only saved myself by my elbows from disappearing altogether. I hoped he would not see this last piece of foolishness of the day, as I kicked and scrambled to get out; but such things seldom pass unnoticed and he came back to give me a haul up. I felt ashamed (probably no one has fallen even halfway into a crevasse on the Lewis Glacier before) but the excitement banished fatigue, and I came in at a good pace, immensely exhilarated.

By the time we reached camp the sun had set. A new tent had sprung up in our absence and Mr. Carr had just arrived. He very kindly lent me an oil stove which, in that intense cold, was a blissful luxury. No one was feeling sociable that evening, and for my own part I sneaked into my tent at the first opportunity, feeling suddenly very ill. Siki (who had not accompanied us on the climb) welcomed me from her warm nest in my blankets, and we shared an egg flip together. She was just as much off her food as I was, and probably the altitude had upset us both.

During the night, the wind rose with such violence that I expected the tent to blow down at any moment. It was like a ship in a hurricane, but whereas a ship can point her nose into the gale and yield to it, the tent received the full onslaught on her broadside and was anchored to the wooden floor. Gallantly did she stand, though straining and shivering under the sudden claps that swept down the glacier, or slyly took her by surprise on the other flank ; while I lay in the darkness with the one comforting reflection that the ground-sheet was sewn into the walls, so that whatever happened she could not blow clean away without me.

There was something frightening about those fierce charges which I could hear approaching from far off, and I lay tensely waiting—for an age, it seemed—till they smote down in rage upon me. " Kenya is angry at having her peace disturbed," thought I, as the hail struck upon the canvas with a dry hard rattle of fury, and well could I understand, then, the natives' awe and superstition about the mountain.

In the morning I found that the snow had drifted in several inches deep over me and all my possessions. I lit the stove and dried everything as best I could. It was still blowing and snowing, and had I shouted with all my might none of the porters could have heard, or even if they had they would not have faced that bitter blast. Small blame to them, either, for nothing in the world would have dragged me from those few feet of friendly and comparatively warm shelter.

At eleven o'clock one of the climbers came to ask if I intended to make a start. It never occurred to me that any one could dig the porters out to face it ; but they were willing enough to leave this nightmare place at any cost, so I quickly packed up.

The tent ropes were as thick as halyards with solid ice, and the iron pegs were an ordeal to take hold of in one's bare hands. In a trice the wind had swept through my clothing, robbing me of the last remnant of natural warmth ; and it must have been fifty times worse for the unfortunate half-naked porters, who were numbed and stupid with the cold, neither listening nor understanding any command and ever leaving off what they had begun in order to wrap their blankets more closely about them.

In spite of the bad weather, Mr. Carr heroically determined to remain in that perishing place for a week or ten days to see the hut rebuilt, and had brought a young man and two Indian carpenters for the work. The climb in itself, to a man of over sixty, seemed to us a gallant achievement, and he made less of the cold than we did. He loved the mountain, and had built the two huts at his own expense for the use of climbers, for which his name will ever be remembered with gratitude.

We had planned to climb Point Lenana—a nice easy shoulder running up above the Curling Pond to a height of 16,300 feet —and to go down from there instead of by the ordinary route ; but nothing could have prevailed upon the porters to wait another day for the weather to clear.

As it was, Point Lenana might not have existed for all that we could see of it. Driving mists and occasional flurries of snow shut us in so that it was difficult to find even the path.

There was something inexpressibly melancholy about that grey blanket of fog, a twilight out of which porters emerged with their unwieldy loads and frozen, badly knotted ropes, seen a moment against the black rock, to disappear stumbling among the boulders now treacherously slippery under ice and sleet. Their stoicism smote us as we followed the little trail of blood left by their poor bare feet over the snow.

As we descended, the sleet turned to rain ; we pounded through mud and slush for a couple of dreary hours and were soon wet to the skin. The mist was so dense that we lost our way below Hall Tarn, till by luck and the unaccountable instinct that wakens in emergency, I remembered a certain stretch of marsh, and striking left, found the path again. The climbers had not camped at Hall Tarn, but by a huge boulder in the giant groundsel valley, and when we reached it we called a halt and divided up our last apple.

A few minutes later we stepped into brilliant sunshine.

Like a dream our troubles were over, and one thought then that after all they had been very bearable, though at the same time mentally shaking oneself like a dog, mightily glad to be out of it.

We dawdled pleasantly, and by the time we had reached the long crest above the Nithi Valley there was not a cloud left in the sky, and Kenya looked down upon us clear and ethereal under the fresh snow. The long-legged shadows already strode up the valley towards her, the precipices framed her on either side and Lake Michaelson laid a green mirror at her feet. We all took photographs, hoping to catch something if not of the wonder of those fresh colours, at least of that perfect composition.

It was sunset by the time we reached the hut, and much against their will I insisted on the climbers sleeping in it. I was very happy in my little tent and preferred moving in at my leisure next day. Everything (self included) needed a thorough scrub before being restored to ordinary life again.

We collected round the hut table once more, and wound up the evening with a memorable brew of punch, in which I proposed a toast to the conquest, and we raised our glasses to one of the noblest of mountains.

After dreaming all night of climbing knife-edged arêtes through swirling mists, I awoke to quiet sunshine and leafy patterns through the canvas, and the birds chirping round me. It was good to be home again, and when the climbers had left I set to work to put my house in order. Hezekiah scrubbed out the hut while I spread the blankets to dry in the sun, and spent happy retrospective hours greasing the ice-axe and mountain boots, saddle-soaping everything that was made of leather, and putting everything away in its right place.

Nothing is so satisfactory as patching up and restoring old things, far more so than buying new ones. One looks upon old things—especially if it is a bit of leather to polish—with particular affection, for they have been through the same adventures as oneself and stand as a record of great days.

It was late in the afternoon before everything was put to rights, and then I had my reward in a voluptuous bath, steaming hot, in the beautiful, new, full-sized, tin bath which Mr. Carr had told me I should find on my return. I tarried in it a full hour, with the sun streaming in through the window. That bath and the luxurious delight of smooth white sheets (I had looked longingly at them all day) brought me as high as physical well-being can go ; and it is worth doing without these things for a while, if only for the edge it puts on one's appreciation of them.

Chapter XV

LAKE MICHAELSON.   THE NITHI VALLEY AND THE TUSSOCKS

NOTHING was pleasanter than to wake in the hut and to watch the leaf patterns trembling over the warm wood, and the dust floating up in specks of sapphire and gold on the shafts of sunlight.   The first thing to catch my eye on waking was a spray of maidenhair reaching out above me to the sun and shining against the shadow.   Looking at it was like lying at the bottom of the sea and looking up to a chain of transparent green bubbles.   At the top of the post supporting the bunk above me I had tied a jar of water, out of which flowers and maidenhair and asparagus ferns climbed as freely as in the grotto.   There were at least two disasters with this jar every day, but they were worth it for the sake of that first waking impression.

Probably every one who has led for a time this simple kind of life cries with Thoreau : " Simplify, simplify ! " and feels that he has made a great discovery.

In the first flush of this discovery I wrote down my conviction that life could be made much happier by a more general return to simplicity.   A man must spend his life toiling and moiling for his family, it is true, but so much of what he gives his life and mind to are things which bring him little real happiness or even pleasure.   So much is sacrificed to convention or for effect, and the possessions he works for end by enslaving him.   Time is so short, yet these are the things which steal his time and his thoughts from the things that are vital and enduring. . . .   The wider your doorstep (my diary continued) the more you are surrounded by walls and boundaries and the farther you are from Nature. Losing touch with Nature often means losing the desire to be quiet, and to consider. Here, in a one-roomed hut, my door opens straight onto the hillside, the leaves like friendly messengers drift in with the morning breeze, and the birds hop down fearlessly at my feet. I cannot help thinking one gets a sweeter thrill of joy from these things than from the load and responsibility of possessions that cut one off from them.

If we were not so positive that to-morrow the sun will rise, with what reverence and joy should we welcome him. And this happiness is there for all, as the sun himself shines for all, but just because it is there we pass it by, perversely denying ourselves.

We feel gratitude only where we feel the obligation, we prize what is difficult to come by or is paid for in visible coin so that we can own it. What belongs to all belongs to nobody, and we look at what pleases us with more regret than pleasure because we do not possess it. And yet, what is to be gained through possession? You have laid an unrest and believe you are satisfied. But the spirit of delight is intangible as the iridescence brushed from the wings of the butterfly you have captured.

It is a delusion that when the jewel is your own you will constantly look at it; for the moment you possess a thing you put it behind you, locked safely in the treasure-house, and turn your face towards new conquests, new acquisitions.

" ' You like flowers ? ' he said." (I am quoting from *Will o' the Mill*.)

" ' Indeed, I love them dearly,' she replied ; ' do you ? '

" ' Why, no,' said he, ' not so much. They are a very small affair, when all is done. I can fancy people caring for them greatly, but not doing as you are just now.'

" ' How ? ' she asked, pausing and looking up at him.

" ' Plucking them,' said he. ' They are a deal better off where they are, and look a deal prettier, if you go to that.'

" ' I wish to have them for my own,' she answered, ' to carry them near my heart, and keep them in my room. They tempt me when they grow here ; they seem to say : " Come and do something with us " ; but once I have cut them and put them by, the charm is laid, and I can look at them with quite an easy heart.'

" ' You wish to possess them,' replied Will, ' in order to think no more about them. It's a bit like killing the goose with the golden eggs. . . .' "

One afternoon, Mr. Carr, his work achieved, arrived back from the glaciers. He was delighted to find his hut cared for, admired the improvements down to the smallest detail till I tingled with pride, and told me I might remain in possession for as long as I wished. And then, although he loved the mountain, and the hut was the apple of his eye, he suddenly asked me how I could bear the solitude. I could only wave my arm vaguely round and ask : " How could one feel lonely in all this ? "—which had never yet convinced any one.

It was impossible to explain the friendship of the place. The very tree at my door—a Brayera with woolly, bright chestnut green leaves—was full of friendly rustlings and often gently reminded me of its presence so that I had to look up and greet it. This was no idle fancy, for it was when I was reading or writing and not thinking about it that I was made most aware of it.

It was obviously fantastic to tell Mr. Carr about it, and after he had gone I seized my pen that evening and wrote : Solitude closed over my head once more and I ran off and rolled in the heather and lay so deep in meditation while the mist floated up, that the birds hopped round, wondering, perhaps, whether they should collect leaves to cover me with. Lonely ? I reiterate again and again : How is it possible to feel lonely in one's own element ? This is the same warm and understanding earth from which I sprang, of which I am composed and to which I shall return ; and the trees and flowers and animals and birds are my own blood brothers, living together under the same sky, warmed and rejoiced by the same sun, loved and redeemed by the same God. . . .

People denounce solitude as bad because they seek in life and in others a refuge from themselves. Yet there is no ultimate escape, and it is themselves they must meet at last. " Know Thyself." There is no danger of exaggerated introspection : that lies only on the borderland of self-knowledge ; for as soon as you know anything completely you look for something else.

In Nature, you learn to know yourself as the thing nearest at hand with whom you must live and work, after which you can forget your very existence in the million beautiful and interesting things around you. And it is the supreme test, because in Nature nothing false can exist. All that is superficial you must shed like a husk, for it has no place there. You are close to life and death, to real things that are fine and sane and simple, and until you have simplified yourself and found out by yourself what is truth for *you*, you are only on the edge of it : away from civilisation, alone in the wilds, no wonder people pity your loneliness, for this being on the edge—lost to the one, not yet accepted of the other— is indeed the greatest loneliness on earth, unfathomable and terrifying. . . .

And when, after anguish of spirit, you perceive an inkling of the truth, *believe* in it, follow it, in spite of opinion.

Thought and action begin with the individual and through him to society, the state, nations, worlds; so that it is only reasonable that he should look thoughtfully into his own heart and sow there the best seeds he can find. Only by making his own this feeling of oneness—truth, harmony, call it what you will—can he transmit it.

The way to it is, after all, unimportant. To some, solitude and Nature may be the way, whilst there are others already so mature and beautiful that it is there within themselves, and they can find the way back to the fountain head without any of those blessed opportunities for solitude to help them.

" Men seek retreats for themselves, houses in the country, sea-shores and mountains; and thou, too " (wrote Marcus Aurelius) " art wont to desire such things very much. But it is altogether the mark of the most common sort of men, for it is within thy power whenever thou shalt choose to retire into thyself. For nowhere either with more quiet or more freedom from trouble does a man retire than into his own soul, particularly when he has within him such thoughts that by looking into them he is immediately in perfect tranquillity. Constantly, then, give to thyself this retreat, and renew thyself; and let thy principles be brief and fundamental, which as soon as thou shalt recur to them will be sufficient to cleanse the soul completely, and to send thee back free from all discontent with the things to which thou returnest."

The hut still lacked pictures on its walls, and I spent long hours in making water-colour sketches, and even longer in making frames for them out of packing-case wood stained with permanganate.

But I could not leave the mountain alone. Like great

music it spurred one to action. That was the reason why you came to love it : you had to give it your best always, and a bit more. It would not tolerate softness either, but was ever challenging you to embrace hardship and endurance and a primitive simplicity of living. It was arbitrary in unexpected ways : it compelled me, for instance, to give up smoking. It fought down the artificiality and false values of civilisation, and brought you face to face with the miracle of life itself. If you turned a deaf ear to its exacting creed, or fell away from its spartan discipline, the mountain subtly withdrew its companionship, and you had to bear failure alone. The very flowers cried shame, for nothing on the mountain was faint-hearted. Peace of the spirit was to be won only at the price of renunciation ; and then the spirit lived. This was to be born again ; and for the first time fully awake you breathed in the sharp, salt tang of life : the drenching sunshine, the anger of the tempest, the crispness of frost that stiffens in the nostrils, the whole-heartedness of rain, and the sweetness of dew-fall and of birds singing in the dawn.

I planned to go up the Nithi (sometimes called Gorges) Valley to see Lake Michaelson and to collect flowers.

It was to be a stroll, a pleasant picnic ; but I should have learnt by then that no expedition on the mountain was ever a picnic ; and this one proved the hardest of them all, for it was one unending battle with the tussocks.

I set off very early (leaving the boys to tidy the hut and catch up with me at their leisure), the stars shone brightly overhead, and when I looked back, the light in the hut window still twinkled among the trees.

Walking with your back to the east, you are made almost more aware of the coming of dawn than when you face it. Climbing up, with my eyes on the mountain, it was as though a succession of screens were being drawn back from the light ;

suddenly it became several degrees brighter, a kind of move-ment in the sky behind me that was as deliberate as the opening of the eyes. The light became so lurid that I fancied I could detect my own shadow. The east was now flaming orange and the west an unearthly green that imparted a greenish colour to the very rocks. Overhead, the two skies met in a clearly defined arc of blue and lilac, and under this strange illumination the dandelions glowed like suns, but the purple scabious were blanched.

" Now the sun will come up," I thought expectantly ; but instead of growing brighter, earth and sky slipped back again into the enfolding night. These flaming banners were but out-riders of the sun ; they came and passed, and still there was a long pause, and the earth waited in ashy silence.

Suddenly the tip of the peak burned crimson, and the sun shot up blinding bright over the horizon of fog. There was something about watching his coming—alone in the unbroken silence and the deep solitude—that was as old as the world ; and probably every primitive (or civilised) man has at such a time offered up some kind of prayer.

Leaving the road, I followed up the crest towards Hall Tarn, then striking down left to a terrace by five huge mono-liths, I thought to skirt above the Nithi Valley midway between the floor and the top of the cliffs, thus taking up gently to the head of the falls below Lake Michaelson, and avoiding any unnecessary climb. It was a trap, and I should have done better to climb up by the path all the way to the giant groundsel valley below Hall Tarn, for my easy-looking route was soon cut short by a precipice that drove me down to the very floor of the valley among the tussocks.

These tussocks played such an important rôle in life on the mountain that I must describe them in some detail. The word tussock is misleading, for it calls up snipe bogs and tufts of matted grass or peat which offer stepping-stones above the water. But these tussocks had rarely anything to do with bogs. In fact they had tantalizingly nice hard ground between them where, if one could only have followed it, one would have been perfectly happy. It looked all right. You started along a little path, and in three steps you met a tussock. There was no way round, so you climbed on top. This seemed to be the solution, and you now chose the overhead route instead, walking or leaping from tussock to tussock. It worked admirably for three or possibly five tussocks, and then there would be a gap too wide to jump. So you dropped down again. And, of course, they were not just ordinary tussocks, but (like all else on the mountain) they were giants. They varied from anything up to a yard in diameter and waist-high, like haycocks.

The mountain was everywhere protected from intrusion : by the impenetrable forest below, by the slipping shale and volcanic dust above, but the best protection of all was this middle zone of tussocks. They covered practically every slope and valley, and the moment you left the path to explore, you were at their mercy. You wasted hours ploughing through them, and they broke your back, your heart, and your resolve. Speed was impossible. They were exasperating as the doldrums ; indeed I cannot paint them too harshly. And yet I had a sneaking affection for them. Unlike lots of inanimate objects, they had no particle of spite. But then, I could never look upon them as inanimate. Like the trees, the curiously shaped rocks, the friendly giant lobelias and groundsels, they were very much alive and had strong personalities of their own. They gave me the toughest times I can remember, and yet to the end they persisted in remaining friendly. They had comfortable shapes, they were rough and warm and smelt of moors, and when you sat among them all snugged down and out of the wind's eye, they fitted into the small of your back better than the very best arm-chair.

But there was no time for dawdling now, and I set myself patiently (it was no good trying to hurry) to cross the rough acres that stretched before me.

As I threaded my way, I saw something ahead that cheered me forward : the ground, studded with celandine, looked quite flat and as trim as sward closely nibbled by sheep. I laboured hopefully towards this Mecca over the last of the choppy cross-sea of tussocks; but alas ! for my hopes, the ground was everywhere undermined by an army of moles or rats, and broke through at every third step like breakable snow-crust. Still, after the tussocks even this was paradise.

The river ran over the shallows, winding hither and thither as though it loved this place and was loath to leave it ; and higher up it tumbled with a joyful song from boulder to boulder where the scarlet gladioli hung their heads above its banks. The cliffs rose up steeply on either side like a canyon, so that you had to throw your head back to see the top, and against their shadow the tree groundsel sent up flowers of pure gold.[1]

Long ere this, the boys had caught up. They told me that on the way they had watched a leopard in full chase after a duiker, close above the hut.

We now began the arduous climb to the top of the falls, battling our way through the heather that reached far over our heads, stumbling among tussocks, falling into hidden holes and generally getting the worst of it. I worked upward to a boulder on the skyline, promising myself that if I could only reach it we should have a couple of hours lazing in the sun by the lake shore.

And then, when I emerged at last, scratched and bleeding

---

[1] There were three kinds of groundsel : tree groundsel and giant groundsel, and a groundsel that grew low and bushy, like huge cabbages. The tree groundsel threw out branches and was the more graceful, the giant groundsel with single trunk and topknot was the more human.

from the clutches of the heather, there was no sign of the lake. It was too much of a disappointment to bear comment. Without looking back at the boys I began skirting this second valley, floundering through more acres of tussocks and stopping to drink at a dozen little cascades which fell over the path. This ice-cold water was so pure that it had a taste.

As I stepped round an out-jutting rock, I beheld the peak framed in by the Hall Tarn precipice, and there before me lay Lake Michaelson. It had been more than worth the six-hour climb, so calm it lay at the foot of those savage cliffs, and still shield-like, almost round, its inviting shallows made me long to launch a canoe or to swim out to the deeps.

By then, the inevitable mists had gathered, and I climbed up to explore what one might imagine were the ruins of a vast temple in the cliffs. There were deep recesses, and arches supported by high rugged columns. It was a place full of mystery. A curious feeling of desertion hung about it, as though it had once been something more than this, and the walls seemed to echo a great and forgotten past.

Our voices were awed to whispers, and when I left the boys to light a fire, and climbed up to a cave, I approached it over a deep carpet of moss that deadened my footsteps. It was vivid green streaked with yellow, like sunshine, and so velvety that I had to kneel down and rub my face against it. There was a sudden fragrance, indescribably sweet, and I looked into the mouth of the cave across a bank of white arabis—wave upon wave of it against the darkness. The roof arched sixty feet above my head, and near the top a second cave led out ; but try as I would I could not reach it, for the walls were slippery with wet moss. It was the home of the Hall Tarn swallows, and the ledges were buried under old droppings and feathers.

As I looked down through this colossal doorway to the lake, a shaft of sunlight plunged like a sword to its very depths, lighting the gloom with emerald. Next moment it was gone. The face of the lake was clouded with raindrops and the mists gathered a little closer around it.

But there was more in this place than external beauty : I was in the presence of something ; on the edge of a great discovery. This presence was so strong that it filled the cave. The slow drip, drip of water patiently repeated over and over again something I could not understand, the living rock struggled with dumbness in an effort to reveal it to me. I sat till I was cramped with cold, trying to make my mind a blank to receive this message. Nothing happened. The monotonous dripping hammered out the minutes, and the white vapour drifted slowly into the cave, touching me with chill fingers.

I could have wept with disappointment. This experience was real as the mountain before me, in a sense far more real. Yet what was it ? As I climbed down I tried to find the answer. Had this rock been one of the secret hiding-places of the Holy Grail ? With this thought, the Grail *motif* in *Parsifal* came into my head, till the cliffs echoed it. The Good Friday music would have sounded magnificent in such a place ; above all I could hear the four deep reverberating notes of the bell ; the cliffs tossed them to and fro, the valley resounded again, as I stood looking up at the rock, waiting for it to open to me.

The boys had made a fire with some dead lobelia and groundsel stems, and sat huddled in their blankets stretching out their hands to the smoke. Groundsel is good fuel, but when alight it smells like a glue factory.

The boys did not think much of my idea of a picnic (it was now raining fairly persistently) so in order to create a diversion I offered a prize of fifty cents to the one who could throw a stone into the lake. It was a long throw from where we were sitting above it, but they became so expert that both of them won. We thereupon discussed the quickest way home. They held for climbing up to the giant groundsel valley below Hall Tarn, but I was bent upon exploring another cave which I had seen on my way up ; so we divided forces : they climbed the steep ascent, while I ran down past the lake. It was to be a race back to the road from where we had left it a couple of miles or so above the hut. On the face of it you would have voted for the Nithi Valley, for it was a very long climb up to the Hall Tarn path ; and I started off full of optimism, confident that I should win.

The most delicious sensation was to walk through the plantations of young cabbage groundsel ; their silvery woolly leaves were soft as moles' fur against one's bare knees which had been scratched and torn by the heather.

Looking under the hackles of the lobelia I found that they were in full flower ; they had a sweet pungent smell that went to the back of one's throat like the cry of a bat, and made me think of the *orchis vanille* of the Alps, with a drop of vinegar added.

My cave undermined the rock by twenty feet, and was about ten feet high, and full of a white powdery deposit which also lay about in lumps. It tasted like soda, and the animals evidently liked it, for there were everywhere claw-marks (the size of a weasel's) where they had scratched for it.

I hurried on, still thinking about the race, and climbed down to the top valley which spread out like a terrace above the falls. I followed the stream and leaped from tussock to tussock. They were very difficult to balance on and for once they were in marshy ground, so that when I missed them and fell between, I was bogged to the knee, and once fell in almost up to my neck.

I scrambled and rolled my way down the steep drop by

the falls, and arrived at the bottom, torn, breathless and wet through. Now I was back among the innumerable dry watercourses whose banks were starred with celandine but undermined by the rats. As I made my way, I thought that it must be a wild place during the rains when the air would be full of the roar of torrents. As it was, a hundred flowers charmed the eye—camomile and scabious, gladioli, immortelles, various flowering heaths, Michaelmas daisies, harebells, thistles, a sort of cows' parsley, white anemones and a kind of cineraria.

I made the most of them, for afterward came the tussocks. They were the unkindest and waist-high variety, and I floundered and floundered among them for nearly two hours, till my heart nearly broke, and I could scarce lift my knees over them any more. If Bunyan had met tussocks like these he would have substituted them for the Slough of Despond. To escape them I even waded down the stream, but the icy water blistered my toes and forced me back to the tussocks.

At last I reached the bend of the valley and took up left-handed to the road. It proved rough going among heather and boulders, with steep cuttings in the hillside that had to be circumvented ; but after the tussocks, anything was bliss. It was still a long way to the road ; I set a tack across and up the face of the slope, though inevitably I fell away from it. A ten-minute rest and a piece of chocolate would make all the difference, I thought ; so I sat down, and my fatigue was soothed away by the little sun-birds that hovered about me, coming always closer and closer till I believe that had I remained long enough, they would have settled on my shoulders. The cock bird seemed but little larger than a wren, and with his two long, curving tail feathers and glowing green breast, he was exquisitely beautiful. That particular region was a favourite haunt of theirs, for the slopes were covered with giant protea (a shrub about the size of an azalea bush with a pinkish-yellow bloom not unlike St. John's Wort, but larger) from whose flowers they sucked the honey.

When I struck the path again, I heard the boys' voices just ahead of me, and I was much cheered by the thought that the race, after all, had been a close one ; but they watched my coming with a slightly superior air of " What did we tell you ? " and said that they had waited for well over an hour.

Well, anyway, no one else had ever walked the length of the Nithi Valley, and (as far as I know) the cows' parsley and the camomile were my own discovery. And I extracted what comfort I could from this doubtful glory as I limped home in the falling darkness.

Chapter XVI

THE FIRE

THE boys came round next morning looking the picture of woe and asking if they could go home at once.

They both complained of feeling very ill indeed. Hezekiah had simply caught a chill ; but Magadi's symptoms were suspiciously like jaundice ; so I gave him some gargle and sent him back to bed with three extra blankets and a large dose of castor-oil.

Hezekiah, fortified with aspirin and the minimum amount of work, was told off to look after him, and I set out with Siki down the valley to prospect for the site of my new house. I was itching to lay the foundation-stone, for I had already bought the land and planned every inch of the house in my mind's eye.

A couple of miles below the hut, however, the Mara stream beguiled me from my purpose, and I threw myself down on the bank beside it. Round the bend it came slipping towards me over its golden brown bed, clear as the very air, except where the current dimpled its azure surface. Ferns trailed their finger-tips in it, lending it their sweet vivid green, a dragonfly darted above, and a tiny blue butterfly hovered among the flowers by the brink. Most exquisite of all was the sound of this little brook, a gentle gurgling song— unhurried and purposeful as Time—sung in the silence for all eternity to the listening mountains. Lying beside it on propped elbows, and picking out the dreaming melodies, you might think of all the world rushing about so busily to the sound of motor horns, steam whistles and jazz bands, while every moment a thousand rivers play their winning music, and no one can spare time to pause and listen.

Above me was a hill-top from where I thought I should see over a new stretch of country ; so I went to climb it.

I found some delicious little berries like sloes growing on a kind of yellow barbary, but after that, I became inextricably tangled among brambles and giant heather. I fought my way standing upright and crawling on hands and knees by turn, and when I reached the top, the jungle rose thickly above me and I could see nothing but an oblong of sky where two white eagles circled overhead.

Deceptive little paths ran down again, which would start off promisingly only to peter out before a wall of impenetrable undergrowth that lacerated my bare knees and brought me to a breathless standstill. What cruel stuff, I thought, as I tore my way through. One calls Nature cruel, but what a fallacy ! Nature is neither cruel nor kind, she just *is*.

Scrambling and tumbling, I came out at last on the banks of my stream. A waterfall twice my own height fell into a pool near by, and beckoned so irresistibly that in two seconds I had stripped and stepped in under it. One moment of icy spray, and then the weight of white water dashed over my shoulders like ice or fire. Gasping for breath I plunged out onto the sunny bank, and the wind, warm and fragrant among the heather, dried me. Few things are more delicious than to feel the sun and wind upon one's body. I curled up in the sun, and the music of the waterfall drew farther and farther away till I fell asleep.

When I reached home at sunset, I found the boys much restored and quite cheerful again, and I made poor Magadi a comforting bowl of soup in atonement for the castor-oil.

They had both caught cold (it was really nothing more) and what they needed to put them right was a good hot drink of Unicorn's milk. This is a concoction of my own, made with sugar, yolk of egg and milk (like ordinary egg-nog) and brought up to unicorn standard by the addition of cinnamon, cloves, ground ginger and nutmeg, and a generous dollop of kirsch or rum. I may add with all modesty that it has always proved infallible.[1] I drank some myself, just as a precaution; and lighting the lamp, I settled down for the evening.

I loved the evenings in the hut almost best, for it was then that it looked so home-like. I could shut the door and draw the curtains and, with the stove burning, the room became comparatively warm. The alarm clock ticked busily on the wall, and the lamplight threw a cheerful glow over the red wood.

The acoustics were far better than they had been in the tent, and I looked forward all day to the concert after supper, and constantly changed the programme beforehand. Mindful that it might be years before the composers would have another hearing up there on the mountain, I tried to be just. I felt oddly guilty for cutting down Schubert in favour of Brahms. Schumann ran him very close, Haydn and Mozart tied. Then there was César Franck's symphony; and Bach's Brandenburg concertos made the rafters dance for gladness. Fine as they all were, it yet seemed to me that none of them understood the mountain as Beethoven did. His ruggedness and gloom and sudden tempestuous joy, above all his great-heartedness that would drive through to the summits with the irresistible energy of an Atlantic breaker: all this was the very soul of the mountain.

Uplifted on the wings of his greatness, I felt that I could look out over the whole of life from the top of the peak.

---

[1] A useful second string is Iguana's milk. The ingredients are: Langdale's cinnamon, honey, cloves, lemon, whisky and boiling water. Proportions to taste.

It was all simple and splendid : worth living for to the last drop of life, or worth dying for at any moment.

With my mind in the clouds, I tidied up everything for the night, and then—and this was almost the cream of the day—I would go out and wander along the path under the stars. The nights were clear and breathlessly still, and the whole earth caught in a trance of loveliness. Orion strode high in the sky, Cassiopeia lay near the northern horizon, and the Pleiades shone so brightly overhead that I could count each star. I went out thinking of other things, perhaps, when a branch of heath, velvet with dew-drops, would brush against me as I passed by and draw me back to the listening beauty of the night. Then I was compelled to lie down in the dew and gaze and gaze into the gloriously lighted heavens, and exclaim in wonder. Mind projected itself so far that I was I no longer, but dissolved into a silvery essence that belonged to earth and sky, that could float out over the forests or up to the glaciers and rest upon the summit.

Returning to myself again—that circumscribed little prison—I thought : on the one hand I am nothing ; on the other I am fire, strength, love itself, because I also am It. As a single individual : less than the dust ; as a part of the whole : strong as the hills and endless as the stars.

Looking up into the sky, I thought that each of us is revolving like one of those spheres in space, moving at his own speed, carrying with him the atmosphere of his own thoughts and individuality. Things from without filter through, but not without in some measure taking the colour of this atmosphere, or being distorted by it. To hear, see and feel them truly, it is necessary to project a part of oneself outside the mist and the hum of these revolutions, into the utter stillness of space.

Next day the boys were well again, and I offered them a

holiday, for they wanted to go to their gardens for more potatoes. But to my surprise they said that they preferred not to become de-climatised, and even suggested that the work was too much for me alone ; by which I guessed that they must now be feeling quite happy and settled on the mountain.

It was without doubt a happy place. Even Hezekiah began to sing at his work—no one could have helped singing—and a kind of irresponsible joy flowed into one's blood till one longed to turn somersaults for sheer well-being.

Work was filled with new glamour, even doing the washing (most prosaic of occupations !) had a certain poetry about it, and the sheets on the line had a way of billowing out over my head like clouds on a summer's day. The poet who sang that " Honest labour wears a lovely face," and added a " hey-nonny-nonny " for the primitive joy of work, would have been puzzled by our modern craze for labour-saving. We may save labour, but we rob work of its dignity and ourselves of that " sweet, O sweet content " which is its blessed reward.

The machines are to blame. They have taken the heart out of work till we have forgotten how to work with affection.

One of the rare quarrels between the boys was on this very subject of work. It arose through the question of firewood, and whose job it was to bring it in ; and words ran so high that it soon grew to be one of the more difficult Labours of Hercules. I on my side warmed up to such a pitch that I told them that they might go and I would fetch the firewood myself. I even went so far as to appeal to Hezekiah's Christian spirit and better feelings. It was just because they had not nearly enough work that they complained of overwork.

They were disarmingly contrite, and cut firewood in fraternal company all the afternoon ; and in the evening I looked round the corner to see them lying on the bank with their heads together over the Bible, Hezekiah (the scholar) reading it out, while Magadi (the untutored savage) painstakingly pronounced each word after him.

I suppose that the secret of that extraordinary exuberance was that one felt so well. Malaria was a thing of the past. The years vanished, and I felt again as I had felt at eight years old, when the miracle of every day had the first bloom of creation upon it, and the blackbird sang in the fir as I crept out of doors at sunrise to run barefoot in the dew.

The mountain was a health resort. There were no mosquitoes, no flies; a riddance which perhaps only those who have come to accept them as the inevitable ingredient of life in the tropics can fully appreciate. The nights were cold, and the days clear, crisp, singing with colour past describing. The air had that absolute purity and wine-like exaltation of a September day on the moors and hills of Scotland. Added to that, was the wonderful quality of the light which belongs to the south.

One evening the boys called me to see a grass fire which was running up the mountain-side and girdling it with flame in the darkness.

It advanced in bright, uneven scallops, and the thick volumes of smoke were combed back by the wind like an angry mane. Its progress was thorough and terrifying, to be stayed by nothing till it bit on snow and ice, and was quenched. A second fire threw up in sharp relief the brow opposite the hut, while high above it the red and crimson and purple smoke darkly intermingled and poured onward, towering up in the blackness of the night like some fantastic cloud round a magician's castle.

I expected to see the flames leaping over the top of the brow at any moment, but the fire must have been miles off, for the smoke persisted through that night and all the next day without appreciably altering its position in the sky. In the evening it was played upon by the westering sun and the flames at once, and coiled and uncoiled its vast billows of smoke in gorgeous effects of opal and copper and purple. It was a wildly daring experiment in colour, more weird and beautiful than anything one could have imagined.

I had planned a trip to Carr's Lakes on the following day, for they lay in the same direction as the fire, which I was longing to see close at hand, and I thought thus to kill two birds with one stone. I accordingly set the alarm clock (more dependable than Hezekiah's elastic notions of time) for four o'clock in the morning; for though the water was often frozen in the buckets, and getting up was a miserable business, I loved an early start.

I awoke with a jump to the metallic and deafening whirr of the alarm, and buried the wretched thing hurriedly under my pillow. Nothing can be more aggressively tactless than an alarm that goes on waking you when you are perfectly wide awake already.

And then I noticed that instead of my waking to pitch darkness, a lurid light pierced through every crack and crevice of the well-ventilated hut. I ran to the door and opened it to a blazing wall of fire advancing down upon me in one long line over the brow less than a quarter of a mile away.

I dashed round to waken the boys (but for the clock we might all have been trapped in our sleep) and then jumped into my clothes.

I debated between the alternatives of defending the hut by cutting a wide moat in the grass below it, or by deliberately firing the grass on the far side of the gorge and driving it up to meet the advancing fire, so as to save a few acres from the burning.

I decided upon firing the grass. We then directed it uphill away from the hut and towards the advancing fire by beating out the flames on our own side and controlling the line as we went along. It was easy enough, at first, for there was a drenching dew and what breeze there was helped us.

We cut flails from the giant heath and worked like blacksmiths guarding our line, now and then the smoke rolling back on us in choking waves, and sometimes, as a bush caught fire, the flames leaping up over our heads into the dawn.

There was something glad and primitive about this battle with the fire, the sun rising steady and remote over the faraway horizon at our backs and we fighting the fierce flames before us. One was plunged from the contemplative into the very actual; the calm beauty of the sunrise was pale and silent and abstract; one's blood leapt to a more urgent rhythm with the work in hand: these fierce, living, scorching flames that had to be subdued. Here was the beauty of reality, the thrill of fear; and we laughed and sang as we wielded the flails, for the joy of putting out our full strength. The same joy which animated the leaping flames strove in us to quench them.

We worked away for a couple of hours or more, by which time the two lines of fire had met and mingled.

All that lay behind us was safe, for a belt of black waste now divided it from the oncoming fire. But the line was, after all, only a few hundred yards long, and now that we tried to attack the real fire, we found that we were not staying it but retreating yard by yard before it.

The sun rose higher in the sky and the dew was all dried up. It is one thing to drive a young, still timid fire the way you will when you can give it an outlet, and are only denying it pasture on one side to encourage it to browse freely upon the other; but it is quite another thing to deal with a wall of determined fire that goes coursing from hill to hill, that has gathered strength of three days' unthwarted career, that has tasted the full glory of destruction and is now mad and insatiable, with a mind created for one thought only and a strength and purpose that are irresistible. Not only that, but there was no alternative with which to bribe it : it must hold on or be utterly quenched, for it left nothing behind it.

However, the main thing was that with our own fire we had turned it aside. It was by no means quenched, but it had wheeled about and now went roaring down the hill parallel with the Mara.

It had already passed the line of direct attack upon the hut, and sooner or later the Mara must give it its quietus. The line (about a mile wide) swept diagonally across the valley below us, and the landscape was beyond our help.

Hezekiah remarked that we could make a first-rate vegetable garden among the ashes. We found, in a tongue of swamp that was still intact, some tall dried plants like elder, which Hezekiah cut into lengths ; and he drew forth from them enchanting shepherd's piping while we made our way back to see how the top end of our line of fire was progressing.

This brought us to the road leading up in the Hall Tarn direction, which, though only an overgrown track, made a fairly safe boundary above (and west of) the hut, should the fire break out again.

I sent Magadi back for the cinema camera, and we had an amusing rehearsal of an Ordeal by Fire. The boys then threw themselves down with a yawn preparatory to going to sleep again. They had worked with a will for nearly three hours which, for them, was almost a record. In fact, the sounds I grew most accustomed to were yawning and snoring. I might have added spitting, but that it would have implied a certain wakefulness. To stir them into some show of activity I suggested that they should have a race back to the hut, which idea appealed to them at once—it having nothing to do with work—and they were off like hares.

I found when I got back that I was as black as a chimney-sweep, my hair was singed, my face burnt, and my hands blistered ; so I had a reviving tub and change before I sat down to breakfast. And I had only just started on my porridge when the boys ran in to tell me that the fire was *coming back*. They set off at once with their axes to cut a moat through the tree heather below the hut.

I did not think much of it, except that having got clean, it was an unwelcome thought to have to change into my smoke-blackened clothes again. At all events I could finish my breakfast.

But at that moment I looked up and saw that our own line of fire opposite had burst into flame again and was spreading with a contagion unbelievably swift over nearly half its length. There was no question of eating breakfast or of changing, either : I cut a fresh flail and dashed to the spot.

It had caught a fair hold of the strip which I had hoped to save, and was now running down to the lip of the gorge. The original fire, which we had turned off at right angles down the valley, had leapt the Mara at a bound and was now racing back up our own bank, leaving a detachment behind to wheel about and make a clean job of the far one ; so that in the twinkling of an eye we were menaced by three armies at once, drawing the net closer and closer about the hut.

Both the road and the gorge, with the stream flowing at the bottom of it, stretched in front of the hut and between it and the fire. I did not believe that the fire would leap the stream, and I hoped to use the road as a defence also. The fire that I had myself started before dawn was to prevent the big fire from coming down to the gorge. Though I cannot show the hills and valleys, the accompanying diagram map may help to show the relative positions of the hut, river, road and fire.

While the boys worked at our defence, hacking and hewing

a lane through the twelve-foot-high heath, I kept guard on the road where it took a wide bend below the hut towards the plains, for, if the fire once crossed it, the circle would in a short space be completed. But the main army was the menace, and when it drew near we all rallied to the point of danger behind the moat we had made, and waited for it with our flails ready.

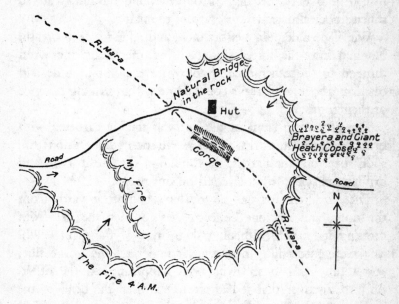

You could hardly have imagined a more pitifully inadequate resistance. The moat was unavailing as a child's sand-castle before the tide. The fire came charging up the slope, roaring through the tall dry heather, sending up whole branches into the air on the whirlwind of its own fury, as though it took hold of the very earth and shook it ; and the flames leapt up into the air with long fierce tongues mixing with the sky's trembling light. We stood there like pigmies before a tidal wave, and before we had time to raise our flails for one futile stroke, the fire gathered itself up, took the moat in its stride, and buried us under a blinding, choking torrent of smoke. The wind drove the whole scorching blast over us, and we had no thought then but to escape and breathe.

When we fought our way out from under the wall of smoke, it was to find ourselves at the very door of the hut. The moat was gone, our line gone, and the trees of heather fifteen or twenty feet high, grouped round the hut, were so much tinder almost within grasp of the flames.

We made a desperate effort then, and taking a deep breath, plunged into the bitter smoke. And mercifully the wind jumped to the other quarter, blowing the smoke aside and the flames back, so that we could come within striking distance of their roots.

The ground in front of the hut was thickly carpeted with grass, heath and tussocks, and here we soon (though none too soon) beat out the flames, thus dividing the fire in two, and driving it back to right and left on our flanks.

The road ran in front of the hut about four yards from the door, and my one concern was to keep the fire from crossing it ; a very difficult task because of the giant heath. We were succeeding in getting it under on the gorge side, and I ran back to see what was happening on the other, only to discover that it had already crossed the bend of the road lower down, and was now taking us in the rear (east) where the hillside sloped down steeply above the hut and was close-set with a copse of Brayeras and heather thirty feet high.

We left the gorge side (where we should have put out the fire could we have spared another five minutes) and dashed back to make a clearing behind the hut. We were working against time in a kind of despair, and every time that we were forced to abandon a position, it was to retreat with our backs nearer and nearer to the hut.

Most disheartening of all was it that the ground won from the enemy would spring into flame again the moment our backs were turned, for the heather roots were burning away deep underground. I realised the danger of this when the front piece burst into flame a second time, and was slyly creeping up to the door while we were battling among the trees on our east flank ; and thereafter I decided to patrol our winnings and never take my eyes off them. I went up and down over a line of a hundred yards, stamping out the flames as they reappeared ; and it was gentle work after the other, like keeping sheep from straying.

The earth took sides with and against us ; what was already burnt was now (comparatively) our friend. Here and there, it is true, the fire had cunningly left a brand to smoulder un-seen ; but I think that the beds of thistles were the worst, for they burned unwillingly, so that you were tempted to trust them, but they held the fire all the longer and would flower into flame just when you had decided that they were safe.

And so it went on. We were always retrenching, beaten back and back till I thought that all must be lost and (with how much reluctance) I gave the order to cut down the giant heath trees nearest the hut, for their very proximity would have been enough to set the tarred roof ablaze if once they caught.

But there was no time to carry out that order.

If the fire relented on one side, it closed in upon the other. The copse above us now sent up flames sky-high, and the world was full of roaring and searing and rasping and wrenching and crackling, as each tree or dry patch of underwood was in turn seized and devoured and discarded for the next. A solid body of flame came towering steeply downhill on the very top of us, and we could only watch it in utter helplessness, and pray that at our hastily-made clearing it might hesitate.

It was horrid anxiety. Yet, in the midst of it all, I could not help taking the other point of view. This was not merely *a* fire, it was the Spirit of Fire ; not just a blind element let loose, but a mind expressing itself in a reckless joy. To us it had come to be a force diabolically astute, full of tactics and forethought, working on a systematic plan of campaign. It accepted defeat in one place so as to give us an inch of hope for the glorious satisfaction of crushing it out of us.

" Very well," it seemed to say, " I don't mind *where* I take you, but take you I must "; and leaving go of the east flank by the copse, it plunged straight into our weakest point on the north where the heather grew in a high matted jungle, choked with bushels of dry brown needles. Once there, it wearied of humouring us and, invoking the gale to its aid, it was for making the final charge home and so ending it.

We were three against a half-circle of two hundred yards of flame, easily twenty and thirty feet high, fanned back on us to a white heat and tearing up the bushes in fierce angry bursts. Before, it had been half playing with us, always laughing at us, but now it was in grim earnest : this was the last point of the circle, the decisive hour of the whole day's battle.

But the fire gained in strength, whereas we were steadily losing ours. The boys worked on in a kind of stolid hopelessness, their faces drawn, lips parched and cracked, hair and clothes singed and burnt. As for me, I could hardly raise my arms to swing the flail, my head was spinning and I was in so much pain from lameness that I groaned aloud to stop myself from fainting or from bursting into tears. It was utterly hopeless, the odds were overwhelmingly against us, and now that we were fighting the flames in giant heath yards above our heads, we were losing at every point. We called out to one another in turn for help at our several posts, but always the answer came back : " It's worse here ! "

I looked at my watch for the first time. It was three
o'clock. No wonder we were exhausted. Time had ceased
to be, yet in reality we had been engaged in this battle,
without respite, for more than ten hours. This was the final
effort, and we must win. Hezekiah staggered over to me,
muttering that he could do no more. But looking at the
time had given me an idea. It was worth giving the fire
five minutes' play in order to rally our own strength, and I
dashed into the hut for a can of water, cake, biscuits—any
food I could lay my hands on. We felt faint and sick, but
forcing ourselves to eat restored us miraculously and revived
our hope.

The end came unexpectedly. At one moment we were
lost, and then, quite simply, we found that we had control.
It had been anybody's victory all day long, but when it was
really ours it seemed too good to be true. There was a
sudden cessation of that flaming and roaring : the spirit of the
fire had left us and passed on.

I did not for a moment believe that we had conquered it
—it was too strong, too indomitable, a power that filled one
with respect and a glorious admiration—for, of course, had it
meant to, it had made a mouthful of us. I think that at the
last it gathered itself up to real anger, and then realising its
own strength it forebore to make proof of it. It was a noble
thing, great as the Sud or the desert or the deluge, and it
had given us a wonderful vision of itself. During those ten
hours I felt that I had come to know the personality and
significance of fire, to meet it face to face.

It was an uplifting experience, immensely terrifying, and
I was fervently grateful for our escape. Had the boys taken
the holiday I had offered them, or had I not planned an early
start for Carr's Lakes, the beloved little hut might never have
been saved. As it was, when I looked round at the black
desolation that stretched on every side, it seemed to me

incredible that the tiny island of green upon which it stood should have been spared.

The boys had shown perseverance that amounted to little less than heroism. I took back (mentally) all the black marks against them for their laziness ; for whatever their faults, they could rise to an occasion.

I made some strong tea, about a quart each with plenty of sugar and milk and (unbeknown to the boys) well laced with brandy. Then I took down the medicine chest and oiled and bound up our wounds. We had many burns and blisters. Hezekiah had burned his heel, and though I had scarcely noticed it at the time, the palms of both my hands were flayed.

After that, we went carefully over every inch of our boundary, poured water on some suspicious bits and generally made sure that all was safe.

After dark the boys climbed into a tree and cut down a burning branch ; and I set the alarm clock to waken us at midnight and again in the small hours, to make sure that we were not betrayed. This, as it turned out, was a very necessary precaution, for the wind had called up the flames again in two places, and we had easily lost all, even then.

Chapter XVII

NOAH'S ARK

THE little oasis of about half an acre which we had wrested from the jaws of the fire was like Noah's Ark, for it had become a refuge to all the animals and birds on my side of the mountain.

This, at last, was the dream come true : not only to be surrounded by all these birds and beasts, but to know that they looked to me for sustenance. Now I felt I might truly sing with the poet :

> Birds and beasts and jewelled insect free
> Know me full well ; one brotherhood are we.

They were pathetically tame through fear and hunger, and when I strolled out in the starlight, the branches overhead were filled with timid rustlings and the path with scurrying feet. I lit a match to find out what had made such a commotion among the dry leaves, and a little mouse sat up looking at me.

Luckily I had plenty of rice and maize-flour, and was able to provide ample breakfasts and suppers for them all. I sank tins of water into the ground, for water was quite as important to them as food.

In a single day disaster had overtaken these hundreds of living creatures ; their lairs, their nests, even their young, perhaps, were all gone ; yet the birds sang as joyously as though nothing had happened. The three crows returned as eagerly for their breakfast, the doves cooed as languorously from the few remaining trees, and the eagle's cry rang out through the silence above the same hill-top. Their acceptance of what had happened was immediate and unquestioning. It was this that wrung my heart with compassion. Again and again earth's teaching was always that the inevitable must be endured. It is our own fault if we suffer more than our due of pain because we rebel against it, or dwell too much upon the thought of it.

I had made up my mind to devote the last three weeks of my stay to collecting the flowers; but now I might course over thirty square miles of country and not find a single blade or leaf. I was doubly glad that I had often paused to enjoy the greenness, that I had spent a last morning in the fairy dell.

Another sad event caused by the fire was the burning of a beautiful Dombeya tree at the bend of the road below the hut. I had hoped to be able to save it, and we threw into the hollow trunk buckets of water that hissed up from the roots in a cloud of steam. Hezekiah cut a bamboo pole and plunged it down into the embers to a depth of over five feet, so that nothing I could do could save the tree.

The fire still pursued its unrelenting course. Below the hut, the bamboo forest had caught, as I could hear by the continual explosions like pistol-shots. Above, three fires raked the crests and valleys, the road winding up in the distance still keeping a boundary, so that there was a zigzag of fire like forked lightning, very fine and weird in the moonless dark.

The effect of these fires was extraordinary, reminding me of the curious pall that hung above the Kivu volcanoes. The sun was dimmed to the gentle radiance of a February day in the north; a soft coppery light rested upon the hillside, touching with gold the withered leaves of some bush that had partly escaped burning, and transforming with lovely changeful hues of violet, blue and lilac, the stark and desolate waste of ashes that surrounded me upon every side. There was a lingering sadness, an ineffable quiet beauty about the landscape like a soul that has come through sorrow purified and serene. The spirit of it came to you unbidden, with the caress of wings, a sudden and sweet consolation. I know not if it was more like spring or like autumn. Perhaps, after all, they are not dissimilar, and that the same tenderness which protects very young things comes back at last to the old after the joy and bitterness of life.

The fires created draughts that amounted to gales, which whirled about clouds of débris. Now and then there were real wind-devils, but they announced their coming by an ominous roaring in the distance, and I had time to shut the door and windows. But I was sometimes too late, and then the hut, which had been scrubbed and dusted, would in a moment be filled with a cloud of ashes.

The boys had discovered an abandoned hive of honey, and went off each day with a rope to climb the tree and rescue it. At last they were successful, and they presented me with a piece of honeycomb full of dark and perfumed honey delicious to taste, though the comb itself was too tough to eat. It would have outlasted the best chewing-gum.

Besides the reed flute played with an unceasing monotony that robbed it of its early charm, they started Olympic games, throwing the spear at a neatly devised target. I longed to join in.

Only a precious fortnight remained of my two months, and I knew that so long as the boys were there I could make nothing of my Noah's Ark (the tameness of those fat little doves was already becoming an unbearable temptation to them, and I had some dark suspicions), so I sent them away again, inventing as a pretext some urgent letters for the mail.

They filled up my water supply and left early next morning.

It was a weight off my mind, for I worried how to keep them occupied and happy. The silence when they had gone made itself felt, indeed, you could almost *see* it, as though it were a part of the blue lambent air and those far-away peaks trembling in liquid light till they all but dissolved into the purity of the sky.

With a huge sigh of content I took Grant's *Walk Across Africa* out into the heather. Grant was a lovable companion ; he fitted in with that place.

Presently a lizard ran over my knee and stayed a little to sun himself. Looking up from my page I watched him as with each quick movement he turned the sun's rays from his sides with glinting bronze. My eyes wandered from him to the Brayera's green leaves above me, enveloped in the incredibly blue sky, or out to the cloud-roof below, woven with a shining texture that would bear one up, and filled with rainbows ; till the intense beauty of everything took my spirit unwares.

My reading was spasmodic, yet I knew that I was not irrevocably bound to reading so many volumes or to walking so many miles in a given time, and therein lay the real benefit of the experiment. Time. Time to let one's mind expand and unravel itself, time to live gently and with affection, and for a while to feel Nature round one, and her influence alone, and to listen to her.

In my diary I wrote that this was happiness. Happiness —not pleasure, which we often mistake for it, running hither and thither to pursue it amid a whirl of excitement that helps to save us from ourselves—happiness must spring from its own seed, it cannot be grafted in the mind or heart from without. And the first condition of happiness is serenity of mind. All philosophy, all religion, all morality aims only at this. . . . In that quiet state where you know peace of mind it is easy to listen. And this is what Nature teaches you : To walk openly, to look upon all things with affection, and to learn the patience which can spring only from infinite love. . . . Of all things worth gaining, which is worth most ? I think it is Compassion. It is the final lesson including all the others, including an understanding heart.

In this quiet state the boundaries of Time and Space fall away, and more than that, the limitations of the individual, and so the spirit is freed at last.

The spirit puts forth itself in a million different expressions. When it draws back unto itself, what matter if this atom was I, or another, or a tree, even, or a wild flower ? Not the individual, nor the claims of the individual . . . but to give back the spirit in full measure, and pure.

Next day I felt that I ought to make another attempt to reach Carr's Lakes. But the burnt and blackened country looked very uninviting and I compromised instead by climbing up to the Gates of Kenya—the twin dome-shaped hills with the rocky gorge between them already mentioned— an hour's climb above the hut.

The Gates proved difficult to reach. I left the road too soon, striking across a forest of burnt twigs where clouds of ashes rose up at every step, and I was forced back to the road again. I stepped onto it where it crossed the river over a bridge, and being half choked by the ashes I could not resist a dip. Up there, within sight of the glaciers, it was the coldest dip of my life, for it was still early and the frost lay in the shadows. Yet it was inspiriting there on the open moor, with the river as clear and brown as any highland stream, and that huge amphitheatre rising up to the peaks.

Perhaps this stream came from a lake hidden among the numerous folds of the valley and hitherto overlooked, and I had half a mind to give up the day to searching for it. Lake Vivienne had a rather picturesque sound in my ears, but a nightmare army of tussocks soon drove all such vanity out of my head and turned me back to my original plan.[1]

I took the Gates of Kenya in the rear, and from them I saw what I had passed within a stone's throw a score of times and had never discovered : a waterfall over a drop of perhaps a hundred feet. I knew it must be the Nithi Falls, and making my way across to the top of the cliff over which they leapt, I looked down to an irresistibly lovely glade fresh as an emerald under the spindrift. I clambered down first through suffocating ashes and then through green bushes and creepers into this dewy paradise.

The water fell in two leaps from the top into a wide pool, at the edge of which I found a stratum of the red ochre stone called by the natives Nondo, which they use in their hairdressing and for painting themselves. Natives never came up as high as this, so that the porters must have discovered it here on one of the mountain expeditions, and they had pounded it in a hollow slab of rock near by.

The pool suggested only one thing, which was another bathe. I waded in as close to the waterfall as I dared, and when I came near I found myself more than half surrounded by a little rainbow. Despite the gale of wind and the icy spray, I crept a little nearer to see it better, for it was the most beautiful thing you could fancy, dancing through the spray like a shower of rhinestones burning in the sunlight ; and against the dark shadow on the water it was so bright and clearedged that it seemed I could clasp it in my hands.

From this big pool the water gathered up its purpose once more and sped from pool to pool with a swift current and miniature falls among the boulders. I lay flat on a boulder in mid-stream with my chin scarce above the level of the water, and watched how the two currents meeting and mingling

[1] Some years later, I had the privilege of being permitted to give my name to the falls below Lake Michaelson.

made a perfect honeycomb. The shadow of the honeycomb fell through onto the golden floor, and sometimes the left-hand current predominated and sometimes the right, endlessly weaving the long crystal lines of the surface.

I plunged into one pool after another, they each looked so inviting ; and the plunge took away my breath yet brought such a tingling glow with it that I waited impatiently for the sun to dry me that I might repeat the experiment.

Exploring round the big pool, where the sun's rays were tempered by the gentle fall of spindrift, or lying quite still on a boulder where the swallows darted to and fro, skimming within an inch of my face—so that I always waited in the hope that they might brush me with their wings in passing—I found that the hours went by like music, all unperceived.

Listening to the drowsy sound, I gazed up with shaded eyes to the fall itself leaping out over the cliff from the blue sky like a little cloud, shimmering with swift-dropping crystal ; and I followed its fall from top to bottom, unbroken save where it spurted off an out-jutting ledge that checked its career midway. And when I looked at the solid rocks beside it, they seemed to move upward. It put me in mind of being once caught in an avalanche, when I had watched in bewilderment the rock slipping up, before I realised that it was my own stretch of snow that was slipping down ; the same optical illusion one is never tired of playing on oneself in a station when the other train moves out first.

Among the tender green were soft purple orchids and golden starry flowers, and many others—a place so verdant and beautiful that I could not drag myself away ; and it was not until the sun dipped behind the shoulder of the mountain that I acknowledged the necessity for getting into my clothes and coming home.

I arrived back grimy from head to foot after a struggle through the charred undergrowth, and decided on the greatest of all luxuries : a hot bath. I lay and scalded very happily, and it was only when I began a brisk rub down that I found I was literally rubbing the skin off my back and shoulders. A bath was the last thing to have tried, for though I was unaware of it at the time, I had been badly caught by the sun, and any movement was afterward an exquisite torture.

Although it was practically on the equator (and I have since been told that it was folly) I never wore a hat while I was on the mountain. I used to wear it tucked into my belt in case I felt the symptoms of sunstroke coming on (I know now that it does not always announce itself so obligingly), but except that my hair was bleached to various shades of gold and tawny, which I fondly believed to resemble a lion's mane, nothing worse befell me.

The question of sunstroke or accident had been already discussed, for no one else looked upon the hut as a health resort, and friends had asked me what I should do if I fell ill up there. But in the enumeration of the possible misfortunes that might overtake me, no one had thought of toothache. And one morning a miserable molar completely changed my outlook on life. I tried cloves, tied up my head in a scarf, did everything imaginable ; but a couple of days went by and still the pain raged unabated. There was only one thing to be done, and that was to take the wretched tooth out.

Ever since that day, a visit to the dentist has been a pleasure, for it is not until you have tried to pull out your own tooth that you can appreciate your dentist at his proper value. A painless injection, an adroit turn of the wrist and he tells you that it is all over, " and now take a little water please ! " It seems so easy.

But tie a fishing-line round the tooth, attach the other end to a beam (remembering to hold tight to your lower jaw with both hands to prevent its being dislocated) and then jump. This, more than volumes of dental literature, will open your eyes to the skill, strength and artistry of the dentist.

Even then, all that happened was that the line broke. I sat on the edge of the bed and thought things over till an idea came to me.

I then tied the line to the top of the door, so that it was taut when I stood on tiptoe. It answered admirably, for even the pain in the tooth was less agonising than standing on tiptoe for nearly two hours ; and the more I sank onto my heels, the better the pull. But it failed to pull the tooth out, and by then the pain was so intolerable that I took the pliers from the tool chest and eventually finished off the job.

I felt faint and very sick, but the offender was out, roots and all, after a struggle of three hours and forty minutes. I timed it exactly, for I was proud of the achievement ; and as a reward I put the trophy away in the lofty company of some odd teeth of crocodile and lion, keepsakes which I had picked up on safari.

The ordeal safely over, I sat outside the hut in the deck chair and began to enjoy my Noah's Ark. The pair of doves, (especially now that the boys had gone away) had never been so tame. They walked unconcernedly round my chair, hopped onto the rung, and the little hen, walking under my crossed leg, even bumped her head against the sole of my foot.

She was tamer than the cock bird and had a gentler disposition. Indeed, he was extremely dictatorial, always saying : " Come here, my dear, I keep telling you not to take risks ! " Or if she found a tit-bit, he unceremoniously drove her off and ate it himself. But this was only that discipline might be maintained, for he was incurably in love with her and never let her out of his sight. They made the air drowsy all day with their sweet, hoarse cooing.

Now that I could observe them closely, I saw that they had

ruby-orange eyes with black centre and outer ring, and red feet, and that their heads were almost cobalt blue, tinged with lavender. They had a dark half-ring on the neck, and a bar or two of cinnamon on their dark wings.

I had never seen doves so dark, and when next I had the opportunity I went to South Kensington to identify them. Nothing so far obtained tallied with my colourful description, and I began to wonder if, after all, I had found a new species. Then, from one of the many thousand drawers, they took down a long cardboard box filled with specimens of a very drab little bird. He certainly had what might at a pinch be described as cinnamon bars on the wing. And his name was *Streptopelia lugens,* one of the commonest kinds of African doves.

" But where are those lavenders and cobalts ? " I exclaimed reproachfully ; " I didn't invent them ! "

" Ah, but you see these are only dried specimens," was the reply ; " birds look so different when they are alive."

I agreed sadly, yet I knew that that was only half the truth. As shells or pebbles shine with a peculiar bloom and lustre through their natural medium of water, yet once you take them home and dry them they look faded and common-place, so these little doves, I believed, owed much to the golden ambience of that magic light.

I was still watching them and sprinkling rice in the dust, when I looked up and saw a duiker walking with timid, hesitating steps up the path. He saw me quite well (he had already come many a time for the rock-salt I laid out for him) and, though he was no longer alarmed, it was traditional for him to pretend that he was. It was a kind of game : he would listen intently, turn swiftly to an imaginary sound, retreat and advance again. All the while, the westering sun made a halo round him, or shone red upon his satin flank as he turned towards it. And always he came a little nearer, so that I could see not only the vertical black bar from his nose to the top of his forehead, but also his delicate hooves and the warm texture of his skin, and just how wet and cold his little grey nose was. At last, within a few paces of me, he would boldly stoop his head to lick the salt ; and I felt, then, that I would gladly wait years if he would only take it from my hand.

The sun set ; and above the black outline of the hillside the sky warmed with soft, rosy colours of the afterglow, and the little parrots called to one another as they flew home to roost. Darkness fell, and the dew, and a breeze came up from the plains stirring the leaves before they found repose in another breathless, starry night.

So the days came and passed, strung together like pearls. Time flew ; yet I waylaid eternity.

One day I made a find on top of the cupboard, for stored away at the back were a number of books.

They catered for all tastes, and the discovery was as exciting as exploring a wreck. They ranged from two interesting articles on Conrad and Sargent to copies of a magazine called *Sunday at Home,* which mesmerised me by its sheer dreariness.

But if there was a sickening banality about the story of the young couple " whose romance was salvaged by a verse from the Psalter," and the homely little chats on morality, my hot rebellion was quelled when I turned to the advertisements. In these lay the gist and kernel of business ; their human and anguished cry dismayed and haunted me. To think that there could be so much misery in the world that all those armies of Missions, Leagues, Charities and Relief Funds should be necessary. . . . And to think, too, how one goes blithely through life glorifying God in Nature (and Nature in God) without having so much as an inkling of crowded poverty or of real black misery and despair.

There were novels, too, but what caught my fancy most

was a book called *The Prisoners of the Red Desert*. It was a harrowing record of the privation and sorrow suffered by the crew of the *Tara* patrol ship (torpedoed during the War off the coast of Egypt) when they were taken prisoners at Port Bardia by the Turks. Food, usually such a tedious subject in books, here rises to epic strength in the story, and the reader is made to take as keen and anxious an interest in it as the poor prisoners themselves.

I was plunged so deep in their adversities that when I looked up and saw my palatial hut, and good bed and plenty of blankets and books and brazenly full store cupboard, I blushed for shame and fasted for twenty-four hours by way of atonement ; after which I carefully meted out the same meagre ration of plain boiled rice which was all that the prisoners were given. The altitude made one ravenous ; and I read all day without stopping, hunger gnawing realistically at my vitals the while.

Stores had failed before now. In the Congo we had once gone nearly six weeks without tea, flour, sugar and salt ; but there had always been *soap*, whereas those unfortunate prisoners had had to do without even that, and were literally herded together like cattle in their own filth.

Yet all is relative, and my next dip into the hut library (a novel of Seton Merriman's) surrounded me with so much comfort and luxury and all the amenities of civilisation that when I looked up to the ramshackle little hut, hundreds of miles from anywhere, with no chance of getting even bread or meat or milk, I began to think that my way of living was very simple and that I was almost roughing it. At the end of that book I had *foie gras* for supper.

All the same, I loved the books of privation best, and the odysseys of life. It is they that bring one down through the surface of superficial mirage and aimless groping to the real hard bed-rock. Life reduced to its lowest terms :

what is indispensable ? A little food, water (and soap), clothing, and if possible some kind of shelter. Living like the brute beast, and yet it is then that you have the strongest contrast between the beasts and man, for it is then that man lives vitally near to the spirit.

Forced to live near the earth, robbed of our cotton-wool possessions and taught-from-without creeds, faced with real hunger, thirst, cold, living close to life and death and danger—then the spirit transcends all material things and God becomes an inseparable part of everyday life, as Allah to the Bedouins, because we *need* Him. No longer is He the impersonal abstraction beyond the shining heavens, but mingled with the very earth we touch, the water we drink, the fire that warms us, the air we breathe—all around us, yesterday, to-morrow, now at this minute.

The whole difficulty (my diary continues) is that the conception of God is like the conception of space and infinity : the mind stretches to breaking-point, it cannot grasp the *idea*. The idea of the stars. Our own solar system and we but a grain of dust in the Milky Way. For a time one struggles with the thought of it, trying to figure to oneself what the astronomer's rows of noughts really mean in space ; but sooner or later one lapses back to the idea of the sun ninety-five million miles away and we, Earth, held to it by gravitation and from falling into it by centrifugal force ; one may also dwell with composure on the thought of the other seven planets bigger and smaller than we, heavier and lighter, with different lengths of days and nights. After that, one thinks (already more vaguely) of the billions of stars, " thick inlaid like patines of bright gold " in our dome of night. But to contemplate infinity is an effort of tremendous concentration possible only during rare and inspired moments. It can never be, for ordinary minds at least, the exercise of every day.

And in the same way, in moments of great exaltation, brought about by the achievement of something, perhaps, or merely by seeing a flower for the first time with real intuition, one has a sudden glimpse, and for a fraction of time can apprehend God. But more often at the word God, the mind substitutes a personality in its own image, quarrels with the absurdity of the supposition and instead of broadening the conception, loses the point of the argument to the extent of denying God's very existence.

The divine law, the divine force and the divine protection are all there, but the idea is too big for most of us to grasp. The frog trying to give an idea of the size of a bull, and bursting with the effort. Our minds being the size of frogs, the fear of bursting compels us to reduce everything else to the size of frogs also. It is a great simplification. But the things themselves remain the size of bulls or elephants or Himalayas, nevertheless, and it is only the link between them and our own vision that is needed.

Chapter XVIII

"NATURE NEVER DID BETRAY . . ."

THE GATES OF KENYA had given me a glimpse over country beyond my own valley, across a broad-backed rolling moorland down to the forest. It had looked so invitingly green after the prevailing world of ashes, that I set off early one morning to spend the day there.

As usual, it was deceptively far off, but proved easy to approach by a long estuary of tussocks. They were the real heartless kind, but since they had undergone the fire I had the advantage of them.

The forest was reward enough for hours of tussock-fighting, and after wandering along game paths between sweet-scented hedges and among bamboo—where I found some fresh rhino droppings—I came to a grove of tall trees with a stream murmuring deep down under mossy banks. The trees, bare but for the wisps of beard-moss hanging from their branches, stood up darkly as firs against the surrounding green; and there was a smell of resin there, also, the delicious smell all forests have when the sun is so hot that you can hear the seed pods popping round you.

I lay looking up through the bright green leaves of a Brayera, and watching a pair of bush-crows as they spread their scarlet wings and flew off to a neighbouring tree and back. That sudden splash of scarlet, transparent against the sun, made you catch your breath—it was so unbelievably bright and exotic among the luminous green.

This sanctuary in the midst of the primeval forest was the innermost abode of peace. It may never before have seen a human being, for ordinarily it was cut off by miles of pathless jungle and tussocks, and the fire alone had made it accessible.

Buffalo and rhino might have wandered there, or a bush-buck; but nothing came except a flock of tiny birds that chirped like blue tits, and a dove or two. The wind stirred in the trees, sending the shadows momentarily tossing; indeed the breeze gave a voice to the whole forest, not break-ing in upon the silence but calling up everything to a kind of conscious joy of being. If the djin of the forest had told me to wish then, it would have been to come back to that quiet place. And because it was so near the last day and my heart ached already with the coming regret, I strove especially to engrave it in my memory, so that whenever I wished years afterward, " in all the uproar and the press," I could with-draw my mind and sit again beneath those trees and listen to the bird that whistles three bars out of Chopin's Third Ballade, and see the flame of crimson wings.

At length I continued on my way, and following a path through thick jungle I put up two coveys of partridges.

Having come so far, I thought that by striking through the forest I could make the third side to the square and meet the road below the hut. Could I have foreseen the result of this decision I should have been content to retrace my steps among the tussocks to an inch. The forest thickened impenetrably, hidden precipices barred my way and, when I escaped from it, there was no alternative but to fight through a forest of burnt twigs that grew so close together that I had to crawl on hands and knees among the choking ashes. On and on stretched this forest of charcoal, and I wormed my way and panted and cursed and broke the sticks that held me back, and tore my knees against the stubs till I was ready to sit down and howl like a dog in despair. Impenetrable forest, even the tussocks, anything, I thought, was better than these ashes whirled about me by the gale in a blinding, suffocating cloud.

I climbed slowly upward to a ridge which I hoped would be bare and lead me more or less in the direction of home ; but when I reached the top it was thicker than all the rest, and there was nothing for it but to plunge back into the forest. The relief of escaping from the ashes, and of being able to draw breath among sweet green-stuff again was grateful beyond telling, and when I came to a little bower roofed in by bamboos close to a hollow tree, I lay down with a sigh of happiness, and slept.

Nothing is so sweet as going to sleep in a forest. Gradually the sound of the whispering leaves and the flutter of birds' wings lull you to rest ; and when from a long way off you come back, wondering for a moment where you are, sun-dappled tree trunks and the shifting design of leaves take shape again before your waking eyes.

I was by no means home, and I had such a struggle with a patch of giant heath that had escaped the fire—tearing my way through brambles and falling waist-deep into the thick and rotting undergrowth—that I began to regret even the ashes ; and I realised more strongly than ever how but for the fire all this country had been absolutely inaccessible.

I now endeavoured to make my way back to the estuary of tussocks, but seeing a bare hill-top on my right I climbed it to take my bearings. And it rewarded me with the most welcome of all sights, for there below me was the little hut. Even then, it took me more than two hours to reach it, by which time it was dark.

It was on occasions like this that the joys of solitude might almost have been outweighed by finding supper ready for me. But when I caught sight of myself in the glass, I was on the whole relieved that my two faithfuls were not there to greet me—I was so completely and desperately black.

It was my last expedition on the mountain, and I had no heart for music that evening.

I looked at the calendar for the twentieth time trying to juggle more successfully with the dates, and to squeeze in a few more days before I was to sail. One ought never to make plans ahead. My forest djin was well out of earshot, or I should have begged him to cancel them all with one wave of his wand and give me another two months' grace. But when I awoke next morning to the sun's level rays striking through the window in leafy patterns, and the drowsy rustle of leaves shaken out of their sleep, the inexorable reminder dropped into my consciousness like lead that this was my last day.

Putting the thought resolutely behind me, I jumped out of bed and flung wide the doors to another dawn. I could never quite get used to the miracle of it. Always I ran up the path straight into the sun, where the feathery grasses floated up in a fiery cloud of dew-drops ; and the vanishing rime, still crisp among the shadows, ran out in a mist of silver, and was gone.

I came back, made some camomile tea, with a slice of lime added—a clean, bitter drink to begin the day with—and took it out into the heather where I could lie in the sun and watch a hawk quartering above the hillside for his breakfast ; and the little birds in choirs of three and four, who always sang the same two bars out of the Brahms Piano Quintet, would fly into a tree-top and burst into a brief ecstasy of song. Turning my face to the sun, I played with a kaleidoscope of flaming orange and scarlet and yellow by shutting my eyes more or less tightly, and every now and then a bird winging by would throw a passing shadow of purple.

Those early mornings lifted me into happiness so exquisite that I did not know whether to sing or cry. Life became suddenly simplified to the only real need—shared with all created things—which was to give praise.

Nature gave herself out in a kind of lavish exuberance :
everything was thrice as full of sap and colour as it need
have been, the sky's blue overflowed into every shadow and
reflection on the earth, and earth was caught up in a song
of light. The contagious joy of it cried out to me, also,
to give in full measure, and over and above, never to hold
back or to reason by miserly logic. "You are *you*," it said,
"taken at your just value, neither more nor less, as a tree
is a tree and a rock is a rock and nothing else. How idle
to seem to be more, how futile to protest that you are less !
Be natural, and when all the earth swings on to the eternal
rhythm, go with it gloriously."

It was true, and example and precept were there all round
me. Everything that lived, lived generously and for the
day. Everything cried out to me that the past and the
future were abstract ; immortality was the present, and
only the present was mine. They lived in the present
and found it good. To have looked at it askance, or to
have wished it different, would have seemed like disparaging
God.

The things round me were ever trying to tell me something
more, gently toppling over theory after theory and leading
me back to first principles. Not philosophy but simplicity.
I missed much, for nothing is harder than to unlearn one's
preconceived ideas. One should start off fresh without any.
Things may be quite different from what they seem or from
how we see them. As Montaigne wrote : "When I play
with my cat to amuse her, how do I know that it is not she
who is trying to amuse *me* ? "

There was still a good supply of maize, rice and oatmeal
left, and I went to prepare a big farewell feast.

When I stirred the bucket, the signal was greeted as
promptly as in any farmyard, for we kept very regular hours.

The birds flocked down, and the three crows with white capes had thrown away discretion long ago, and greedily chose their own menu straight out of the bucket while I was helping the rest. What made me feel most like Noah (or Alice) was the punctual arrival of two little mice and a kind of beaver-rat. Wild mice are easily tamed, and as a child in Norway I had had several pet lemmings who lived wild but often came to me for their meals.

My most difficult guests (on account of their diet) were half a dozen chameleons that lived permanently on top of the bunk-frames. I supplemented their meagre hunting, and they ate flies out of my hand ; but though the flies were dead, the chameleons never allowed that to hurry them. The stalk was just as painfully conscientious, their ball-bearing eyes looked just as many ways at once, and after an incredibly long wait their tongues would shoot out like lightning to snatch the fly.

Having fed them for the last time, I took them gently up one by one and put them in the Brayera tree. They hated being picked up, and always distended themselves to twice their normal size and hissed at me like tiny fierce dragons. The largest was about eight inches long and the smallest less than one, though he blew himself out and hissed like a grown-up. They were drab brown, but they could vary to yellow, orange, browny-red and very dark brown, according to what you put them against. Their natural colour varies with different chameleons, and the changes at their command can only be variations on their original colour. On the Uasso Nyiro I once caught a splendid chameleon who was pea-green. He could manage pale lemon yellow, bright emerald or dark blue-green ; but when I put him on a red blanket, the nearest match he could do was a lovely shade of lavender with mottling of a darker purple. The brown ones on the mountain found red easy, but their attempts at green were very muddy, and they specialised in marbled effects rather than uniform shades.

As I sat writing inside the hut, forlorn with the sense of inevitable departure, a little brown bird the size of a bullfinch flew in through the open door and hopped over my table. I sat holding my breath while he pecked at the blotting paper, cocked a beady eye at me, then fluffed himself out and set to work to preen himself. Though the birds were very tame, none had ever before ventured inside the hut. It was my last day, and had the mountains bent their heads in farewell, I could not have felt more elated or more moved.

Hezekiah and Magadi arrived with the porters late in the evening with a very discouraging report of the road, saying that it was doubtful whether they could take the loads down through the burnt forest to Chogoria in the day.

So I was determined to make an early start, and was up at four next morning. But by the time everything was packed and the porters had wrangled over their loads, and the hut was swept and tidied, it was nearly seven o'clock.

Mtu Massara, as charming as ever, was not a good head man. It had happened before and it happened again : the porters sneaked off before he had given the word, so that some of them went only half loaded, while there remained much behind and no porters to carry it. He looked at the pile with a deprecating grin, and shrugged his shoulders as one who indulgently recognises that after all boys will be boys. But I had no mind to share this view, and though well aware that he was above carrying anything but a walking-stick, I hardened my heart and made him pay for his inefficiency by carrying the biggest load that was left. I slung the cameras round me while Hezekiah carried the rest, and at last we were ready to take the road.

I remained behind for the melancholy business of shutting

up the hut. Its friendly walls were already warm in the early sunshine; the sky, bluer than ever above its roof, spilled over into the shadows which were edged with sparkling dew. The noise of the caravan had faded, silence took possession once more, though it seemed to me now like the silence of desertion, and the choir of little birds sang again the familiar snatch out of the Brahms Piano Quintet. And, above it all, the mountains, bathed in light, trembled in the golden morning. There was no excuse to linger, the key scraped protestingly in the lock, and I turned my back and ran as hard as I could down the path. . . .

Siki frisked ahead, snuffing the crisp, glad air; the dew in the heather and cobwebs went flashing past us, the stream ran crystal among the shadows, partridges called and presently the bamboos stood out feathery and golden in the sunlight. This brought me to the plateau with the grove of junipers, a couple of miles or so below the hut, where I had so often planned to build my house. It was going to be made quite simply with three thicknesses of bamboo (cut from the forest close by) and lined with beaver-boarding to make it draught-proof. The garden was laid out already, and clumps of tall bamboo and gracefully disposed groups of Juniper, Dombeya, Cedar and Brayera trees were there to shelter the house, yet not to hide the supreme view of the mountain, or the plains far below. I struck off to right and left looking for the exact site, yet I could not make up my mind, for each was more enchanting than the other, and when I rejoined the path my mind was filled with a hundred plans. Departure ceased to hurt, so sure was I then of coming back.

At the edge of this plateau—which belonged to the mountain, yet looked out over the world as well, I sat down to have one last look at the peak and the rolling moorland filled with sun and the ineffable serenity belonging to it. Then I set off down into the forest.

The dew lay thickly upon the violets and tiny blue lobelias and pink *Impatiens* that carpeted the ground; but I soon came to the ravages of the fire, and then the real hard work began.

The road was impassable. Hundreds of bamboos had fallen across it. A few minutes later I overtook the porters, who were trying to find a path through; but the forest was so thick that we were compelled to go far out of our way. The stems were ranked close, so that you had to squeeze between them, shouldering sideways, and I could never understand how the porters managed to pass through with their unwieldy loads on their heads. All day I admired in wonder their stoicism and patience. Hour after hour they struggled, lifting their loads over the fences of fallen timber, or kneeling down to pass under the low arches. Soon there was no way round, for the whole width of the forest had been burnt, and we advanced like tight-rope walkers along the swaying slippery platform of bamboos fallen athwart the path about six feet off the ground. There were more gaps than footholds, and I, slithering on the lacquer-like surface of the bamboo poles in my nailed boots, more than once fell through. Every time this happened there was a roar of applause; this mode of walking became a new kind of game and every one took special pride in his own agility.

But after a time even this overhead path gave out—the gaps were too frequent—and there was no choice but to crawl on hands and knees through the hot ashes along the tunnels of charred débris. We sat down in the midst of it, begrimed to the eyes, our lungs full of ashes and our hearts of despair. For five hours we had fought and toiled to cover a distance that would ordinarily have taken less than one. But there was no help for it; even if we could not reach Chogoria that day, we could only go on fighting our way through that nightmare of ashes, doubled up beneath the tree trunks pressing tyrannically down upon us.

After this, we came to the fire itself, and lost the path altogether in the surging flames. It was very exciting, for not only were we surrounded by burning trees and the flames licking up stealthily upon either side, but the noise of the burning bamboos was as deafening as gunfire. Shot after shot rang out upon all sides till there was a steady volley.

Picking our way between two converging walls of fire, like the children of Israel between the waves of the Red Sea, we would feel a scorching heat, and look up to see a huge cedar or camphor tree like a column of white flame towering above us. That none ever fell upon us was little short of a miracle.

Suddenly the two fires ran together and closed in front of us. There was no possible retreat : all behind us was now a roaring furnace. We made a dash for it, and were immediately cut off from one another, lost and blinded in smoke. We ran hither and thither to escape, but on every side more flames met us, leaping out with savage tongues from the dim twilight of smoke and shadow. We called to one another desperately, and at length the porters who had gone ahead with axes to hew out a path, heard us and ran back to show us the way through.

It was the supreme moment of our deliverance, and unforgettable was the feeling of relief when we ran out of that raging inferno into the sunlight, and then stepped into the cool green virgin forest again. How broad and good seemed the road now at last unbarred before us !

Leaving the fire at a safe distance in our rear, I called an hour's halt. We were close to the halfway camp, and every one could go to the river and drink his fill. Our throats were parched almost beyond speech, and we were not only painfully singed and burnt, but the fire had sucked from us all moisture and vitality.

Hezekiah brought me my luncheon, and I sat down in the green jungle beneath a tree and bathed my bare feet in the cool green leaves. I was miserably lame, and poor Siki lay beside me licking her pads, which were badly burnt. The hour soon went by and all were ready to start off again. Hezekiah was loath to leave me behind unarmed in the forest (even Siki followed the caravan), but I reassured him and continued to rest long after they had all gone.

Silence resumed its sway, till presently I heard some animal moving cautiously towards me through the undergrowth. It might have been a bushbuck or a pig, or it might have been a leopard. I never knew. I lay there idly wondering, and feeling happy in that perfect security which the forest seemed to extend. This, I thought, is the summit and glory of going into the forest alone and unarmed ; the world can hold nothing more beautiful than this feeling of protection, nothing that can so uplift one to humility.

Refreshed by the rest, I continued on my way at a swinging pace down through the last of the bamboo and across the open places filled with immortelles and butterflies, where the sun drew out the scents, aromatic as spices, on the still, hot air. Then down through the tall forest, and where I had toiled panting on the way up I now had enough breath left over to sing with. After the drenching sunlight it was vault-like, coldly green and dim ; but as my eyes grew accustomed, the little blue pea flowers (*parachetus communis*) twinkled among the shadows, and the silver boles stood out like lovely columns from the dark shining leaves. Or you would come to a bare giant trunk with deep buttresses or partitions (ideal for playing hide-and-seek in) and corrugations that were withal so smooth that you might think the tree was moulded in pewter. This Muna tree with his tremendous bole, and his crown of branches eighty or a hundred feet above your head, often stood in a clearing apart, and was, perhaps, the king of the forest. I could never pass one without stopping almost reverently to pat him.

By and by I, too, felt constrained to observe the profound silence, to step ever more softly among the leaves, with ears pricked and eye alert, picking my way easily, delicately almost, like a buck. Now a bird called liquidly *tink-tonk*, or the crooning of a colobus monkey came drowsily through the hot afternoon. Against the dark stagnant depths, the sun here and there plucked out a living arch of green as pellucid as the curve of a toppling wave ; and every now and then I paused in mid-stride to sniff, as some tree like a wild magnolia strewed its creamy waxen buds across my path with a fragrance that was hurtingly sweet.

I caught up with the porters at the stream by the tree-ferns, and climbing down to a pool beneath their gracious fronds I paddled in the ice-cold water. Each stream held out the same possibilities of refreshment, and at the last one, in the glade where the bridge was, I lingered behind long after the men's voices had died away. With Chogoria (so I thought) only an hour away, I would not be hurried over my leave-taking. Though I promised I would come back to it all some day, deliberately to unclasp one by one the fingers that held me was a bitter moment, and none ever looked more intently upon the beloved features, seeking to memorise them imperishably in the heart, than I as I gazed upon the current of that little stream and upon the tall, still trees dreaming in the sunset.

A golden cloud of locusts flew overhead, unhurried, yet with a set purpose as little to be stemmed as Fate. And I followed them, for they, too, were bound for the plains.

My heart was heavy, and I limped in so much pain that I could have wept ; yet even then, in the amber dusk and the still beauty of the forest, pain seemed a little thing ; and for nothing in the world would I have curtailed those last hours of marching beneath the trees.

But when the forest thinned out and fell behind, and I found myself on the long, dusty road, I would have given much to have been at the end of my journey. The road was bitter long—having motored on the way up I was not aware how long it really was—and I was by then so lame that I would gladly have gone on all fours. But I kept meeting batches of natives coming home from work, and for pride's sake I had to make some pretence of a jaunty step. When they had gone by, I sat in the ditch humbly enough, screwing myself up to the last weary stretch ; and I eventually crawled into the Mission at eight o'clock in the evening, thirteen hours after leaving the hut.

As I came round a bend in the road, the Mission lights shone among the trees. With the end in sight, there was no need to hurry any more, and I sat down where a tree bulked friendlily beside me in the darkness. Above the forest the peak had come into view again, soaring up infinitely remote among the stars. I could guess at a faint gleam of snow under the summit. I said to myself that it was over, to-morrow I should be back in civilisation. . . .

Gazing up at the peak, I went back in imagination over my journey from the beginning when, nearly ten months before, I had set out from Kiu station to the water-hole at Selengai ; and it seemed to me that, as when you march all day in the heat and the dust and have your reward in the brief beauty of the sunset that transmutes the very dust itself, so this quest of solitude—which may sometimes be a lonely ordeal—is rewarded a thousandfold by its rare and fleeting visions. For a little moment all is simplicity ; the mists roll up, revealing the peaks serene and strong before you.

It was those visions that I wanted above all else in the world to bring back and to share ; for at the root of all our lives is a great and terrifying loneliness, from which first or last there is no escape.

Yet by going out to meet it halfway, one discovers that its terrors are illusory. Solitude is an ally, there is nothing to fear, for truly " Nature never did betray the heart that loved her."

With infinite and loving patience she reassured me over and over again with symbols brighter than words : " You are not a stranger walking the earth to clutch at this friendship or that to be comforted. As surely as you will return to me at last, so surely while you live am I interwoven with every fibre. You are never lost or alone so long as you can claim kinship with everything that is. You are no more alone than the river is alone or the mountains are alone, or anything in the universe, for you are *a part of the whole* and not a single unit of nothing, aimlessly drifting. Don't build up the walls of loneliness about your spirit. Keep flowing, so that every day you can come out and meet yourself in the sky's reflection or the dew lying in petals, or any other natural thing. Renew yourself in these things, identify yourself with them ; for all is fashioned from the same material, shaped by the same inspiration and animated by the same life-breath."

Earth and spirit proclaimed with a thousand tongues the unity of the spirit. It is not life, nor Fate, nor Providence that is unkind, but we ourselves who persist in dividing instead of uniting. The same love of dividing that makes us cut ourselves into fifty religious sects all seeking one and the same Truth, or that makes for the sifting and sorting into different social layers, or divides us into different political parties, or nation versus nation : it is this same mania for dividing and separating that finally revenges itself upon the individual. Yet we are, after all, only superficially divided. Spirit will ever be like mercury, ready to run together again at the first opportunity.

Nature may be a cruel contradiction—life for ever warring against life—but her ultimate message is the friendship of God. Secure in that friendship we cannot be afraid. Life is the glorious experiment, and Death the great adventure, when the mists shall at last lift long enough for us to see clearly.

For a complete list of books available from Penguin in the United States, write to Dept. DG, Penguin Books, 299 Murray Hill Parkway, East Rutherford, New Jersey 07073.

For a complete list of books available from Penguin in Canada, write to Penguin Books Canada Limited, 2801 John Street, Markham, Ontario L3R 1B4.